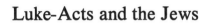

Luke-Acts and the Jews

SOCIETY OF BIBLICAL LITERATURE
MONOGRAPH SERIES

Adela Yarbro Collins, Editor
P. Kyle McCarter, Jr., Associate Editor

Number 33
LUKE-ACTS AND THE JEWS
Conflict, Apology, and Conciliation

by
Robert L. Brawley

Robert L. Brawley

LUKE-ACTS AND THE JEWS
Conflict, Apology, and Conciliation

Scholars Press
Atlanta, Georgia

LUKE-ACTS AND THE JEWS

by
Robert L. Brawley

© 1987
Society of Biblical Literature

Library of Congress Cataloging-in-Publication Data

Brawley, Robert L. (Robert Lawson)
  Luke-Acts and the Jews.
  (Society of Biblical Literature monograph
series ; no. 33)
  Bibliography: p.
  Includes indexes.
  1. Bible. N.T. Luke—Criticism, interpretation,
etc. 2. Bible. N.T. Acts—Criticism, interpretation,
etc. 3. Jews in the New Testament. I. Title.
II. Series.
BS2589.B73   1987   226'.4067   87-9574
ISBN 1-55540-125-2 (alk. paper)
ISBN 1-55540-126-0 (pbk. : alk. paper)

Printed in the United States of America
on acid-free paper

CONTENTS

ABBREVIATIONS

2 Apoc. Bar.	Syriac Apocalypse of Baruch
b.	Babylonian Talmud
BA	*Biblical Archeologist*
BAG	W. Bauer, W. F. Arndt, and F. W. Gingrich, *Greek-English Lexicon of the NT*
BDF	F. Blass, A. Debrunner, and R. W. Funk, *A Greek Grammar of the NT*
Ber.	*Berakot*
Bib	*Biblica*
B. Meṣ.	*Baba Meṣiʿa*
BZ	*Biblische Zeitschrift*
CBQ	*Catholic Biblical Quarterly*
C.E.	Common Era
EncJud	*Encyclopedia Judaica (1971)*
1 Enoch	Ethiopic Enoch
ʿErub.	*ʿErubin*
ETL	*Ephemerides theologicae lovanienses*
EvT	*Evangelische Theologie*
HTR	*Harvard Theological Review*
HUCA	*Hebrew Union College Annual*
Int	*Interpretation*
JBL	*Journal of Biblical Literature*
JEH	*Journal of Ecclesiastical History*
JSNT	*Journal for the Study of the New Testament*
JTS	*Journal of Theological Studies*
Jub.	Jubilees
LSJ	Liddell-Scott-Jones, *Greek-English Lexicon*
LXX	Septuagint
m.	Mishna
Mak.	*Makkot*
Menaḥ.	*Menaḥot*
Midr.	*Midraš*
MT	Masoretic Text
Neot	*Neotestamentica*
NovT	*Novum Testamentum*

NRT	*La nouvelle revue théologique*
NTS	*New Testament Studies*
Pesaḥ.	*Pesaḥim*
Q	The Synoptic Sayings Source (*Quelle*)
QL	Qumran literature
1QS	*Serek hayyaḥad (Rule of the Community, Manual of Discipline)*
RB	*Revue biblique*
RevExp	*Review and Expositor*
Roš. Haš.	*Roš Haššana*
RTP	*Revue de théologie et de philosophie*
Šabb.	*Šabbat*
Sanh.	*Sanhedrin*
SBLSP	Society of Biblical Literature Seminar Papers
Šeqal.	*Šeqalim*
ST	*Studia theologica*
Str-B	H. Strack and P. Billerbeck, *Kommentar zum Neuen Testament*
Sukk.	*Sukka*
t.	Tosepta
TDNT	G. Kittel and G. Friedrich (eds.). *Theological Dictionary of the New Testament*
TLZ	*Theologische Literaturzeitung*
TS	*Theological Studies*
TZ	*Theologische Zeitschrift*
VT	*Vetus Testamentum*
y.	Jerusalem Talmud
Yoma	*Yoma (= Kippurim)*
ZNW	*Zeitschrift für die neutestamentliche Wissenschaft*
ZTK	*Zeitschrift für Theologie und Kirche*

ACKNOWLEDGMENTS

I gratefully acknowledge a debt to a variety of sources for help in completing the project represented by this book. Memphis Theological Seminary provided me with a sabbatical leave to permit me time for the study. The Association of Theological Schools awarded me a Younger Scholar's Grant to finance my research. President Thomas W. Gillespie of Princeton Theological Seminary gave me an appointment as a visiting fellow for the term of the grant, and Librarian Charles Willard opened the facilities of Speer Library to me. SBL Monograph Series Editor Adela Yarbro Collins and two anonymous readers provided critiques of an earlier draft and gave me opportunity to respond to their criticisms in a revision.

Of course I depend on an array of scholars whose credit the annotations reflect only partially. I lean even more heavily on colleagues, friends, and family whose credit likely does not appear in the annotations, and whom I must credit in a more personal way than these lines allow.

Chapters 3 and 4 contain some materials which previously appeared in my article, "Paul in Acts: Lucan Apology and Conciliation," in *Luke-Acts: New Perspectives from the Society of Biblical Literature Seminar*, edited by Charles H. Talbert. These are used by permission of the Crossroad Publishing Company.

CHAPTER ONE
INTRODUCTION

In the history of the interpretation of Luke-Acts, an extraordinary confluence of streams of thought has swept scholarly attention away from Luke's portraits of Jesus and personages in the early church. F. C. Baur[1] and the Tübingen school attempted to recover the history behind Acts with a well-known Hegelian bias. Wilhelm Wrede[2] and the history-of-religions school forswore the bias but aspired to the same goal, namely, the history behind the text. One particularly influential result of the comparative history of religions was discovering the importance of an eschatological perspective for interpreting the NT. Johannes Weiss and Albert Schweitzer demonstrated that eschatology was constitutive for the NT worldview.[3]

Although the Bultmannian school appropriated the methodology of comparative history of religions, it regarded the recovery of the history behind the text as a false goal (not to say false god). Not only had the vision of faith of the early church obscured the facts of history, but the task itself was misdirected. Since faith stands

---

[1] F. C. Baur, *Kritische Untersuchungen über die kanonischen Evangelien* (Tübingen: Fues, 1847) 394–95, 428–34, 520–30; idem, *The Church History of the First Three Centuries* (London: Williams and Norgate, 1878) 77–82; idem, "Über Zweck und Veranlassung des Römerbriefs und die damit zusammenhängenden Verhältnis der römischen Gemeinde," *Tübinger Zeitschrift für Theologie* (1836) 59–178; idem, *Über den Ursprung des Episcopats in der christlichen Kirche* (Tübingen: Fues, 1838) 142; idem, *Paulus der Apostel Jesu Christi: Sein Leben und Wirken, seine Briefe und seine Lehre* (Stuttgart: Becher & Müller, 1845) 5–12.

[2] W. Wrede, *Über Aufgabe und Methode der sogenannten neutestamentlichen Theologie* (Göttingen: Vandenhoeck & Ruprecht, 1897). English translation in R. Morgan, *The Nature of New Testament Theology: The Contribution of William Wrede and Adolf Schlatter* (London: SCM, 1973).

[3] J. Weiss, *Jesus' Proclamation of the Kingdom of God* (Philadelphia: Fortress, 1971); A. Schweitzer, *Das Abendmahl im Zusammenhang mit dem Leben Jesu und der Geschichte des Urchristentums* (Tübingen: Mohr [Siebeck], 1901) 1.77; idem, *Paul and His Interpreters: A Critical History* (London: Black, 1912) 216–17, 226, 240; idem, *The Quest of the Historical Jesus: A Critical Study of its Progress from Reimarus to Wrede* (London: Black, 1954) 237–40, 349–401.

independently from history, the interpreter needs rather to discover the theology of the biblical authors.

Another tributary both flows against the current and converges with the stream. The *heilsgeschichtliche Schule* offered an alternative to the historical reconstruction of the history-of-religions school. Although there were older antecedents, Adolf Schlatter[4] and the Erlangen school emerged as its modern proponents, Oscar Cullmann[5] becoming its champion. Against the comparative history of religions, the *heilsgeschichtliche Schule* opposed the alleged impact of Hellenism and paganism on the evolution of the church and traced strong continuity between Christianity and the history of Israel. Against the Bultmannians, the *heilsgeschichtliche Schule* controverted the dichotomy between faith and history and claimed an essential core of historical event as necessary for faith.

When Hans Conzelmann, a pupil of Bultmann, took up the eschatological and theological tasks, he proposed that Luke had accommodated to the delay of the parousia by setting out a specific view of *Heilsgeschichte*.[6] According to Conzelmann, Luke considers his own present as the time of the church and sets out to explain how the church of his time stands in continuity with the original community. Luke's ecclesiology responds to the problems of eschatology.

This theological reading of Luke-Acts resulted in a striking congruity with the *heilsgeschichtliche Schule*. Whereas the *heilsgeschichtliche Schule* had hotly debated the Bultmannian bifurcation of faith and history, Conzelmann's hypothesis of a Lucan *Heilsgeschichte* sidestepped the historical question, with the exception of the one historical datum of the delay of the parousia. The precedence of Luke's theology of history over his presentation of history cleared the way for a scholar such as Jacques Dupont,[7] an ardent opponent to Bultmann's appropriation of comparative history of religions, to interpret Luke-Acts in terms remarkably compatible with Conzelmann's reading.

The question of the relationship between faith and history thus

[4] A. Schlatter, "The Theology of the New Testament and Dogmatics," in Morgan, *Nature of New Testament Theology.*

[5] O. Cullmann, *Christ and Time: The Primitive Christian Conception of Time and History* (Philadelphia: Westminster, 1950); idem, *Salvation in History* (New York: Harper & Row, 1967).

[6] H. Conzelmann, *The Theology of St. Luke* (New York: Harper & Row, 1961).

[7] For the opposition to the Bultmannian appropriation of comparative history of religions, see J. Dupont, *Gnosis: La connaissance religieuse dans les épîtres de saint Paul* (Louvain: Nauwelaerts, 1949). His interpretation of Luke-Acts appears in several works. See esp. "Le salut de gentils et la signification théologique du Livre des Actes," *NTS* 6 (1959–60) 132–55.

avoided, a strong consensus emerged among former disputants that Luke depicts the development of the church into a gentile entity that gives up on the Jews. With that, Lucan ecclesiology took on such proportions as to control the entire reading of Luke-Acts. The image of the Jewish mother abandoning its offspring until the offspring repudiates its mother so dominated as to color the interpretation of the rejection of Jesus in Nazareth (Luke 4:16–30) and Paul's final word to the Jews in Rome (Acts 28:28), and, consequently, everything in between.

It is in this fashion that the history of interpretation has been diverted from Luke's portraits of Jesus and personages in the early church. Luke's primary characters have been regarded as pointing beyond themselves to the unfolding story of the church. Thus, ecclesiology has swallowed up christology and gentile Christianity has consumed Paul. I have thought it necessary, therefore, first to erase some of the extraordinarily bold underlinings of negative assessments of the Jews that have led to the hypothesis in current scholarship that Luke gives up on them. Erasing involves the recovery of the portraits of Jesus and Paul. Thereafter, I have tried my hand at drawing the lines of interrelationships between Jews and Christians that are perceptible in Luke's two volumes.

In addressing the problem of Luke's perspectives on the relation between non-believing Jews and believers (both Jews and gentiles), I am adding my voice to a growing chorus of scholars who are protesting the notion that Luke depicts the triumph of gentile Christianity at the expense of Jews, and who are formulating a construct of Luke's thought in relation to his life in an environment where inner Jewish questions are still viable.

Antecedents of this approach go back as far as F. C. Baur. Although his description of early catholicism as a development out of antitheses between Jewish and gentile Christianity has been correctly rejected as a Hegelian distortion, the question he was asking about the relationships between Jewish and gentile Christians were hardly marginal. Nevertheless, other scholarly concerns largely overshadowed those issues until the Scandinavian Jacob Jervell revived them.[8] Another Scandinavian, Nils Dahl, furthered the debate with his essays "The Story of Abraham in Luke-Acts" and "The Purpose of Luke-Acts."[9] Among more recent contributors Luke Johnson has advanced the discussion significantly by detecting a consistent Lucan literary pattern of a division of the

[8] J. Jervell, *Luke and the People of God: A New Look at Luke-Acts* (Minneapolis: Augsburg, 1972).
[9] These two essays now appear in N. Dahl, *Jesus in the Memory of the Early Church* (Minneapolis: Augsburg, 1976).

people in the face of Jesus the prophet.[10] David Tiede has produced one of the most thoroughgoing attempts to locate Luke's thinking in inner Jewish struggles.[11] Donald Juel has agreed with Tiede, on his own terms, that Luke-Acts fits into the literature produced as a response to crises within the Jewish community.[12] Jervell has recently renewed his argument that Jewish Christianity strongly influences Luke's milieu.[13] Marilyn Salmon adds her voice to the debate in a recent dissertation. Because she confines her discussion to Luke's presentation of the Pharisees and Jewish law, her results are necessarily modest. Nevertheless, she claims that intra-Jewish controversy accounts for the way Luke deals with the law and the Pharisees.[14]

The rejection of Jesus in Nazareth so obviously sets the stage for Luke-Acts that it is imperative to locate its focus and determine its function. Accordingly, chapter 2 reconsiders this much debated pericope and demonstrates the primacy of the portrait of Jesus within it. The programmatic character of Acts 1:8 demands similar attention. Chapter 3 examines it anew and discloses its relation to the sanction of subsequent events, particularly the legitimation of Paul. The legitimation of Paul is a key to Acts, and chapter 4 shows how Luke wrote in an environment where he could appropriate Hellenistic literary devices and use them in order to sanction Paul. Chapter 5 then gives evidence that Luke exonerates Paul as thoroughly Jewish against both external Jewish detractors and internal Christian opponents.

The discussion then shifts to particular categories of Jews and Jewish institutions in order to investigate how Luke envisions them. Chapter 6 develops the thesis that for Luke and his audience the Pharisees are respected and authoritative representatives of Judaism who provide a foil for Jesus and who contribute to Luke's vindication of Christianity, the apostles, and Paul. In contrast, chapter 7 contends that Luke views Sadducees and the high priestly party as inauthentic Jews unworthy of representing Judaism. On the other hand, ordinary priests can merit a positive evaluation from Luke. Moreover, although Jerusalem and the

[10] L. Johnson, *The Literary Function of Possessions in Luke-Acts* (Missoula: Scholars, 1977).

[11] D. Tiede, *Prophecy and History in Luke-Acts* (Philadelphia: Fortress, 1980).

[12] D. Juel, *Luke-Acts: The Promise of History* (Atlanta: Knox, 1983) 7, 31, 68, 100, 101–12, 115–20.

[13] J. Jervell, "Paulus in der Apostelgeschichte und die Geschichte des Urchristentums," *NTS* 32 (1986) 378–92.

[14] M. Salmon, "Hypotheses about First-Century Judaism and the Study of Luke-Acts" (Ph.D. diss., Hebrew Union College, 1985).

temple come under judgment, they function implicitly as the point of contact between earth and heaven. Chapter 8 analyzes the Jewish people at large and argues, against widely accepted methodology, that the roles of Jewish crowds must be individually differentiated.

Although there has been some loss of confidence in the two-document hypothesis for the composition of the Synoptic Gospels, comparison of Luke with the hypothetical sources possesses at least heuristic value in highlighting Luke's peculiar perspectives. But Luke's view of the Jews does not hang on the redaction of individual detail. Rather, this study deals with Luke-Acts as an integral literary product. Luke's thought is reflected in the entire work. Beyond that, the methodology takes clues from the literature of antiquity as to how literary devices function. This is especially apparent in the study of legitimating devices and in the implication that the temple and Jerusalem mark the point of contact between the divine and human worlds.

This outline of issues stakes out the boundaries for and provides an anticipatory glance at the study that follows. But the solutions, some hinted at already, do not come into view beforehand. They come after the study and represent an attempt to piece together a puzzle.

CHAPTER TWO

THE IDENTITY OF JESUS IN LUKE 4:16–30 AND THE PROGRAM OF LUKE-ACTS

By way of a synagogue service in Nazareth, Luke sets forth his basic characterization of Jesus. This significant function of Luke 4:16–30 has long been neglected by the scholars who place undue stress on anticipating the era of the gentile church. It has become rather standard to allege that the aftermath of the inaugural sermon in Nazareth foreshadows the rejection of Jesus by the Jews and prefigures the reciprocal irrevocable transfer of the gospel from the Jews to the gentiles.[1] Commentators who interpret Luke's tableau in this manner run aground because of the common methodological fallacy of exaggerating Luke's *Heilsgeschichte* rather than focusing on his presentation of Jesus and his mission. Preoccupied with the course of the gospel into the gentile world, they have tended to overlook the identity and ministry of Jesus which the pericope advances. A few scholars have recognized that the person of Jesus stands at the center of the pericope, but they proceed to view Jesus as the rejected one who in turn rejects unbelieving Jews.[2] Surprisingly, they make the inaugural sermon of Jesus a forecast more of the accession of gentiles in Acts than of the story of Jesus in Luke.

The drama in Nazareth opens with a customary synagogue service that astonishes no one. When Jesus reads from Isaiah,

---

[1] This view proposed by R. Lightfoot (*History and interpretation in the Gospels* [London: Hodder and Stoughton, 1934] 196–205) and advanced by H. Conzelmann (*The Theology of St. Luke* [New York: Harper & Row, 1961] 34, 114, 194) and by E. Haenchen (*The Acts of the Apostles: A Commentary* [Philadelpia: Westminster, 1971] 101, 414, 417–18, 535, 724, 729–30) has won virtually universal acceptance among scholars.

[2] H. von Baer, *Der Heilige Geist in den Lukasschriften* (Stuttgart: Kohlhammer, 1926) 63; Conzelmann, *Theology*, 33, 103; M. Rese, *Alttestamentliche Motive in der Christologie des Lukas* (Gütersloh: Mohn, 1969) 148; J. Dupont, *Les béatitudes: La bonne nouvelle* (Paris: Gabalda, 1969) 2.131, n. 3; U. Busse, *Das Nazareth-Manifest Jesu: Eine Einführung in das lukanische Jesusbild nach Lk 4, 16–30* (Stuttgart: Katholisches Bibelwerk, 1978) 50–51.

things are as usual until he announces the fulfillment of the text even as it is being read. That is, Jesus appropriates for himself the anointing of the Spirit of the Lord which the text originally applies to the prophet. The prophecy promises release of captives and healing of the blind. Thus, Jesus' claim anticipates that he will proceed to cast out demons and heal with power. Certainly, therefore, the claim foreshadows this kind of ministry. But surprisingly Jesus suppresses any such activity in Nazareth. He will not satisfy the curiosity of his hometown folk to see his works (Luke 4:23). Thus, although Luke anticipates the ministry of Jesus, here one of his prominent interests is the claim of Jesus that the Spirit of the Lord is upon him. Luke appropriates the citation of Isaiah for identifying Jesus as well as for prefiguring his mission and ministry.

Recognizing that Luke's interest centers on the story of Jesus checks a premature vault to the gentile era of the church and makes it clear that the standard view of the Nazareth pericope as a paradigm of Luke's rejection of the Jews in favor of the gentiles must be revised. Luke transforms a potentially embarrassing response of the people of Jesus' hometown into a confirmation of Jesus' identity. This insight opens the door for a new way of reading Luke-Acts. According to the conventional wisdom, the repudiation of unbelieving Judaism and the accession of gentiles to the prerogatives of Israel colors everything from Luke 4 to Acts 28. The following discussion demonstrates how inadequate such a view of the Nazareth incident is, develops the thesis that this scene advances Luke's portrait of Jesus, and shows in what way the pericope may be programmatic.

What Is the Meaning of "Nazareth"?

It is only in retrospect, after one has read to the end of the Lucan corpus, that the rejection in Nazareth can be viewed as anticipating the program of Luke-Acts. Therefore, the paradigmatic significance of Luke 4:16–30 depends to a high degree on how Luke-Acts is read. The crux of the matter for this discussion is Luke's attitude toward the Jews and his view of the gentile mission. Does Luke turn against the Jews and demonstrate how the gospel falls virtually into the sole possession of the gentiles? Or does Luke remain open to the Jews and envision the church in broader terms than its gentile manifestations? Current scholarship is dominated by the view that Luke chronicles the movement of the gospel away from the Jews until gentiles assume the place of the people of God. Under this view Luke 4:16–30 is understood as anticipating the turning of God's promises from Israel to the nations. In spite of the scholarly consensus, the thesis that Luke-Acts relates how the gospel passes definitively from recalcitrant Jews to responsive gentiles proves to be a poor interpretation.

In reality, Acts shows surprisingly little interest in the gentile mission *per se*, although that mission is often taken to be its principal theme. The passages most frequently cited as evidence that, for Luke, the gentiles supersede the Jews (Acts 13:46, 18:6, 28:28) help to explain one of the reasons why Paul turns to the gentiles (see chapter 5). Although the Jerusalem Council legitimates the mission to gentiles as gentiles, the last half of Acts contributes little to the story of the universal extension of God's salvation. Luke traces Paul's career rather than the gospel's. He actually shows no concern with how the church is established in Rome and surprisingly little concern with Christianity's extension beyond Paul's mission in the diaspora. Thus, it hardly proves true that Luke develops a motif of the definitive transfer of the gospel to gentiles. Rather, Luke focuses single-mindedly on Paul's ventures. In particular, Luke defends Paul from the charges that he abandons Judaism and explains why he nevertheless engages in a gentile mission. If Paul diverts his mission to include gentiles, it is not that he has renounced Judaism. On the contrary, some Jews who reject Paul's gospel motivate him to turn to the gentiles. (There is a simultaneous explanation that Paul's gentile mission is ordained by God.)

In view of the apologetic function of Luke's presentation of Paul, what is the meaning of the Nazareth pericope? Since Paul's declarations that he turns to gentiles in the face of obdurate Jews actually reflect Paul's mission among gentiles rather than unfold a pattern of the passing of Israel's prerogatives to the nations, Luke 4:16–30, viewed in retrospect, can no longer be understood as projecting programmatically the diversion of the gospel from Jews to gentiles.

After Jesus' initial presentation in the synagogue in Nazareth, Luke describes the mood of the worshipers with additional words of Jesus: "Doubtless you will say (ἐρεῖτε) to me. . . , 'Physician, heal yourself.' " Some scholars take ἐρεῖτε here as a literal future which predicts what will happen after Jesus' ministry in Capernaum. Supposedly, then the Nazarenes will call for acts similar to those done in Capernaum. But it is significant that before referring to Capernaum Jesus first quotes the proverb, "Physician, heal yourself." The axiomatic nuance of the saying applies at that moment, and thus the proverb prevents the future ἐρεῖτε from being construed literally. Rather, it allows Jesus to express the disposition of the people of his hometown at that very moment.[3] When Jesus articulates the attitude of the people in Nazareth, he contrasts Capernaum with his hometown: "What we have heard you did at Capernaum, do here also ἐν τῇ πατρίδι σου" (v 23). But when he alludes to Elijah and Elisha in order to illustrate that no prophet is acceptable ἐν τῇ πατρίδι αὐτοῦ (v 24), πατρίς appears to refer to the Jewish nation. In order to show that Elijah and Elisha were not acceptable ἐν τῇ πατρίδι αὐτῶν, the widow of Zarephath is explicitly contrasted with "many widows in *Israel*" (v 25), and Naaman the Syrian is explicitly contrasted with "many lepers in *Israel*" (v 27). Whereas in connection with Jesus, πατρίς means Nazareth, in reference to Elijah and Elisha it means Israel. Is πατρίς, therefore, a mediating term which equates the hometown with the homeland so that Nazareth becomes a symbol for Israel?

The answer depends to a large degree on the function of the references to Elijah and Elisha in Luke's argument. If Luke intends for Jesus to duplicate the ministries of those venerable prophets, then he may well envision a pattern whereby the salvation of gentiles comes about by means of Israel's rejection of God's grace. That is, is Jesus a recapitulation of Elijah and Elisha? The answer on the basis of the text must be in the negative. Luke gives no indication that he thinks that Jesus reproduces the ministries of those ancient prophets. Rather, he cites the cases of Elijah and Elisha to prove that no prophet is acceptable ἐν τῇ πατρίδι αὐτοῦ.

The parallel structures of vv 24 and 25 bear this out. In v 24 Jesus introduces the saying that no prophet is acceptable ἐν τῇ πατρίδι αὐτοῦ with the phrase, "Truly, I say to you." A parallel phrase follows in v 25: ". . . in truth, I tell you . . . ."[4]

> "*Truly, I say to you*, no prophet is acceptable in his own country.
> But *in truth, I tell you* there were many widows in Israel . . . ."

Therefore, rather than making a direct equation between the

---

[3] W. Eltester ("Israel im lukanischen Werk und die Nazarethperikope," *Jesus in Nazareth* [Berlin: de Gruyter, 1972] 141) shows further that the future is to be attributed to the diatribe style. Thus the future ἐρεῖτε allows Jesus to express the present attitude of the Nazarenes.

[4] J. Bajard ("La structure de la pericope de Nazareth en Lc. iv, 16–30," *ETL* 45 [1969] 170) shows that ἀμὴν λέγω ὑμῖν (Luke 4:24) is in parallel with ἐπ᾽ ἀληθείας λέγω ὑμῖν (v 25). But he incorrectly concludes that the parallel demonstrates that the meaning of Nazareth is enlarged to Israel. The parallel indicates that vv 25–27 illustrate the axiom of v 24.

ministries of Israel's prophets and the work of Jesus, Luke, in fact, makes an analogy between Jesus in relation to his hometown and Elijah and Elisha in relation to Israel. A schematic representation of the analogy is:

Jesus—Nazareth : Capernaum :: Prophet—πατρίς (outsiders) ::
          Elijah and Elisha—Israel : gentiles

Jesus in relation to Nazareth is to Capernaum as a prophet in relation to his πατρίς is to outsiders as Elijah and Elisha in relation to Israel were to gentiles. The parallel structures of vv 24 and 25 show that Luke draws the analogy between the entire complexes Jesus—Nazareth—Capernaum and Elijah, Elisha—Israel—gentiles rather than between the details (Nazareth : Israel, Capernaum : gentiles) where by some stretch of the imagination Capernaum stands for the gentiles. When the analogy is viewed in terms of the entire complexes, then to interpret the illustrations of Elijah and Elisha as paradigms of ministry to gentiles is to mix the terms to read: Jesus is to gentiles as Elijah and Elisha were to gentiles. But that is an unwarranted confusion which makes Capernaum represent the gentiles (*reductio ad absurdum*) and renders Jesus' ministry frustrated since he carries out no gentile mission in Luke. Elijah and Elisha sanction Jesus in the face of his rejection in Nazareth rather than casting a pattern for the ministry to gentiles. Moreover, to read Nazareth as a cipher for Israel and Capernaum as a symbol for gentiles is to repeat the fallacy of Origen with his allegorical methodology, for in uncovering the hidden mysteries of this text, he too sees Nazareth as a symbol of the Jews and Capernaum of the gentiles (*In Lucam Homilia* 33). How can modern interpreters so quickly name "the Jews" when Jesus confronts only the people of Nazareth? After all, Israel appears in the text only in connection with Elijah and Elisha. Nazareth is no cipher for Israel nor Capernaum a symbol for gentiles.

Yet another factor supports the conclusion that Elijah and Elisha do not provide a programmatic pattern for the rejection of Jews and the acceptance of gentiles in Luke-Acts. In Luke's line of argument, Jesus adduces analogies with the prophets to vindicate his relation to his hometown. That vindication constitutes an argument from greater to lesser. If the relations of Elijah and Elisha to gentiles prove that no prophet is acceptable ἐν τῇ πατρίδι αὐτοῦ, it follows that a prophet known in Nazareth merely as Joseph's son (v 22) will hardly be received hospitably.

Leander Keck and James Sanders see Jesus in Nazareth as an

Elijah figure.[5] But why should there be any focus on Elijah when Luke devotes equal attention to Elisha? Accordingly, Joseph Fitzmyer considers Jesus a fulfillment of both prophets.[6] But that is also inadequate because it fails to consider the parallelism between v 24 and vv 25–27, which shows that Luke draws an analogy between Jesus and Israel's ancient prophets. Moreover, it reads the comparison between Jesus and the prophets backward. The function of the allusions to Elijah and Elisha is to demonstrate that a prophet is not acceptable ἐν τῇ πατρίδι αὐτοῦ. The absence of a gentile mission in Luke shows clearly that Luke does not portray Jesus' ministry as a duplicate of theirs. Thus, in spite of a double meaning (hometown/homeland), πατρίς does not provide the link to justify interpreting Nazareth as a symbol for Israel.

This function of Luke's analogy dovetails precisely with the larger framework of the context. Hans Conzelmann notes that the immediate context provides for the proper interpretation of the juxtaposition of Nazareth and Capernaum.[7] That is, upon his rejection in Nazareth, Jesus does indeed go to Capernaum (Luke 4:31). He then proceeds to proclaim good news under divine necessity to other Jewish cities.[8] Quite simply, far from anticipating the extension of the gospel to gentiles, the rejection in Nazareth eventuates in its extension to other Jews.

The Identity of Jesus in Luke 4:16–30

Luke gives the incident in Nazareth a position of decisive importance. He structures the order of events so that in contrast to Mark and Matthew the rejection in Nazareth inaugurates the ministry of Jesus. In addition, whether or not Luke has a special

---

[5] L. Keck, "Jesus' Entrance upon His Mission," *RevExp* 64 (1967) 481; J. Sanders, "From Isaiah 61 to Luke 4," *Christianity, Judaism and Other Greco-Roman Cults; Studies for Morton Smith* (ed. J. Neusner; Leiden: Brill, 1975) 1.100.

[6] J. Fitzmyer, *The Gospel According to Luke (I–IX): Introduction, Translation, and Notes* (Garden City, NY: Doubleday, 1981) 537.

[7] Conzelmann, *Theology*, 38. Conzelmann does support a secondary meaning of the contrast between Nazareth and Capernaum as a symbolism of turning to the gentiles.

[8] H. Combrink, "The Structure and Significance of Luke 4:16–30," *Neot* 7 (1973) 38. The divine necessity for Jesus to preach to Jews is frequently taken as a part of Luke's version of "to the Jews first, then to the gentiles." See Fitzmyer, *Gospel*, 529. B. Reicke ("Jesus in Nazareth—Lk 4,16–30," in *Das Wort und die Wörter; Festschrift Gerhard Friedrich* [ed. H. Balz and S. Schulz, Stuttgart: Kohlhammer, 1973] 52) argues that Luke presents an analogy between Jesus and Paul whereby in *both* cases grace is first offered to Jews, then to gentiles. Since Jesus carries out no gentile mission in Luke, Reicke's conclusion must require a contorted logic in which recalcitrant Jews stand for Israel and believing Jews stand for gentiles.

source, he offers the reader a far more elaborate story. There can be little doubt, therefore, that Luke intends the event in Nazareth to be programmatic. But the prominence of the identity of Jesus elucidates the programmatic significance. Luke shows his hand by setting off the Nazareth incident and Jesus' ministry at Capernaum with an inclusion about the growing reputation of Jesus (Luke 4:14, 37). Luke gives two summaries in which he reports the increasing fame of Jesus where the Marcan parallel has but one. He introduces the section in v 14: "And a report concerning him went out through all the surrounding country." The conclusion in v 37 is virtually identical: "And reports of him went out into every place in the surrounding region." Thus, Luke sets the entire section within brackets about the reputation of Jesus, and he offers the reader thereby a clue to his interest in the person of Jesus in the section. Furthermore, the exorcism in the synagogue in Capernaum headlines Jesus' ministry there, and the key to it is that the unclean demon identifies Jesus as the Holy One of God (v 34). Hence, in the immediate context of 4:16–30 significant emphasis falls on the identity of Jesus.

How, then, does Luke portray Jesus? Luke's desire to present Jesus as one who is filled with the Holy Spirit emerges as early as Luke 3:22 where the Spirit descends upon him at his baptism. Luke repeatedly emphasizes the life of Jesus in the Spirit (4:1, 14). But Jesus' ministry in the Spirit is set over against the competing possibility that the demonic will determine the behavior of Jesus. So the inaugural sermon in Nazareth is juxtaposed to the temptations in the wilderness. Because Jesus, full of the Spirit, withstands the temptations, he proves himself to be endowed with the Spirit. Only then does he embark upon his ministry in Nazareth in the power of the Spirit (v 14). All of this is a prelude to the reading of Isa 61:1. "The Spirit of the Lord is upon me." When Jesus rolls up the scroll and claims, "Today this Scripture is fulfilled in your hearing," he appropriates for himself the anointing of the Spirit in Isa 61:1 and alludes both to his baptism and his conquest of the devil.

Jesus' claim to be anointed resounds with striking messianic overtones. References in two speeches in Acts provide a Lucan commentary and show that the evangelist understood ἔχρισεν in Luke 4:18 in messianic terms. First, ἔχρισας in the prayer in Acts 4:27 interprets the meaning of the anointed one in the quotation from Psalm 2 LXX (Acts 4:26), so that it should be translated "made messiah."[9] Second, in a Petrine speech in Acts 10:38, ἔχρισεν αὐτὸν

    [9] K. Lake and H. Cadbury, *The Beginnings of Christianity* (London: Macmillan, 1933) 4.47; Haenchen, *Acts*, 226–27.

ὁ θεὸς πνεύματι ἁγίῳ alludes both to Isa 61:1 and Luke 4:18. This passage in Acts, when viewed in conjunction with the baptism of Jesus in Luke 3:22 and with Luke's notices of Jesus' life in the Spirit in 4:1, 14, indicates that the evangelist understood that God anointed Jesus at his baptism with the Holy Spirit and thereby designated him messiah.[10] And so Jesus' announcement that he is anointed is nothing less than a demand to be recognized as messiah.

Luke's citation of Isaiah sets the spirit-filled and messianic identity of Jesus against the background of the eschatological Jubilee year. James Sanders has shown that rabbinic traditions link Isa 61:1–3 with the eschaton and the QL associates it with the final Jubilee year.[11] Thus, Luke employs the Isaianic passage against an established eschatological background. According to August Strobel, Luke may have even calculated the time of the beginning of Jesus' ministry by an apocalyptic calendar which would make the year of Jesus' sermon the tenth and final Jubilee from Ezra's return.[12] Even if Strobel's computation should prove incorrect, the evidence remains compelling that Luke portrays Jesus as the anointed one who announces the messianic Jubilee year.

The audience in Nazareth also engages in speculation about the identity of Jesus: "And all spoke well of him, and wondered at the gracious words which proceeded out of his mouth; and they said, 'Is not this Joseph's son?'" (Luke 4:22). But inspite of an initial positive response,[13] the assembly refuses to accept the

[10] Haenchen, *Acts*, 227, n. 1, 352; Dupont, *Les béatitudes*, 2.132–33. Rese (*Alttestamentliche Motive*, 117) is hesitant to recognize an allusion to Isa 61:1 here on the basis of only two words. But the messianic overtones cannot be doubted. J. de la Potterie ("L'onction du Christ," *NRT* 80 [1959] 240–46) argues that both Acts 4:27 and 10:38 allude to prophetic anointing only, rather than to a messianic anointing. His conclusions are based on a questionable reproduction of the original meaning of OT allusions in their NT contexts and on an equally questionable appeal to the historical Peter. F. Hahn (*Christologische Hoheitstitel: Ihre Geschichte im frühen Christentum* [Göttingen: Vandenhoeck & Ruprecht, 1963] 395–96) accepts de la Potterie's conclusions.

[11] Sanders, "From Isaiah 61," 88, 91; cf. idem, "Isaiah in Luke," *Int* 36 (1982) 151–52. In contrast see R. Albertz, "Die Antrittspredigt Jesu im Lukasevangelium auf ihren alttestamentlichen Hintergrund," *ZNW* 74 (1983) 182–206. Albertz thinks that Luke eliminates particulars from the Isaiah passages which would tie the meaning to particulars of Israel, including the Jubilee year, to give Jesus' ministry a social thrust to the lower classes.

[12] A. Strobel, "Die Ausrufung des Jubeljahrs in der Nazarethpredigt Jesu: Zur apocalyptischen Tradition Lc 4:16–30," *Jesus in Nazareth* (ed. W. Eltester, Berlin: de Gruyter, 1972) 42–44. Strobel's calculation is impressive, but it must remain tentative, since he dates the fifteenth year of Tiberius from his coregency = 26/27 C.E., and since the calculation depends on counting Jubilee years from an uncertain date of Ezra's return.

[13] B. Violet ("Zum rechten Verständnis der Nazareth-Perikope Lc 4:16–30," *ZNW* 37 [1938] 256–57) and J. Jeremias (*Jesus' Promise to the Nations* [Naperville,

elevated claims made by Jesus. They can evaluate him only as
Joseph's son who was brought up in Nazareth. Since their appraisal stops far short of Luke's, it is in competition with his and
constitutes unbelief. How does Luke deal with this competing
view of Jesus' identity?

In the first place, Jesus takes the initiative. He gives utterance
to the contemplations of the people in Nazareth: "Physician, heal
yourself" (Luke 4:23). Bo Reicke argues that this dictum identifies
Jesus as a physician.[14] That Reicke errs in finding the identity of
Jesus as a physician here is clear from the commentary on the lips
of Jesus that explains the proverb: "What we have heard you did at
Capernaum, do here also in your own hometown." This explanation restricts the adage from identifying Jesus as a physician.
Rather, it shows that it voices the desire of the people of Nazareth
to see mighty works that will support the identity of Jesus already
set forth.

But in the second place, Jesus does make a claim for a
particular identity when he associates himself with the prophets (v
24).[15] If Jesus is a prophet, how can this identity be confirmed?
Jesus himself sets the test: No prophet is δεκτὸς ἐν τῇ πατρίδι
αὐτοῦ.

The meaning of δεκτός in this maxim is a vital factor in
understanding it. J. Bajard contends that the verbal adjective here
does not have the passive sense "acceptable," but the active sense
"favorable," "salvific."[16] This constitutes Jesus' answer to the
expectation of the Nazarenes that he should perform mighty works.

IL: Allenson, 1958] 44–45) argue on the basis of supposed Aramaic originals that
ἐμαρτύρουν αὐτῷ is a dative of disadvantage ("to bear witness against") and that
therefore there is no initial positive response to Jesus. The question of Aramaic
originals, however, does not come into play in determining what Luke means. The
response in Nazareth fits into a theme of positive reaction already prominent in the
context (Luke 4:14–15, 32, 37). Moreover, Luke's usage of μαρτυρέω elsewhere
shows that 4:22 is not a dative of disadvantage. See H. Schürmann, "Zur
Traditionsgeschichte der Nazareth-Perikope Lk 4,16–30," *Mélanges bibliques en
homage au R. P. Béda Rigaux* (ed. A. Descamps and A. de Halleux; Gembloux:
Duculot, 1970) 188.

[14] Reicke ("Jesus in Nazareth," 49–50) bases his conclusion on the association of
the idea of healing in the proverb with the cleansing of Naaman (v 27) and with the
reference to healing the broken hearted (v 18), a disputed variant found in the
koine group of MSS.

[15] Here Reicke ("Jesus in Nazareth," 50) is correct. Cf. A. Finkel, "Jesus' Sermon
at Nazareth (Luk. 4,16–30)," *Abraham unser Vater: Juden und Christen in
Gespräch über die Bibel; Festschrift für O. Michel* (ed. O. Betz et al; Leiden: Brill,
1963) 108–109.

[16] Bajard, "La structure," 167–70.

And so Bajard envisions Jesus provoking his audience by denying them acts of benevolence.[17] Such an understanding, however, creates a severe tension between the proverb and the sermon of Jesus in the synagogue. In the sermon Jesus announces the fulfillment of benevolent promises to the congregation: "Today this Scripture is fulfilled in your hearing" (Luke 4:21). If δεκτός implies a refusal to offer Nazareth acts of benevolence, Jesus should have proclaimed rather that the promises were *not* to be fulfilled in the hearing of his audience. In addition, although the parallel between ἐμαρτύρουν αὐτῷ and ἐθαύμαζον ἐπὶ τοῖς λόγοις τῆς χάριτος demonstrates that λόγοι τῆς χάριτος signifies primarily "gracious words," Luke's use of the same phrase in Acts 14:3 and 20:32 (cf. 20:24) shows that at least on a secondary level he understands it as the message of grace.[18] Thus, the Nazarenes comprehend Jesus' sermon in a benevolent sense.

Moreover, Bajard's hypothesis that the maxim means that no prophet is favorable to his own country deprives Jesus' entire career of authenticity. The context throughout Luke and a large part of Acts shows how wide of the mark that is. Acts 10:38 summarizes Jesus' ministry by claiming that he went about doing good. Luke portrays Jesus as precisely the one who is benevolent toward his people. Jesus' benevolence for his own is nowhere more poignantly expressed than in Luke 13:34: "O Jerusalem, Jerusalem, killing the prophets and stoning those who are sent to you! How often would I have gathered your children together as a hen gathers her brood under her wings, and you would not!" In addition, it is thematic in Luke that prophets are unacceptable rather than unfavorable. The blood of all the prophets shed from the foundation of the world is required of Jesus' compatriots because they concur in their forebears' rejection of the prophets (11:47–51).[19] The evidence weighs heavily against the active

[17] Admittedly, the verbal adjective ending in -τος is ambiguous with respect to voice; see J. Moulton, *A Grammar of New Testament Greek* (Edinburgh: T. & T. Clark, 1949) 1.221–22. But the ordinary usage of δεκτός with respect to human beings is passive (BAG; LSJ. Cf. *BDF* §65(3), 112, 117). Unless Luke drastically alters the meaning of Mark 6:4, his use of δεκτός in place of ἄτιμος would favor the passive sense. Also Acts 10:35 has the passive meaning. See Busse, *Nazareth-Manifest*, 35.

[18] H. Flender, *St. Luke: Theologican of Redemptive History* (Philadelphia: Fortress, 1967) 153. See also Violet, "Zum rechten Verständnis," 264, 268; Jeremias, *Jesus' Promise*, 45; J. Nolland, "Words of Grace (Luke 4:22)," *Bib* 65 (1984) 47.

[19] D. Moessner ("Luke 9:1–50: Luke's Preview of the Journey of the Prophet like Moses of Deuteronomy," *JBL* 102 [1983] 594–604) demonstrates that the rejection

meaning of δεκτός and in favor of its passive nuance. Hence, Luke must mean that no prophet is *acceptable* ἐν τῇ πατρίδι αὐτοῦ. Jesus articulates that adage as a counter-claim to the competing view that he is (merely) Joseph's son. And so in spite of the Nazarenes' inability to accept the Spirit-filled and messianic identities of Jesus, Luke adds a prophetic identity.[20] Yet, the proverb does not merely establish Jesus' claim to be a prophet, it also sets up a criterion that confirms his claim—no prophet is acceptable ἐν τῇ πατρίδι αὐτοῦ. After the two OT examples of Elijah and Elisha illustrate the maxim, the people of Nazareth verify it and thereby the identity of Jesus—they reject him (v 28).[21]

A great deal of scholarly energy has been expended in efforts to account for the hostility of the people of Nazareth against Jesus.[22]

---

of the prophets is thematic for Luke, but he overemphasizes the rejection as "monolithic." As L. Johnson shows (*The Literary Function of Possessions in Luke-Acts* [Missoula: Scholars, 1977] 48–126) rejection is half of a double-pronged pattern of acceptance/rejection.

[20] F. Schnider (*Jesus der Prophet* [Göttingen: Vandenhoeck & Ruprecht, 1973] 166) thinks that Jesus' messianic claims exclude a prophetic identity. The two identities are not mutually exclusive but complementary.

[21] The emphasis upon Jesus' identity does not stand against Johnson's view (*Literary Function*, 95) that Luke uses the people of Nazareth as a type of those who reject the prophet. That is, there is a pattern of rejection throughout Luke-Acts that legitimates the prophetic identity of Jesus and his successors.

[22] Jeremias (*Jesus' Promise*, 45) contends that the audience was offended that Jesus' reading stopped short of the announcement of God's vengeance in Isa 61:2. That is an atrociously weak argument from silence that fails to consider that the incident as it stands is what Luke makes of it. Recently H. Baarlink ("Ein gnädiges Jahr des Herrn—und Tage der Vergeltung," ZNW 73 [1982] 204–220) has renewed support of Jeremias, albeit on the level of Lucan redaction. He argues that Luke reserves Isa 61:2b until Luke 21:22 as a part Luke's theological structure of first to the Jews and then to the gentiles. His arguments, though impressive, nevertheless fall because he fails to consider the brackets around the pericope in Luke 4:15, 36 where the response to Jesus is patently positive. There are two widely accepted explanations of the reactions of Jesus' audience: (1) The people of Nazareth reject Jesus because he has made exalted claims for himself, and they can accept him only as Joseph's son. See K. Rengstorf, *Das Evangelium nach Lukas übersetzt und erklärt* (Göttingen: Vandenhoeck & Ruprecht, 1952) 56; Keck, "Jesus' Entrance," 478; Flender, *St. Luke*, 156. (2) They reject Jesus because he announces the extension of God's promises to strangers and foreigners. So Bajard, "La structure," 170; R. Tannehill, "The Mission of Jesus according to Luke 4:16–30," *Jesus in Nazareth* (ed. W. Eltester; Berlin: de Gruyter, 1972) 61–62; D. Hill, "The Rejection of Jesus at Nazareth (Luke 4:16–30)," NovT 13 (1971) 168–69, 178. A. Leaney (*A Commentary on the Gospel according to Luke* [New York: Harper & Row, 1963] 52) argues erroneously that it is the prophet Jesus who rejects his own people. Nolland ("Words of Grace," 44–60) suggests that "words of grace" is Luke's notice to the reader to account for the Nazarenes' astonishment, the reason for which they themselves are unaware. Thus, Nolland explains the tension between the intial acceptance and the final rejection of Jesus. But Nolland fails to

James Sanders, using comparative midrash, has proposed one of the most impressive of these clarifications.[23] He argues that Jesus' sermon occasions the offense. The pivotal point comes with Jesus' hermeneutics, that is, the way he interprets the citation from Isaiah. On the basis of hermeneutical principles evident at Qumran (and in the early Christian community), Sanders concludes that the people in Nazareth would have expected God's wrath to fall upon outsiders and God's mercy to fall upon themselves. But the allusions to the relations of Elijah and Elisha with outsiders reverse these expectations. Thus, Jesus' compatriots reject him because of his prophetic challenge to their self-understanding.

Sanders' approach is constructive in that it does not make Nazareth a cipher for Israel nor Jesus anti-Jewish. In fact, David Tiede, developing Sanders' ideas, concludes also that Luke is not anti-Jewish.[24] Luke's program is not the rejection of the Jews and the accession of the gentiles, but Jesus' obedience to God which entails a prophetic critique of any community claiming God's promises.

But for all the scholarly effort to explain the hostility against Jesus in the plot of Luke 4:16–30, in actuality it is insufficiently motivated. Luke himself remains otherwise silent as to why Jesus encounters animosity, because, according to the criterion on the lips of Jesus, no prophet is acceptable ἐν τῇ πατρίδι αὐτοῦ. That the antagonism lacks additional literary justification proves all the more the truth of the maxim. The people of Nazareth reject Jesus simply because he is a prophet.

It is important for Luke to show that the rejection is no slight case of antagonism but an effort to lynch Jesus. Charles Talbert has shown that in antiquity both pagans and Jews highly regarded the martyrdom of an innocent person as a sign that legitimates the martyr's claims.[25] The crowd at Nazareth attempts to execute Jesus

---

perceive that the lack of motivation of the anger of the Nazarenes plays a dramatic role in the function of the pericope to identify Jesus as a prophet. That dramatic role makes such circuitous explanations superfluous.

[23] Sanders, "From Isaiah 61," 92–100. Cf. Sanders, "Isaiah in Luke," 151–54.

[24] D. Tiede, *Prophecy and History in Luke-Acts* (Philadelphia: Fortress, 1980) 48–49, 55–63. L. Crockett ("Luke 4:25–27 and Jewish-Gentile Relations in Luke-Acts," *JBL* 88 [1969] 177–83) claims that because Elijah's visit to the gentile widow is beneficial to both, the Nazareth incident anticipates beneficial relations between Jews and gentiles in Luke-Acts. His intuitions are helpful, but certainly Luke makes nothing of mutual profit between Elijah and the widow.

[25] C. Talbert (unpublished lectures, Stetson University, ca. 1981); idem, *Reading Luke: A Literary and Theological Commentary on the Third Gospel* (New York: Crossroad, 1982) 221–24. Overeagerness, however, on the part of the martyr to incur martyrdom is a cause for caution as to its legitimating effect.

with insufficient cause. The absence of motivation underlines the innocence of Jesus. Luke portrays Jesus here almost as a martyr. Thus, the attempt on the life of Jesus vindicates all the more his claims. But since his claims are about his identity, the lynch mob confirms all the more *his* authenticity. Nazareth rejects Jesus because he is a prophet.

Only, Luke's line of reasoning is the other way around. In response to the competing view that Jesus is (merely) Joseph's son, Jesus first refuses to prove his identity by mighty works. But then he does establish a basis for judgment: No prophet is acceptable ἐν τῇ πατρίδι αὐτοῦ. Dramatic irony is at work. The people of Nazareth, who cannot accept the exalted identity of Jesus, reject him, but in so doing they demonstrate nothing other than the exalted identity of Jesus.[26]

The Identity of Jesus in the Program of Luke-Acts

Establishing that the identity of Jesus is one of the primary emphases of the incident at Nazareth now makes it possible to reconsider the way in which the pericope betrays Luke's plan. Luke does give the rejection of Jesus in his hometown programmatic prominence and thereby employs it as a blueprint for his leading ideas about Jesus. The way in which Luke 4:16–30 is programmatic depends on how these major themes are developed throughout Luke-Acts.

The discussion above has already shown how the context of the baptism of Jesus and his temptation in the wilderness sets the stage for the identity of Jesus as one who is anointed with the Spirit. In fact, it is significant that in Luke 4:1 Jesus is not led ὑπὸ τοῦ πνεύματος, as in Matthew 4:1, but ἐν τῷ πνεύματι.[27] Thus, for Luke, Jesus operates in the Spirit in contrast to being led by the Spirit.

Outside of the accounts of Jesus' entrance upon his mission, Luke alludes to Jesus' relationship to the Spirit only at Luke 10:21. Nevertheless, the references at the beginning of Jesus' task are vital to Luke's view of Jesus. The descent of the Spirit upon Jesus in Luke 3:22 and the repeated characterization of Jesus as Spirit-

---

[26] Reicke ("Jesus in Nazareth," 51) thinks that the effort to execute Jesus means that the people of Nazareth evaluate Jesus as a false prophet to be stoned in accordance with Deut 13:1–11; 17:2–7. That would heighten the irony—the rejection of the true prophet as a false prophet would confirm that no prophet is acceptable ἐν τῇ πατρίδι αὐτοῦ. But Luke 4 lacks sufficient evidence for Reicke's conclusion.

[27] Conzelmann, *Theology*, 28, n. 1.

filled in Luke 4:1, 14 show that the gift of the Spirit is not a matter of temporary inspiration but of permanent endowment.

Because Luke so strongly establishes the identity of Jesus as one anointed with the Spirit at the beginning of Jesus' ministry, he is able to assume it through the rest of the Gospel with little need for additional references. But when Luke has Peter recall that God anointed Jesus with the Holy Spirit in a speech before Cornelius (Acts 10:38), Luke demonstrates how important it is thematically in spite of the lack of frequent references. Not only does Peter name the Holy Spirit, but he relates that Jesus was anointed "with the Holy Spirit and with power." If Holy Spirit and power are synonymous, references to the power of the Lord upon Jesus in Luke 5:17, 6:19, and 8:46 also allude to the Spirit. Luke's portrayal of Jesus as one anointed with the Spirit fits his program for Jesus' entire career.

Luke equally establishes the messianic identity of Jesus, and yet it continues to surface throughout Luke-Acts. Demonic spirits know that Jesus is the Christ (Luke 4:41). Whereas Peter's confession in Mark 8:29 remains ambiguous as an identification of Jesus, Luke's parallel epitomizes the genuine identity of Jesus (Luke 9:20). Further, Peter's sermon on the day of Pentecost contains an announcement to Israel that God has made the crucified one "both Lord and Christ" (Acts 2:36).[28] Again, in a sermon before the temple, Peter identifies Jesus as the messiah (3:18, 20). In addition, 4:26 interprets Ps 2:1–2 messianically and takes it as a reference to Jesus. On other occasions, Paul, like Peter, identifies Jesus as the Christ (Acts 9:22, 17:3, 18:5). Finally, Apollos demonstrates from the Scriptures that Jesus is the Christ (18:28).

In two passages Luke reveals his concern with the messianic character of Jesus in a more subtle way. First, at the descent of the Mount of Olives, Jesus' disciples proclaim him to be the king who comes in the name of the Lord (Luke 19:38). In comparison with Mark, Luke wishes to spell out more clearly the messianic kingship of Jesus. But the Pharisees oppose this periphrastic messianic confession. Their opposition affords Jesus himself opportunity to confirm his messianic nature. He retorts that the confession is such a divine necessity that if it were not on the lips of his disciples, the stones would cry out. His witnesses are right!

Second, Luke 7:19 employs a similar messianic periphrasis in

---

[28] de la Potterie ("L'onction, 240–42) claims that Acts 2:36 shows that for Luke it is only at Jesus' glorification that he is designated Messiah. But against his own argument, he cannot deny the identity of the earthly Jesus as the Christ in Peter's confession (Luke 9:20). Furthermore, the earthly Jesus suffers as the Christ (Luke 24:26, 46; Acts 17:3).

the inquiry of John the Baptist: "Are you he who is to come?" Jesus refuses to give a direct answer. Rather, he responds by referring to his deeds. John can supposedly deduce from Jesus' works that he is indeed the one who is to come.

Like Luke 4:16–30, 7:22 highlights the messianic identity of Jesus against the background of the eschatological Jubilee release. Here, Jesus describes his accomplishments in terms which are surprisingly similar to the announcement of the eschatological Jubilee in 4:18–19: "The blind receive their sight, the lame walk, lepers are cleansed, and the deaf hear, the dead are raised up, the poor have good news preached to them." The Jubilee release provides the background for Jesus' exorcisms and healings and for his concern with the poor and oppressed throughout Luke.[29]

This christological focus comes to a climax in Luke 24:25–27, when the risen Jesus clarifies his own messianic identity in face of the scandal of his suffering. He interprets the Scriptures so as to explain to Cleopas and his anonymous companion the necessity of the messiah to suffer. He repeats the interpretation of the Scriptures to the eleven who have been joined by the two disciples from Emmaus (vv 44–46). Paul Schubert has shown how closely related this passage is structurally to 4:16–30 by the proof from prophecy motif.[30] In Nazareth, Jesus appropriates for himself the messianic prophecy of Isa 61:1 (Luke 4:21). On the way to Jerusalem, he expands his claim to be the fulfillment of everything written of the Son of Man by the prophets (18:31). In Jerusalem, the risen one now provides the hermeneutic for his followers to understand christologically Moses, all the prophets, and the Psalms (24:27, 44–45). But the proof from prophecy demonstrates nothing other than the messianic identity of the risen one who is also the suffering one. At the beginning and end of his Gospel, Luke evidences his concern to offset the offense of the rejection of Jesus in his hometown and the scandal of the crucifixion of Jesus at the instigation of his compatriots.

In Luke 4 the Spirit-filled and messianic identities of Jesus are juxtaposed to the competing view that Jesus is Joseph's son (v 22). Elsewhere, Luke commits himself to dispute the contention that Jesus is (merely) Joseph's son. In the annunciation Mary's promised son is already identified as the Son of God (1:32, 35). In the

---

[29] H. Cadbury (*The Making of Luke-Acts* [London: SPCK, 1958] 262, cf. n. 7) provides the insight that Luke's attitudes about the poor and oppressed are largely rooted in apocalyptic hopes. Hence, the apocalyptic Jubilee atmosphere extends beyond Luke 4 to wider reaches of Luke-Acts.

[30] P. Schubert, "The Structure and Significance of Luke 24," *Neutestamentliche Studien für Rudolf Bultmann* (ed. W. Eltester; Berlin: Töpelmann, 1954) 165–86.

story about Jesus as a lad in the temple, Luke portrays Jesus as dedicated to another father (2:49) and thereby implies that Jesus is God's son. The genealogy traces the origins of Jesus back to God, albeit incongruently through Joseph who is merely the alleged father (3:23–38). Although the voice at Jesus' baptism is directed to him personally, it informs the reader that Jesus is the Son of God (v 22). The stage is already set *before* the inaugural sermon for Jesus' identity to exceed the Nazarenes' evaluation of him as (merely) Joseph's son.

On subsequent occasions Jesus continues to demonstrate his commitment to God above family. When his mother and brothers come to see him, he redefines familial relationships by disregarding the claims of kinship and confederating himself with those who heed the word of God (Luke 8:19–21). In a related incident, Jesus declines to visualize blessedness in the personal reciprocal bond between mother and child and shifts to a communal image where he stands with others in the bond of hearing and keeping the word of God (11:27–28). Luke completes his presentation of the relationship of Jesus to his family by portraying Mary and his brothers as part of the original number of the primitive church (Acts 1:14).[31] Here the order of domestic honor is reversed. The family now defers to Jesus rather than Jesus revering the family.

Luke 4 climaxes with the identity of Jesus as a prophet. This is certainly a programmatic theme for Luke-Acts. After the raising of the son of the widow of Nain, the crowd acclaims Jesus a great prophet (Luke 7:16). When Simon the Pharisee hosts Jesus at his table, he disputes in his own mind the prophetic nature of Jesus: "If this man were a prophet, he would have known who and what sort of woman this is who is touching him" (v 39). In response to Simon's skepticism, Jesus relates the parable of the two debtors. The parable and its application function in the first instance to vindicate the woman. But then the vindication of the woman exonerates Jesus. The question of Jesus' prophetic identity in the mind of Simon is clearly answered. Jesus does know who and what sort of woman is touching him.

Jesus' prophetic identity emerges elsewhere in Luke from the mouth of Jesus himself. When the Pharisees warn Jesus to flee from Herod (Luke 13:31), their intervention provides a background against which Jesus affirms his identity. He presents

---

[31] Joseph's conspicuous absence is likely due to his death prior to Jesus' ministry; so R. Brown, *The Birth of the Messiah: A Commentary on the Infancy Narratives in Matthew and Luke* (Garden City, NY: Doubleday, 1977) 519.

himself to them as a prophet who stands in continuity with the prophet-martyrs of Jerusalem.

Further, two disciples, albeit disillusioned, identify Jesus as a prophet. When the two men from Emmaus summarize Jesus' ministry, they refer to him as a prophet (Luke 24:19).

Two speeches in Acts, however, demonstrate that Luke considers Jesus not only a prophet, but the promised Mosaic prophet. First, in his speech before the temple, Peter cites Deut 18:15, 18 and proclaims Jesus as the prophet like Moses (Acts 3:22). Second, Stephen cites the same text and makes the same point by implying that Jesus is the fulfillment of Moses' prophecy (7:37). This provides the background for understanding Luke's thematic development of the prophetic nature of Jesus first presented in Luke 4.

Not only does Acts explicitly present Jesus as a prophet like Moses, but, as David Moessner has demonstrated, Luke presents his story of Jesus in a form that recapitulates the Deuteronomic portrait of Moses.[32] The Mount of Transfiguration establishes Jesus as a mediator of God's word like Moses embarking on a journey toward death (Luke 9:28–36). That journey, like the wilderness wanderings, leads to death for recalcitrant unbelievers, but to the promised land for the people of God. Thus, the structure of what Jesus does and teaches, as well as his direct claims, betrays his prophetic identity.

In their rejection of Jesus, the Nazarenes respond with murderous rage to the adage that no prophet is acceptable ἐν τῇ πατρίδι αὐτοῦ. Although their behavior confirms all the more Jesus' prophetic identity, it also foreshadows his ultimate destiny. Thus, Luke closely associates the death of Jesus with his identity as a prophet. In Luke 13:33 Jesus contends that a prophet must die in Jerusalem, and Luke 11:49 and Acts 7:52 view persecution and martyrdom as a part of the course for a prophet. Therefore, Jesus experiences rejection throughout his ministry, and his death confirms his identity.[33] The people of Nazareth then spurn Jesus in the typical fashion of Israel's persistent refusal to heed the prophets.

[32] Moessner, "Luke 9:1–50," 575–605. In my view Moessner overemphasizes both Jewish opposition to Jesus and the vicarious nature of Moses' death.
[33] O. Steck (*Israel und das gewaltsame Geschick der Propheten: Untersuchungen zur Überlieferung des deuteronomistischen Geschichtsbildes im Alten Testament, Spätjudentum und Urchristentum* [Neukirchen-Vluyn: Neukirchener, 1967] 4–99, 267) views Luke's portrayal of the destiny of Jesus as in line with Jewish tradition which developed out of the Deuteronomistic understanding of the fate of the prophets. Steck thinks that Hellenistic Jewish Christianity appropriated a bank of tradition about the constant refusal of Israel to heed the prophets in order to present Jesus as the culmination of the constant refusal of

In fact, as Luke Johnson demonstrates, the dominant dramatic pattern in Luke-Acts is the relation between prophet and people.[34] But, whereas in the overall structure of Luke-Acts the relation between prophet and people involves a pattern of acceptance as well as rejection,[35] the people of Nazareth appear, for Johnson, to be a type of the Jews who reject the prophet, though elsewhere Johnson sees a pattern of acceptance in addition to the rejection. The failure to take note of the pattern of acceptance as well as rejection is a weakness of Norman Petersen's exposition of the literary pattern of confrontation between God's agents and God's people in Jewish sanctuaries. He argues only for a pattern of rejection that results in the extension of the gospel to others.[36]

To characterize the Jews as standing over against Jesus is a serious misreading of Luke. Even beginning with John the Baptist, multitudes are baptized (Luke 3:7, 21). 7:29–30 reiterates the baptism of all the people and the tax collectors by John and makes a sharp distinction between them and the Pharisees and lawyers. This still relates only to John. But the parable of the children in the market place (vv 31–35) applies the division to Jesus as well. In 4:14–15 Jesus' reputation is building. In v 42 people seek him. Emphasis on crowds is repeated in 5:1, 19 and intensified in 6:17–19 and 7:11. Crowds follow Jesus in 8:4, 9:11, 9:37, and 11:29. In 12:1 the crowd is so large that thousands trample each other. In 19:37 the whole multitude of disciples acclaims Jesus. To envision the Jews as rejecting Jesus, therefore, is to ignore a characteristic pattern in Lucan summaries.

Since Luke 4:16–30 portrays only the rejection of Jesus by his hometown, it is not cut from the larger pattern of acceptance/rejection. Luke relates only the rejection because it alone fits the criterion of the maxim: No prophet is acceptable ἐν τῇ πατρίδι αὐτοῦ. In the Nazareth pericope, Luke turns up the lights on the career of Jesus with a fascinating attempt to overcome the pain and embarrassment of the rejection and near martyrdom of Jesus in his own hometown. Ironically, the response of the people in Nazareth does not disconfirm the identity of Jesus but verifies it. Luke crowns his Gospel with a comparable effort to surmount the

---

Israel to believe the prophets. Cf. G. Friedrich, "προφήτης," *TDNT* 6.834–35, cf. n. 348.

[34] Johnson, *Literary Function*, 220, cf. 48–126.

[35] J. Jervell (*Luke and the People of God* [Minneapolis: Augsburg, 1972] 41–74) demonstrates the acceptance/rejection pattern for Acts.

[36] N. Petersen, *Literary Criticism for New Testament Critics* (Philadelphia: Fortress, 1978) 85–91.

offense of a crucified prophet and messiah by introducing a hermeneutic from the risen Jesus himself that interprets the OT. Instead of disconfirming Jesus' messianic identity, the OT, properly understood, demonstrates that the messiah must have so suffered (24:26–27, 46).

In summary, in the rejection at Nazareth, Luke epitomizes his view of who Jesus is. The scene enables the reader to behold Jesus as the Spirit-anointed messiah and prophet who claims the ministry of establishing the eschatological Jubilee. His claim elicits a potentially embarrassing rejection by his hometown. This foreshadows the ultimate destiny of Jesus and anticipates that the sailing will not be smooth. But the alleged other side of the coin fails to turn up. There is no reciprocal rejection where Jesus (i.e., Luke) writes off either the people of Nazareth or the Jews.

Jesus as a Paradigm for His Followers

For Luke, this Jesus is unique. The time of Jesus is a sharply defined period when he alone is filled with the Spirit.[37] He alone is messiah. There is salvation in no one else and by no other name (Acts 4:12). Further, he is *the* Mosaic prophet.

And yet, the Lucan view is that Jesus, for all his uniqueness, does serve as a paradigm for his followers. Jesus promises the apostles the Spirit (Acts 1:5, 8). When viewed in retrospect from Acts, Luke 12:12 appears to presuppose the coming of the Spirit upon the primitive Christian community. Furthermore, Luke's readers can hardly fail to note the parallels between the beginning of the ministry of Jesus at Nazareth and the initiation of the mission of the church on the day of Pentecost (Acts 2). The 120 persons who comprise the nascent Christian community are all filled with the Holy Spirit. Moreover, Acts also repeatedly certifies its heroes by means of notices that they are filled with the Spirit: Peter (4:8), Stephen (6:5, 7:55), Barnabas (11:23), and Paul (9:17, 13:9). The gentile converts associated with Cornelius are authenticated by the coming of the Spirit upon them (10:44–47). A similar legitimation accompanies Paul's baptism of the twelve Ephesians (19:6). Thus, the Jesus who is filled with the Spirit foreshadows his followers who will be filled with the Spirit.

In this regard the prophetic identity of Jesus also typifies his successors. Jesus' Spirit-filled followers take up the prophetic task of proclaiming the good news. The Sanhedrin opposes the proclamation of Peter and John (Acts 4:1–22) and of the twelve (5:17–41), but thereby only serves to show the validity of their

---

[37] Conzelmann, *Theology*, 28.

message. Thus, suffering for the name demonstrates their legitimacy (v 41).

In his speech before the Sanhedrin, Stephen establishes a criterion similar to Jesus' adage in Luke 4:24: "As your fathers did, so do you. Which of the prophets did not your fathers persecute? And they killed those who announced beforehand the coming of the Righteous One" (Acts 7:51–52). As if to prove his point, they kill him, so that at the end of Stephen's story, the reader now understands "As your fathers did, so do you . . ." as applying to Stephen's opponents. So Stephen's martyrdom ironically illustrates his prophetic nature.

The same light illuminates Paul's sufferings. From the time of his experience near Damascus, he is destined to suffer as a divine necessity (Acts 9:16; δεῖ αὐτὸν παθεῖν). Paul must suffer because he bears the name of the Lord as a witness. This prophetic task, according to the Lucan concept, will inevitably arouse opposition. When Paul's sufferings materialize (e.g., 14:19–20), they vindicate his prophetic mission.

Furthermore, the paradigm that emerges from Luke 4:16–30 vindicates Jesus' followers who suffer and indeed may serve as an exhortation to readers anticipating persecution. The harassment of the apostles in Acts 5 legitimates them as worthy (v 41). There are also conspicuous parallels between the events surrounding Jesus in his passion and those surrounding Paul at the end of Acts.[38] And yet, for all the similarities between the destiny of Jesus and that of his followers, Luke minimizes their martyrdom. He details only the stoning of Stephen (Acts 7) and passes over in brief the death of James, the brother of John (12:1). Granted, Luke pictures Paul as a near martyr (14:19, 21:30–32, 23:12–15, 25:3). Nevertheless, by allusions to Paul's demise in the Miletus speech (20:22–25), Luke demonstrates that he obviously knew of Paul's death but refrains from recounting it. Luke, therefore, may have attempted to exhort his readers to avoid a martyr complex[39] and at the same time may have viewed the death of Jesus as a paradigm to vindicate Christians facing opposition. Hence, when proper account is taken of the distinction between Jesus and his followers, Luke 4:16–30 is paradigmatic for subsequent Christian leaders.

Conclusion

This chapter demonstrates the need for a revision of the widely accepted opinion that Luke 4:16–30 establishes a pattern for the

---

[38] Talbert (*Reading Luke*, 186–87) lists numerous correspondences.
[39] R. Maddox, *The Purpose of Luke-Acts* (Edinburgh: T. & T. Clark, 1982) 96–97.

passing over of Israel's prerogatives to the gentiles. If a disclaimer is necessary, I am not suggesting that in itself Luke's interest in the identity of Jesus excludes the possibility that the scene foreshadows the rejection of Jesus by the Jews and also the reciprocal rejection of the Jews. But two additional considerations team up with Luke's focus on the identity of Jesus to eliminate this sort of reciprocal rejection as thematic for the pericope and programmatic for Luke-Acts. One is the larger thematic development to the end of Acts, especially the apology for Paul in the last quarter of Acts. The other is the function of the allusions to the ministries of Elijah and Elisha to gentiles.

Chapter 5 will discuss in detail the concern of Acts with the Pauline mission rather than with the extension of the gospel to gentiles as such. Suffice it to say for the present that when the second half of Acts is no longer viewed as the story of the definitive transition of the gospel from Jews to gentiles, but as an account of the Pauline mission, Luke 4:16–30 loses its alleged programmatic character of prefiguring the problem of unbelieving Jews and receptive gentiles. The failure of Acts to follow a schema of turning the promises of Israel over to the gentiles fits with the immediate context of Luke 4 where in straightforward fashion Jesus leaves Nazareth and journeys to other cities under the necessity of preaching good news to other Jews.

In addition, an analysis of the argument of Luke 4:23–28 reveals that the references to Elijah and Elisha do not foreshadow the gentile stage in the history of the church. Rather, Luke attempts to show that Jesus, like Elijah and Elisha, is a prophet who is not acceptable ἐν τῇ πατρίδι αὐτοῦ. In the argument this maxim controls the reference to the ministries of Elijah and Elisha among foreigners so that they function to show how Jesus stands in line with other prophets who failed to find acceptance among their own people. Not only does this maxim restrict the meaning of the references to foreigners, in the analogy between Jesus and the prophets there is no *tertium comparationis* linking the exclusion of Israel from the ministries of Elijah and Elisha to an alleged rejection of Nazareth by Jesus. Although Nazareth does not accept Jesus, and thereby proves his prophetic identity, Jesus does not reciprocate. For their part, the recalcitrant people of Nazareth anticipate one-half of the response of the people to Jesus in Luke-Acts. Jesus and the proclamation of the early church produce a division among the people. Nazareth aligns itself with that segment of Israel which refuses to believe. But on the evidence of Luke-Acts, there is another segment which believes. Thus, in the argument of Luke 4:16–30, πατρίς is not a mediating term that equates Nazareth with Israel, but a flexible expression that can refer now to Israel in the cases of Elijah and Elisha and again to Nazareth in Jesus' instance. The analogy between Jesus and the venerable prophets of Israel illustrates the truth of the maxim: No prophet is acceptable ἐν τῇ πατρίδι αὐτοῦ. Consequently, although Luke's interest in the identity of Jesus alone does not eliminate the possibility of foreshadowing the ultimate rejection of the Jews, its combination with the larger context of Luke-Acts and with the actual line of argument within the pericope does. The incident at Nazareth alerts the reader to the Spirit-filled, messianic, and prophetic identity of Jesus that Luke elaborates. Thus, Jesus' inaugural sermon is programmatic in the sense that it provides a basic paradigm of who he is and what he will do without prefiguring the irrevocable transfer of the gospel to gentiles.

In a secondary sense Luke's portrait of Jesus prefigures the careers of his followers. There is a qualitative distinction between who Jesus is and who they are. Nevertheless, the more they correspond to Jesus, the more their own relationship to God is guaranteed. Thus, they are legitimated as Spirit-filled leaders who authentically proclaim Jesus as the Spirit-anointed messiah and Mosaic prophet.

CHAPTER THREE
ACTS 1:8 AND THE PROGRAM OF ACTS

The task of determining the literary structure of Acts would be far simpler had Luke outlined the contents of the second volume for us, a rather frequent practice among Hellenistic authors. As it is Acts 1:1–2 provides a summary only of the first volume and leaves it to the reader to discern the structure of the second. Nevertheless, according to a virtual consensus among scholars, Luke reveals the structure of Acts in the promise on the lips of Jesus: "But you shall receive power when the Holy Spirit has come upon you; and you shall be my witnesses in Jerusalem and in all Judea and Samaria and to the end of the earth" (Acts 1:8). Supposedly, this prediction sets the pattern for the geographical extension of God's salvation and anticipates the definitive transition of the gospel from Jews (Jerusalem) to gentiles (Rome).[1]

The next two chapters call the scholarly consensus into question and propound the thesis that the legitimation of significant movements in the Christian enterprise including particularly Paul's mission, rather than the geographical extension of the gospel, is the key to the structure of Acts. This thesis depends on three basic proposals: (1) that Acts concentrates on Paul as Paul rather than making him a symbol for Christianity, (2) that the story of Paul not only dominates the literary structure of the second half of Acts but also rests on major preparation for Paul in the first half of Acts, and (3) that Luke attempts to rehabilitate Paul. These proposals constitute the primary concerns for this chapter and the following one.

---

[1] A selection of prominent scholars documents the consensus. J. Weiss, *Über der Absicht und dem literarischen Character der Apostelgeschichte* (Götingen: Vandenhoeck & Ruprecht, 1897) 3–5; F. J. Foakes Jackson and K. Lake, *The Beginnings of Christianity* (London: Macmillan, 1922) 2.175–76; M. Dibelius, *Studies in the Acts of the Apostles* (London: SCM, 1956) 193; E. Haenchen, *The Acts of the Apostles: A Commentary* (Philadelphia: Westminster, 1971) 143–44; H. Conzelmann, *Die Apostelgeschichte erklärt* (Tübingen: Mohr [Siebeck], 1972) 22.

The Inadequacy of Viewing Paul as a Symbol for Christianity

Martin Dibelius and Ernst Haenchen argue that the Lucan Paul symbolizes Christianity as a whole. According to them, Luke exhibits interest not in Paul as such but in Paul as he stands for the Christian enterprise. Paul allegedly plays a symbolic role in the defense of Christianity in general. Jacob Jervell has recently argued that Paul stands as a symbol of the whole Christian movement, not in the defense of Christianity, but in providing the legacy for the church.[2] When these notions are combined with the standard view that the structure of Acts is based on the geography of the extension of the gospel, Paul becomes the agent who, in the course of his mission, fulfills the promise of Acts 1:8, even though Jesus addresses the promise to the apostles. As the final words of the risen Jesus before his ascension, Acts 1:8 obviously occupies a strategic place in the structure of Acts. The question is whether or not Jesus' promise sets the geographical outline for the extension of the church and makes Paul its agent. Does Paul in fact carry out the extension of the witness to Jesus to the end of the earth?

Five particular texts appear to imply that Luke regards Paul as a symbol for Christianity. One is the charge of Tertullus that Paul is ". . . an agitator among all the Jews throughout the world, and a ringleader of the sect of the Nazarenes" (Acts 24:5).[3] This accusation is closely related to two other texts. In 17:6, the Thessalonians indict Paul and Silas as men who have turned the world (οἰκουμένη) upside down. When that text is paired with Tertullus's accusation, Paul appears to be regarded as a figure of unparalleled influence. But the charge of Tertullus also bears close affinity to the objections of Jewish Christians to Paul in 21:21: "They have been told about you that you teach all the Jews among the gentiles to forsake Moses." Is Paul the primary leader of the church who has worldwide impact?

A fourth text that comes under consideration here is Acts 26:20. This is ostensibly a remarkable parallel to 1:8. Paul summarizes his ministry before King Agrippa with a geographical summary that is reminiscent of 1:8—Damascus, Jerusalem, all Judea, and to the gentiles. Does this summary demonstrate that Paul fulfills the promise of Jesus in 1:8?[4]

---

[2] Dibelius, *Studies*, 149, 160; Haenchen, *Acts*, 328, 691. J. Jervell, "Paulus in der Apostelgeschichte und die Geschichte des Urchristentums," *NTS* 32 (1986) 382–83.

[3] R. Maddox (*The Purpose of Luke-Acts* [Edinburgh: T. & T. Clark, 1982] 77) argues that Paul's arrival in Rome is essential for the establishment of Christianity there since he is a πρωτοστάτης.

[4] So P. Menoud, "Le plan des Actes des Apôtres," *NTS* 1 (1954–55) 50.

The fifth text is Acts 13:47. Here Luke links the motif of a "light for the Gentiles," which Simeon's canticle applies to Jesus himself (Luke 2:32), to Paul and Barnabas and establishes the end of the earth (ἕως ἐχάτου τῆς γῆς) as the goal of their mission—a verbatim parallel to the last phrase of Acts 1:8. Since Rome is Paul's ultimate destination, does 13:47 link the imperial capital with the end of the earth in 1:8?[5]

Attention to the details of theme and plot development shows that the image of Paul as a symbolic figure for the extension of Christianity is more apparent than real. The identification of Paul as a ringleader of the sect of the Nazarenes is a pejorative characterization by his accuser Tertullus. Likewise, the charge that Paul and Silas have turned the world upside down is a complaint from opponents. It cannot be overlooked that this accusation applies equally to Silas, and this robs Paul of any character as *the* symbol for Christianity. Ironically, the opponents may speak the truth unwittingly, but only in an inverted way. The world is not turned upside down politically, and it is not Paul and Silas who do so. Rather, the plan of God is at work. In the end the opposition provides a foil to show how God cares for Paul and his companions and delivers them.[6]

Luke lets the narrative show the fallacy of the accusations of both the Thessalonians and Tertullus. Far from being a ringleader of the sect of the Nazarenes, Paul is a faithful Jew (Acts 24:14–15; 26:4–7, 22). Further, Paul does nothing to disrupt the social order. In Corinth, Gallio vindicates Paul from any legal violation (18:14–15). At Ephesus it is actually the opponents who are in danger of being charged for rioting (19:37–40) rather than Paul (v 26) and his companions (v 29). Moreover, Paul summarizes his innocence by declaring before Festus that he has not offended against the law of the Jews or against the temple or against Caesar (25:8). The larger context exculpates Paul from the charges of the Thessalonians and of Tertullus. And so 17:6 and 24:5 do not identify Paul as a symbol for Christianity.

It does seem likely that Luke's repeated allusions to a rather universal impact of Paul's mission reflect his exaggerated view of the effect of the mission. Repercussions of the ministry of Paul and Silas hardly resounded throughout the οἰκουμένη, as the Thessalonians charge (Acts 17:6). Similarly, the influence of Paul cannot have been so great as to have reached all the Jews who are

---

[5] So Conzelmann, *Apostelgeschichte*, 22, 78; R. Zehnle, *Peter's Pentecost Discourse* (Nashville: Abingdon, 1971) 99.

[6] D. Adams, "The Suffering of Paul and the Dynamics of Luke-Acts" (Ph.D. diss., Yale University, 1979) 56, 62–69, 292.

among the gentiles, as the Jewish Christians in Jerusalem allege. The characterization of Paul as an agitator among all the Jews throughout the world (οἰκουμένη) betrays the perspective of Luke more than that of Tertullus (24:5).

To a degree the overstatement reflects nothing other than the idiom of the Greek language. Koine lost some of the distinction among the positive, comparative, and superlative. Accordingly, adjectives such as πᾶς did duty beyond a strictly absolute sense. Πᾶς could be nothing more than a popular exaggerated way of expressing a large number. Even οἰκουμένη had this same kind of nuance. Οἰκουμένη could describe an emperor's realm, although it obviously constituted only a part of the actual world. Moreover, there was also a popular usage in which it simply meant a lot of people or places, an idiom still preserved in modern French and Spanish.[7]

Luke's exaggeration of his hero's efficacy does not mean that he makes him a symbol of Christianity. The same type of overstatement occurs repeatedly in Luke's Gospel in connection with the ministry of Jesus. To give but a couple of examples, all the people come to hear Jesus in the temple (Luke 21:38), and the risen Jesus himself is the only visitor in Jerusalem who does not know about the crucifixion (24:18). These typical exaggerations occur again and again in Acts. It is unlikely that the sound of speaking in tongues on Pentecost could have drawn a multitude so large that from it 3,000 people would be baptized (Acts 2:6, 41). Before the Sanhedrin, Peter presumes to speak to all Israel (4:10). The Sanhedrin alleges that the healing of the lame man at the temple gate is manifest to *all* the inhabitants of Jerusalem (4:16, 21). The high priest charges that the apostles have filled Jerusalem with their teaching (5:28). In spite of these typical exaggerations, Luke himself is aware that Paul precipitates less than a worldwide reaction. When Paul arrives at Rome, he discovers that his reputation has not preceded him (28:21).

The overblown images of Luke's heroes betray the literary devices of the storyteller and his prejudice for Christianity, but do not make the heroes symbols of their religion.

In spite of apparent parallels between Acts 1:8 and Paul's résumé of his mission in 26:20, Luke probably intended only a derivative relation. Jerusalem is so prominent as the point of origin for Christianity, that had Luke meant for 26:20 to fulfill 1:8, he most certainly would have avoided reporting that Paul preaches in Damascus *first* (rather emphatic in the Greek). Furthermore, since

---

[7] BAG; *BDF*, §60–61; B. Reicke, "πᾶς," *TDNT* 5.896.

15:3 reports Paul's contact with the Samaritans, Luke likely would have alluded to Samaria in 26:20 had he intended a parallel to 1:8.

Rather than a fulfillment of Acts 1:8, 26:20 completes the readers' expectations of the fulfillment of Paul's divine commission, a specific case of the comprehensive mandate in Luke 24:46–47. Since Paul is a second-generation witness, his proclamation stands in a derivative relationship to the apostolic witness which guarantees the authenticity and continuity of the Christian testimony (see Acts 10:41). 26:20 similarly authenticates Paul's claims to the same divine commission described anew in 22:14–15 and 26:16–18. In fact the ὅθεν of 26:19 links the geographical summary of v 20 with Paul's third account of God's call as proof of his obedience. Thus, the geographical references in v 20 identify Paul as a divinely chosen witness (cf. 9:15, 22:14–15, 26:16–18), but stops short of making him the agent who fulfills 1:8.

Does Acts 13:47, however, establish Rome as a symbol of the end of the earth and identify Paul as the agent who fulfills 1:8? Admittedly, there is a strong case for just such an interpretation of 13:47. But there are two important pieces of evidence that weigh in favor of a negative answer. (1) 13:47 applies to both Paul and Barnabas. (2) An *inclusio* provides the clue to Luke's understanding of Isa 49:6.

(1) Although Luke deliberately attaches the motif of a "light for the Gentiles" to the break with obdurate Jews in Antioch of Pisidia (Acts 13:47), he does not thereby make Paul the symbolic figure of the extension of the gospel to the end of the earth (1:8). Isa 49:6 applies after all to both Paul and Barnabas. Through the OT prophecy, the Lord commands both to turn to the gentiles (στρεφόμεθα, Acts 13:46; ἡμῖν, v 47). Barnabas remains a partner in the gentile controversy through the Jerusalem Council. After the role of Barnabas in the Council and in the promulgation of its decree, the allusion to the mission of Barnabas in Cyprus (15:39) certainly anticipates his continued ministry to gentiles. Furthermore, since 13:47 applies to both missionaries, the mission of Barnabas is just as much ἕως ἐσχάτου τῆς γῆς as is Paul's. Luke portrays both Paul and Barnabas as playing *a* role in the wider mission of the church rather than viewing Paul alone as *the* light for the gentiles.

(2) The interpretive brackets which frame the citation in Acts 13:47 demonstrate that Luke understands his version of Isa 49:6 as two lines of synonymous parallelism. Ἕως ἐσχάτου τῆς γῆς corresponds to εἰς φῶς ἐθνῶν as an equivalent. Luke clearly understands the parallelism as synonymous because he introduces the quote in words of Paul and Barnabas, "We turn to the *gentiles* (Acts 13:46,

emphasis added) and epitomizes it in his own summary, "And when they heard, the *gentiles* rejoiced and glorified the word of the Lord" (v 48, emphasis added). Luke's *inclusio* shows that ἕως ἐσχάτου τῆς γῆς is an ethnic rather than a geographical reference.[8] This means that 13:47 does not anticipate Rome as Paul's ultimate destination nor designate Rome as a symbol of the end of the earth.[9]

As is well known, Jesus addresses his promise in Acts 1:8 to the apostles. If we assume that the promise finds fulfillment in Acts, a discrepancy confronts us, and we come out on the short end of the stick either in regard to the apostles or the geography. Etienne Trocmé attempts to resolve the problem by claiming that the apostles carry out their universal witness on Pentecost by preaching to representatives from all over the world.[10] Trocmé's solution has the advantage of restricting the fulfillment of 1:8 to the apostles to whom Jesus addresses his promise but lacks harmony with the geographical data.[11] Philippe Menoud may be said to come up with two short ends by arguing that 1:8 foreshadows three stages: Jerusalem and Judea, Samaria, and the end of the earth.[12] With the dispersion following Stephen's martyrdom, Philip's mission to the Samaritans, Peter's mission to Cornelius, and the mission of Barnabas and Paul to Asia Minor, the gospel has already attained the final stage before the Jerusalem Council, even if the work is not

---

[8] W. van Unnik, "Der Ausdruck ἕως ἐσχάτου τῆς γῆς (*Apostelgeschichte 1:8*) und sein alttestamentlicher Hintergrund," *Sparsa Collecta: The Collected Essays of W. C. van Unnik* (Leiden: Brill, 1973) 1.393. Van Unnik argues that Acts 13:47 is not *parallelismus membrorum*; rather, the reference to the end of the earth extends beyond the meaning of "a light to the gentiles" to embrace the whole world. But he has not taken into account the interpretive brackets provided by Luke's *inclusio*.

[9] Pss. Sol. 8:15 speaks of one who comes from the uttermost part of the earth (ἀπ' ἐσχάτου τῆς γῆς) in judgment against Jerusalem. Van Unnik ("Ausdruck," 395–99) claims that the phrase alludes to Pompey's former period of residence in Spain. In all likelihood it refers to Pompey's provenance as Rome. But the parallelism and interpretive brackets in Acts 13:16–48 show that Pss. Sol. 8:15 does not come into consideration here.

[10] E. Trocmé, *Le Livre des Actes et l'histoire* (Paris: Presses Universitaires de France, 1957) 206.

[11] So the critique of G. Klein, *Die zwölf Apostel: Ursprung und Gehalt einer Idee* (Göttingen: Vandenhoeck & Ruprecht, 1961) 209–10. Zehnle (*Peter's Pentecost Discourse*, 120–21) shows that the list of nations in Acts 2:9–11 corresponds closely to a list from Paulus Alexandrinus of the fourth century C.E. which likely goes back to the fourth century B.C.E.; this list classifies countries of the world according to the zodiac. Therefore, the list in Acts 2:9–11 reflects the universal nature of the audience at Pentecost.

[12] Menoud, "Le plan des Actes," 46.

finished. But Menoud's proposal loses precision with respect to the addressees and splits the geography of Acts up the middle.

These attempts to resolve the inconsistency between the recipients of Jesus' promise and the geographical schema of Acts illustrate the difficulty of interpreting Acts 1:8 as a direct summary of the book. Even if Paul attains the status of a surrogate who fulfills the apostles' commission, his journey to Rome forms no part of it, because Paul himself envisions his mission as complete before his final visit to Jerusalem. In his address to the Ephesian elders at Miletus, Paul's retrospective summary betrays the perspective that his work is finished.[13] The Miletus speech brings Paul's mission to a close. Luke recounts nothing more of Paul's place in breaking ground for the extension of the gospel. After Paul's final journey to Jerusalem, the last quarter of Acts focuses on Paul's arrest and trials and, apart from some of the Jews in Rome who believe, provides no information about the extension of Christianity. Granted, Paul preaches during his trials, but no one accepts his gospel.

In fact, if we ask how the gospel arrives in Rome, we discover a surprising silence in Acts. Luke omits that chapter of the story. When Paul reaches his destination in Rome, it is clear that the gospel has preceded him. In actuality, therefore, Luke holds little interest in how the gospel as such extends to Rome.

Furthermore, the relatively inconspicuous place of Rome in the geography of Acts prohibits it from symbolizing the end of the earth. Rome does not come into view until Acts 19:21. Here the reader anticipates Rome as Paul's ultimate destination, but Rome creates little narrative tension. Jerusalem continues to dominate the story line. Paul presses urgently to go to Jerusalem. He curtails his contact with the Ephesian congregation in order to be in Jerusalem on the day of Pentecost (20:16). An ominous cloud arises. Prophetic predictions of doom haunt Paul's journey to Jerusalem. Paul receives testimony of the Holy Spirit that imprisonment and affliction await him in Jerusalem (20:22). Disciples in Tyre warn Paul through the Spirit not to go to Jerusalem (21:4). In Caesarea, Agabus the prophet mimes Paul's future arrest in Jerusalem (21:11). Hence, in spite of the notice of the journey to Rome in 19:21, the drama focuses on Jerusalem.

Rome does not surface again until after Paul's arrest in Jerusalem. The Lord appears to Paul at night in order to assure him that he will indeed arrive at Rome (Acts 23:11). A similar angelic message predicts that Paul will stand before Caesar (27:24). In the

---

[13] Dibelius, *Studies*, 155.

line of the narrative these notices give impetus to the journey to Rome, but create little dramatic tension. Rather, they serve to show that Paul's movement is divinely orchestrated. After announcing his intention to go to Rome, Paul actually strives to go exclusively to Jerusalem. The journey to Rome requires no resolve on the part of Paul. Indeed, he only seeks to avoid the plot of the Jews against his life, and so he appeals to Caesar. Even at that point the narrative focus falls on the journey itself rather than the destination. After the drama of an arduous voyage, shipwreck, and viper bite, the arrival in Rome is anticlimactic.

Luke actually discloses his view of Rome in the catalogue of the nations in Acts 2:9–11. Rome is neither the head nor the foot of the list, as a symbol of the end of the earth should be, but one among many. Luke would hardly have given a list in which Rome appears inconspicuously as third from the last had he envisioned Rome as a symbol of the utmost extension of the gospel. M. D. Goulder illustrates how severely the position of Rome in this list conflicts with the Jerusalem-to-Rome view of the plan of Acts by emending the text, without any manuscript evidence, to make Rome the climax.[14] The naming of the nations indicates that for Luke the end of the earth extends far beyond Rome. Consequently, Paul's arrival in the imperial capital cannot be the fulfillment of 1:8.

Although Acts begins in Jerusalem and ends in Rome, it is inaccurate to conclude that Jerusalem falls out in favor of Rome. The narrative in Acts actually reciprocates between Jerusalem and the extended mission. When Philip evangelizes the Samaritans, Peter and John come from Jerusalem to authenticate his mission, and then they return to Jerusalem (Acts 8:25). Paul the persecutor obtains credentials from Jewish authorities in Jerusalem and pursues Christians in Damascus. Later when Paul the Christian preacher escapes from Damascus, he returns to join the disciples in Jerusalem (9:26–29). After Peter preaches to Cornelius, he does not return to Joppa but goes to Jerusalem (11:2). The congregation at Antioch, founded by those who were scattered because of persecution in Jerusalem, sends Barnabas and Paul to Jerusalem with relief during famine (11:27–30). Herod's oppression drives Peter from Jerusalem (v 17), but he returns for the Jerusalem Council (15:6–7). Paul and Barnabas leave Antioch for a mission into Asia Minor (13:3), then they return to Jerusalem for the Council (15:2, 4). At the end of his mission, Paul returns to Jerusalem (21:15). Even when Paul is in Rome, his memory reverts

---

[14] M. Goulder, *Type and History in Acts* (London: SPCK, 1964) 152–53.

to Jerusalem to reiterate his fate there (28:17). Hence, Acts does not delineate a movement away from Jerusalem, but a constant return to Jerusalem. In the geography of Acts emphasis repeatedly falls on Jerusalem from beginning to end.

Luke Johnson has described a prophecy/fulfillment pattern in Acts whereby the development of the story fulfills previous predictions. He avows that Acts 1:8 is a key prophetic statement and that the geographical schema of Acts fulfills it.[15] As important as Johnson's contribution is for understanding Acts, it needs to be refined.

Literarily, the prediction device builds narrative tension and sanctions what follows when the prediction is fulfilled. For example, in Acts 1:4–5, Jesus promises the baptism of the Holy Spirit. The prediction creates a two-fold potential of success or failure[16] and of sanction or disconfirmation. Connected with the promise is a command for the apostles to remain in Jerusalem. They comply, and they devote themselves to prayer. But the author then diverts the reader from the promise. Before this fulfillment, yet another fulfillment takes place—fulfillment of Scripture. Judas has to die, and another has to be chosen to take his place. With this development, Jesus' promise of baptism with the Holy Spirit has fallen into the background. When Luke mentions Pentecost in 2:1, a first time reader may have heightened expectations but has no reason to anticipate the fulfillment of 1:5. Luke overtly builds the tension— "... suddenly a sound came from heaven like a rush of a mighty wind" (2:2). When Luke refers to πνοὴ βιαία there is a word play on πνεῦμα ἄγιον. Luke is beginning to play the theme, but the listener cannot yet distinguish it. Not until the earliest Christians are filled with the Holy Spirit does the reader experience a rush of insight. The reader now recalls the promise of 1:5, which for the sake of the drama has been postponed, a common literary device.

Simultaneously, Jesus' prediction sanctions the events of Pentecost when they take place in fulfillment of his words. The function of ratifying the behavior of those who receive the Spirit is clear on the surface level of the narration. That is, some of the

---

[15] L. Johnson, *The Literary Function of Possessions in Luke-Acts* (Missoula: Scholars, 1977) 16–17.

[16] C. Bremond ("Morphology of the French Folktale," *Semiotica* 2 [1970] 248–76) proposes, on the basis of his analysis of French fairy tales, that narrative proceeds by continuous cycles of potential followed by success or failure. When the narrative stands at a satisfactory state, the author must build up a state of tension again in order to continue the narrative.

diaspora Jews dismiss the display as intoxication (Acts 2:13).[17] The occasion for Peter's speech is then the defense of the unusual behavior. He shows first that the prophet Joel predicted these very events (vv 16–21). Second, he claims that the strange occurrences of Pentecost flow from Jesus, who is himself attested by being raised by God. Peter asserts the sanction from Jesus by explicitly referring to the promise of the Holy Spirit (v 33). The verbal parallels of the terms ἐπαγγελία τοῦ πατρός in both 1:4 and 2:33 and of (τὸ) πνεῦμα (τὸ) ἅγιον unmistakably tie the promise referred to in 2:33 to the one in 1:4–5. Clearly, the prediction with its fulfillment vindicates the peculiar behavior of Pentecost.

With the fulfillment of Jesus' promise at Pentecost, the reader relaxes, and the suspense of its potential success or failure appears to be over. The promise/fulfillment theme falls into the background again, but it has, nevertheless, made its impression upon the reader. Therefore, when the theme emerges quickly and faintly in Acts 8:15–17, the reader understands that receiving the Holy Spirit sanctions Samaritan believers, although the text makes no mention of authenication explicitly. The same sort of implicit sanction affirms Paul's conversion and God's commission for him in 9:15–17 when he is baptized and filled with the Holy Spirit.

The case is quite different with the conversion of Cornelius. This time not only does the narrator tell the reader that the Holy Spirit fell upon these gentiles, but he also reiterates it by describing the amazement of Jewish believers who are accompanying Peter (Acts 10:45). Luke emphasizes it a third time by having Peter ask, "Can any one forbid water for baptizing these people who have received the Holy Spirit just as we have?" (v 47). Once again the legitimating force of this fulfillment of Jesus' promise becomes explicit. One ingredient of the amazement of the Jewish believers is a reluctance to accept gentile believers. Peter's question expresses the hesitation by raising the issue of forbidding baptism.

When Peter returns to Jerusalem, the opposition becomes blatant. The circumcision party objects to Peter's social intercourse with gentiles (Acts 11:2–3). Peter defends his behavior by recalling the promise of Jesus in 1:4–5 and the events of Pentecost (11:15–16). Once again the prediction of Jesus sanctions the gentiles as well as the Jews who have broken Jewish taboo in order

---

[17] L. Panier ("Comprenez vous pourquoi vous comprenez! Actes 1,15–2:47," *Semiotique et Bible* 23 [1981] 24) perceives that Pentecost and the story of Jesus reciprocally authenticate each other. G. Kennedy (*New Testament Interpretation through Rhetorical Criticism* [Chapel Hill: University of North Carolina Press, 1984] 117) supports the function of Peter's speech as exoneration by classifying it rhetorically as judicial.

to evangelize them. As is well known, 15:8 makes the same appeal for the legitimacy of gentile believers apart from circumcision and the law of Moses. As a literary device, prophetic prediction builds tension and provides sanction when it finds fulfillment.

Johnson's delineation of the prophecy/fulfillment device requires yet another emendation. Acts not only fulfills prophetic statements but also revises them and even leaves them unfulfilled. A case in point is Paul's prediction that continuation of the voyage from Crete to Rome would result in damage and loss of life (ὕβρις καὶ ζημία τῶν ψυχῶν, Acts 27:10). There is a clear example of revision here because Paul soon alters the prediction and claims that there will be no loss of life (ἀποβολὴ ψυχῆς, 27:22). But this case also offers a clear example of a prophetic statement going unfulfilled. In the revised prediction of v 24, Paul announces an angelic message that he must stand before Caesar. But Acts closes with that prediction unfulfilled.

As in the case of Jesus' promise, Paul's predictions also create the two-fold potential of success or failure and of sanction or disconfirmation. As Luke describes the sea voyage, tension begins to build when he notes that the winds are contrary (Acts 27:4), the arrival at Cnidus is "with difficulty" (v 7), and advancement is "with difficulty" (v 8). By v 9 the situation has become dangerous. It is at that point that Paul makes his first prediction of injury and loss of life (v 10). The tension mounts all the more when the centurion heeds the captain and the owner of the ship and the advice of the majority. They put out to sea again, and their pleasant embarkment soon turns into a violent storm.

At that point Luke breaks away from the narrative tension and allows Paul to assert the legitimacy of his prediction (Acts 27:21). But the interlude provides opportunity for a revision of and an addition to the prediction. There will be no loss of life, and Paul must stand before Caesar (vv 22, 24). The narrative tension now resumes with the renewed potential of success or failure, sanction or disconfirmation. Quickly, this stage of the voyage moves toward a climax. In shallow water, the sailors fear shipwreck and intend to set out in a lifeboat. But this time they heed Paul's advice and stay with the ship (vv 28–32). There is another interlude from the narrative tension, and, in a setting with eucharistic overtones, Paul renews his prediction of the safety of the lives of all aboard (v 34). Then, an attempt to beach the boat fails, and this stage of the voyage comes crashing to a conclusion (v 41). At this point there is a new threat, although Luke does not milk much narrative tension out of it. The soldiers intend to kill the prisoners, but for Paul's sake the centurion saves them all.

This example provides ample illustration of Luke's use of prophetic prediction to create narrative tension and to sanction his protagonist. Luke legitimates Paul as one who is under the providence of God and who has access to divine foreknowledge. The legitimation works all the more when Paul revises his prediction and all 276 persons survive in spite of the enormous dangers. But one prediction goes unfulfilled. Paul does not stand before Caesar. The debate over the ending of Acts testifies clearly to the narrative tension that the prediction nevertheless creates.

Yet another case of unfulfilled prophecy comes at the very beginning of Acts. At the ascension of Jesus, two men in white robes predict, "This Jesus, who was taken up from you into heaven, will come in the same way as you saw him go into heaven" (Acts 1:11). Not only does this prediction go unfulfilled, but Luke has even prepared ahead of time for its failure to find fulfillment. When the disciples ask about the restoration of the kingdom, Jesus responds, "It is not for you to know times or seasons which the Father has fixed by his own authority" (v 7). And so with the promise in 1:11, the parousia is laid aside in Acts.

In light of these revisions of Johnson's theory of a prophecy/fulfillment device, it is no longer necessary to demand the ultimate fulfillment of Acts 1:8 in Acts itself. Similarly, it is no longer necessary to read the geographical schema as the development of the prediction of Acts 1:8.

In brief, Acts simply does not provide the story of the geographical spread of the gospel *per se*.[18] Luke himself is aware of diverse modes of the spread of God's salvation to both Jews and gentiles. He knows of Philip's mission to Samaritans, to the Ethiopian eunuch, and to Phoenicia. He is aware of the evangelization of Phoenicia, Cyprus, Antioch, and Damascus by those who were scattered from Jerusalem by persecution. He summarizes the mission of Barnabas and Mark after the former separates from Paul. He mentions the work of Apollos at Ephesus and Corinth. Luke alludes to Christians in Rome who greet Paul on his arrival there. But the story of the extension of Christianity does not occupy center stage for Luke. Rather, he places Paul in the limelight.

The final chapters of Acts do not bring the gospel to Rome but Paul. He arrives in Rome under arrest to defend himself ostensibly before Caesar; in actuality he defends himself before the Jews of Rome. From the time of the Miletus address, Paul takes advantage

---

[18] This point alone tells against a primary theme of proclamation and the spread of the gospel in Luke-Acts. Cf. P. Schubert, "The Place of the Areopagus Speech in the Composition of Acts," *Transitions in Biblical Scholarship* (ed. J. Rylaarsdam; Chicago: University of Chicago Press, 1968) 237.

of six occasions to give his apology. Dibelius and Haenchen both recognize that Paul's self-justification is the leitmotif of the last quarter of Acts, but they insist that Paul is a cipher for Christianity and that his speeches defend the general mission to the gentiles.[19] Against this view Jacob Jervell has demonstrated convincingly that Paul's defense speeches are biographical and prevent him from being confused with a symbol for Christianity.[20] Paul's own story rather than the universal extension of the gospel dominates the structure of the last half of Acts.

Nevertheless, Paul's arrival in Rome completes the development of two interrelated literary themes. One is that Paul continues his testimony to all. The second is that Paul foresees his destiny and arrives at that destiny by divine providence.

Rome first surfaces as Paul's ultimate destination in Acts 19:21. As a part of the divine guidance in his career, Paul determines that he must leave Ephesus, go through Macedonia and Achaia, and return to Jerusalem. He attaches to that decision a prophetic prediction that he must also see Rome. Paul himself appears to remain in the dark about the meaning of a journey to Rome until further divine revelation informs him that he must bear witness in Rome (23:11). 23:11 shows that Paul's testimony in Rome is to a certain extent a counterpart to his testimony in Jerusalem. Acts exhibits no concern with how the gospel arrives at Rome but considerable interest in showing the reader that Paul preaches in Rome. Significantly, as a counterpart to the testimony in Jerusalem, Paul addresses Jewish leaders in Rome. At the very end of the account the audience expands to include gentiles. Therefore, on the one hand, Paul's arrival in Rome completes his role as God's chosen instrument to testify before gentiles and kings and the people of Israel (9:15).

On the other hand, God's providential care is readily discernible in Paul's safe arrival in Rome. From a time shortly after his call, Paul's life has been under threat (Acts 9:23, 29). At Lystra Jewish opponents stone Paul and leave him for dead, whereupon Paul experiences a remarkable recovery (14:19–20). On other occasions he repeatedly suffers threats and violence from opponents (16:19–24; 17:5–8, 13; 18:12–17; 19:23–41; 20:3; 21:27–36;

[19] Dibelius, *Studies,* 149, 160; Haenchen, *Acts,* 328, 624, cf. n. 3, 722.

[20] J. Jervell, *Luke and the People of God* (Minneapolis: Augsburg, 1972) 154–55. P. Schubert ("The Final Cycle of Speeches in the Book of Acts," *JBL* 87 [1968] 4) calls attention to the "I" style of the speeches in Acts 21–28. The relationship between form and meaning makes this style a strong support for the character of these speeches as apologies for Paul as an individual.

22:22; 23:10, 12–22; 25:3). But in face of the assaults and intentions to harm Paul, God continually delivers him.

In the course of Paul's experiences of hostility, he receives assurances of God's providential care. In the first place, a divine prediction anticipates Paul's suffering itself. A part of his commission is to suffer for the sake of the name of the Lord (Acts 9:16). Suffering comes to Paul, therefore, as a part of his faithfulness to God.

But in addition, divine revelations pledge God's providential care. In a flashback Paul informs us of divine providence in his previous trials. In the third account of his call, Paul relates the divine promise of deliverance from the persecution that is to accompany his mission (26:16–17). In Corinth Paul has a night vision in which the Lord promises: "Do not be afraid, but speak and do not be silent; for I am with you, and no one shall attack you to harm you; for I have many people in this city" (18:9–10). Under the canopy of divine protection, Paul then foresees that he must go to Rome (19:21). In another night vision the Lord assures Paul: "Take courage, for as you have testified about me at Jerusalem, so you must (δεῖ) bear witness also at Rome" (23:11). Dramatic tension builds as to whether or not the prediction will be fulfilled when Paul continues to face plots against his life (vv 12–15, 25:3) and judicial accusations (24:1–9, 25:7). When Festus threatens to cooperate with a plot of the chief priests and the leaders of the Jews against Paul's life, he appeals to Caesar (25:11).

Storm and shipwreck threaten Paul on his journey to Rome. But in yet another night vision an angel of God reassures Paul: "Do not be afraid, Paul; you must (δεῖ) stand before Caesar. . . ." Paul adds to that his conviction: "I have faith in God that it will be exactly as I have been told" (27:24–25). And so, Paul's arrival in Rome safe and sound demonstrates dramatically that he stands under God's providential care.[21]

Paul in the Structure of Acts

Structurally, Acts falls into two parts. In the first 12 chaps. Peter dominates the story line and events center on Jerusalem. From 13:1 on Acts focuses on Paul and his mission in the diaspora. But clearly this twofold division is rough. Stephen, Philip, and Paul are also primary characters in chaps. 6–9. Philip and Peter move beyond Jerusalem to Samaria, Judea, and Phoenicia in chaps. 8–10. Furthermore, the Jerusalem Council, with Peter and James

---

[21] On the motif of God's providential care of Paul see D. Adams, "Suffering of Paul."

in charge, breaks into the story of Paul. Finally, in spite of Paul's mission beyond Judaism, Jerusalem refuses to fall out of the picture.

Although the outline of Acts continues to attract considerable debate, the majority of contemporary scholars prefers a threefold division following the geographical notice in Acts 1:8. A consensus that the Jerusalem section comes to an end with the martyrdom of Stephen is easily reached, but discussion rages as to the boundaries of the second and third stages. Does the mission to the ends of the earth begin before the Jerusalem Council (13:1) or after (15:36)?[22] The prominence of the Jerusalem Council has led many scholars to argue for a primary break at 15:36. According to a rather standard argument, Acts 15 is the watershed of Acts because here the apostles recognize and regulate gentile Christianity.[23]

Two major clues indicate a twofold division: (1) The function of the report of the Jerusalem Council in the structure of Acts, (2) the architectonic features of the structure.

(1) As prominent as the Jerusalem Council is, it does not hold intrinsic interest independently. Through Peter, anonymous witnesses in Antioch, and Paul and Barnabas the gospel has already reached gentiles. There is no necessity for the apostles and elders to recognize gentile Christianity, but for them to legitimate it to its opponents, namely, some men from Judea and some believers of the party of the Pharisees who advocate circumcision and observance of the law. Furthermore, as far as Luke is concerned, the Council impinges only on those gentile Christians within Paul's

---

[22] W. Kümmel (*Introduction to the New Testament* [Nashville: Abingdon, 1965] 107–108) sees a major break at Acts 15:36, but also develops a five part division geographically. R. Pesch (*Die Vision des Stephanus: Apg 7.55–56 im Rahmen der Apostelgeschichte* [Stuttgart: Katholisches Bibelwerk, 1966] 40) argues for a threefold structure with the major division at Acts 13:1, Acts 8:4–12:25 being a transition of the gospel to gentiles. G. Schneider (*Die Apostelgeschichte* [Freiburg: Herder, 1980] 1.66–68) also divides Acts into three parts, but sees the major break at Acts 15:36. P. Rolland ("L'organisation du Livre des Actes et de l'ensemble de l'oeuvre de Luc," *Bib* 65 [1984] 81–86) supports a threefold division with the major break at 13.1. Cf. E. Nellessen, *Zeugnis für Jesus und das Wort: Exegetische Untersuchungen zum lukanischen Zeugnisbegriff* (Köln: Haustein, 1976) 46–47. J. Dupont ("La question du plan des Actes des Apôtres à la lumière d'un texte de Lucien Samosate," *NovT* 21 [1979] 220–31) revises his fivefold division (Jerusalem Bible) with breaks at both Acts 13:1 and 15:36 in favor of a fourfold division in which he views Acts 15:36–16:5 as a transition.
[23] Weiss, *Über der Absicht*, 25–27; Menoud, "Le plan des Actes," 47. C. Torrey (*The Composition and Date of Acts* [Cambridge: Harvard University Press, 1916]) supports a major division at Acts 15:35 on the basis of a hypothetical Aramaic source for Acts 1:1–15:35. Foakes Jackson and Lake (*Beginnings*, 2.122) allow for a division at either chap. 12 or 15.

sphere. The decree addresses gentiles in Antioch, Syria, and Cilicia only, although Paul and Silas also deliver it to some of the congregations in Asia Minor. And so Dibelius certainly provides the decisive clue that the break occurs between Acts 12:25 and 13:1: Luke reports the Jerusalem Council because of its bearing on Paul's mission.[24]

(2) The architectonic features of Acts confirm that Luke himself devised such a twofold division. Chaps. 1–12 and 13–28 share a loose parallel of both *content* and *sequence*,[25] including parallelism between Peter and Paul. For example, Paul's first miracle of healing a cripple in Lystra (Acts 14:8) corresponds to Peter's healing of a cripple at the temple gate (3:2). The descriptions of the two lame men form a precise literary correspondence: χωλὸς ἐκ κοιλίας μητρὸς αὐτοῦ. Paul's exorcisms find their analogue in Peter's (5:16; 8:6, 7; 16:18; 19:11; 28:9). Paul's confrontation with Elymas (13:6–11) parallels Peter's encounter with Simon Magus (8:14–24), *et cetera*.[26]

On the other hand, the two sections are closely interrelated. Two principal lines of the narrative tie the major divisions together. One is the conversion of Cornelius at the hands of Peter; the other is the call of Paul on the road near Damascus. Two accounts of the conversion of Cornelius appear in the first section, namely, the primary narration and Peter's repetition of it before the circumcision party (Acts 10–11). Peter and James make additional references to the Cornelius incident at the Jerusalem Council (15:7–11, 14) tying the first section to the second.

Luke recounts Paul's call with a similar repetitive architectonic device. The narrator describes the initial account of Paul's call in the first section (Acts 9:1–19). But then Paul himself twice relates his call in the second section (22:1–21, 26:2–23), linking the two divisions together.

Other subsidiary complexities of the plot reach from the second section deep into the first. Luke introduces Paul into the narrative suddenly and connects him with Stephen's martyrdom in Acts 7:58.[27] Luke's interest in associating Paul with Stephen

[24] Dibelius, *Studies*, 193.
[25] C. Talbert, *Literary Patterns, Theological Themes, and the Genre of Luke-Acts* (Missoula: Scholars, 1974) 23–24. In addition to parallels in both content and sequence, Talbert lists other parallels in content and language that do not follow the same sequence.
[26] These parallels were recognized as early as M. Schneckenburger, *Apostelgeschichte: Zugleich eine Ergänzung der neueren Commentare* (Bern: Fischer, 1841) 52–58. Schubert ("Final Cycle," 3–4) shows that the speeches in chaps. 1–20 establish a balance between Peter and Paul.
[27] Paul is not an original part of the Stephen tradition. See C. Burchard, *Der*

cannot be doubted when Paul recalls, in a speech composed by Luke, his approval of Stephen's death in 22:20. Luke does not allow the Stephen incident to stand on its own as an intrinsically interesting event. Rather, he makes it preparatory for his story of Paul.

Stephen's martyrdom marks the outbreak of persecution in Jerusalem. The persecution in turn scatters believers, some of whom speak to gentiles in Antioch (Acts 11:20).[28] It appears that subtle irony is at work. Paul's persecution opens the mission to gentiles for which Paul himself will ultimately be persecuted. But Luke cuts the irony short. He does not attribute to Paul the responsibility for initiating the mission to gentiles. Rather he reports the conversion of Cornelius by Peter before relating that those who were scattered turned to gentiles.[29]

The sudden introduction of Paul at Stephen's death also links him closely with Philip.[30] When Luke mentions that Paul is persecuting the church in Acts 8:3, he relates that those who were scattered went about preaching (v 4). Then Luke moves to Philip's Samaritan mission in particular. Paul thus becomes the transition between two events which move toward the opening of the mission beyond Jerusalem, that is, between Stephen's death and Philip's mission. The reference to Paul's contact with the Samaritans in a Lucan summary in 15:3 indicates that the link between Paul and Philip in 8:3–5 is more than coincidental.

The development of Paul's story line has roots that reach further back into the first half of Acts in the person of Barnabas. Because Barnabas is only one of many who sell possessions and contribute to the community, his sudden appearance seems to be insufficiently motivated. Why is he singled out? Luke devotes this attention to Barnabas to place him in full harmony with the apostles and thus to authenticate him in preparation for his role in the story of Paul.[31] Later the church in Jerusalem sends Barnabas to Antioch and sanctions Antioch's mission to gentiles. Hence,

---

dreizehnte Zeuge: Traditions- und kompositionsgeschichtliche Untersuchungen zu Lukas' Darstellung der Frühzeit des Paulus (Göttingen: Vandenhoeck & Ruprecht, 1970) 26–28, and K. Löning, *Die Saulustradition in der Apostelgeschichte* (Münster: Aschendorf, 1973) 21.

[28] E. Richard, *Acts 6:1–8:4: The Author's Method of Composition* (Missoula: Scholars, 1978) 13–14, 312, 352. My argument above should serve as a corrective to Richard's contention that Stephen's martyrdom marks the departure from Jerusalem toward Rome.

[29] See Dibelius, *Studies*, 161–62.

[30] Ibid., 193; Löning, *Saulustradition*, 20–21; Richard, *Acts 6:1–8:4*, 312.

[31] Haenchen, *Acts*, 99–100; Johnson, *Literary Function*, 203–204.

when Paul joins Barnabas at Antioch, Jerusalem has already given tacit approval. Barnabas plays no genuinely independent role in Acts. None of the accounts about Barnabas hold inherent interest. His importance hinges on his relationship to Paul. Thus, Luke gives his Pauline plot foundations in the introduction of Barnabas.

There is even an indirect but clearly perceptible connection between Paul's story line and Pentecost. Peter's role at the Jerusalem Council provides the linkage through the Cornelius incident. Luke views the occasion of the Jerusalem Council as a Pauline problem, that is, as a debate between Judean Judaizers and Paul and Barnabas. Luke betrays his perspective that the Pauline gentile problem occasions the Jerusalem Council by having Paul and Barnabas, along with Jerusalem envoys, deliver the decree of the Council (Acts 15:22, 25–26). Luke even has Paul and Silas introduce the decree to Lycaonia when it is addressed to Antioch, Syria, and Cilicia (v 23, 16:4).[32]

The Jerusalem Council resolves the problem of gentile Christianity by referring to the conversion of Cornelius. Both Peter and James allude to events recorded in Acts 10 and repeated in Acts 11. James claims that Peter has explained how God first visited the gentiles (15:14). In reality Peter only reminded the Council of what they already knew. James, then, is actually alluding to Peter's account in 11:5–17.[33] That is, Luke fashions a well-known flashback by which he refers the reader to Peter's earlier account of the conversion of Cornelius.

But Peter's account in Acts 11:5–17 in turn links the conversion of Cornelius with Pentecost and indeed with the promise of the risen Jesus in 1:4–5. Peter tells the Jerusalem circumcision party that the Holy Spirit fell on Cornelius and his household ". . . just as on us in the beginning" (11:15). Hence, Luke jumps back to his account of Pentecost in Acts 2. But then Peter goes on to recall Jesus' promise of baptism with the Holy Spirit from 1:4–5 (11:16). That is, Peter's account of the conversion of Cornelius takes the reader all the way back to the beginning of Acts.

In fact, Luke betrays his intention to link Cornelius with Pentecost and with the promise of Jesus in Acts 1:4–5 from the very beginning of the Cornelius episode. In the angelic vision God informs Cornelius that his prayers and alms have won special attention before God (10:4). For this reason, Cornelius is to send men to summon Peter (v 5). Both God's favor and the imperative to

---

[32] Dibelius, *Studies*, 99.
[33] Ibid., 96–97.

bring Peter anticipate that Cornelius will receive something.[34] Peter informs the reader what that something is in 10:47: ". . . these . . . have received the Holy Spirit just as we have." We can justly deduce, from the implied promise that Cornelius will receive something, that Luke has Pentecost and 1:4–5 in mind the moment he brings Cornelius on the scene.

Acts develops an intricate plot in which Peter's role in the conversion of Cornelius officially resolves the Pauline gentile problem. In turn, the conversion of Cornelius rests on Pentecost and the promise of Jesus in Acts 1:4–5. In addition, the baptism of the twelve Ephesians reflects Luke's desire to link Paul to this same promise of Jesus and to Pentecost. The themes of both incidents reappear when Paul baptizes the Ephesian converts of Apollos who know only John's baptism. Paul lays his hands on them, and the Holy Spirit comes upon them as at Pentecost (19:1–7).

And so Luke does not merely find Paul suddenly at the scene of the stoning of Stephen, but anticipates and prepares for him from the beginning of his second volume. The story of Paul not only dominates the second half of Acts but penetrates the first half and establishes its footing in the stories of Cornelius, Stephen, and Barnabas, all the way back to the risen Jesus before his ascension.

Although it has been necessary first to grind an ax against those who blow the geographical outline of Acts 1:8 out of proportion, the more substantive issue is the relationship of Paul to the commission in 1:4–8. This in turn relates back to Luke 24:47–49. The commissions in 24:47 climax the Easter experience that moves first from unbelief and disillusion (vv 11, 21) to joy (vv 41, 52) by way of enlightenment that comes when the risen Jesus discloses himself in interpreting the Scripture and in the breaking of bread (vv 27, 31–32, 43–46).[35] Not only does Luke vindicate the Christ as the suffering one by his proof from prophecy,[36] but he also grounds the commission in Scripture: "Thus it is written, . . . that repentance and forgiveness of sins should be preached to all nations" (vv 46–47). Whereas the risen Jesus explicitly charges the apostles in Acts 1:4–8, here he states the commission in terms of a general fulfillment of Scripture without definite agents. This

[34] For this I am indebted to a suggestion by M. Plunkett, "Ethno-centricity and Salvation History in the Cornelius Episode (Acts 10:1–11:18)," SBLSP (ed. K. Richards; Atlanta: Scholars, 1985) 471.

[35] J. Wanke, *Die Emmäuserzählung: Eine redaktionsgeschichtliche Untersuchung zu Lk 24, 13–35* (Leipzig: St. Benno, 1973) 35.

[36] P. Schubert, "The Structure and Significance of Luke 24," *Neutestamentliche Studien für Rudolf Bultmann* (ed. W. Eltester; Berlin: Töpelmann, 1957) 173, 176.

injunction, therefore, is relevant and applicable to the Christian movement as a whole. The comprehensive nature of the charge thus established, the risen Jesus then commissions the company of the eleven as a particular case of the comprehensive mandate, in order that they might play the role of crucial witnesses (Luke 24:48).

Acts clarifies the role of the apostles as crucial witnesses. They have a double warrant for their role. First, their role depends on receiving the power of the Holy Spirit so that their testimony lies dormant within the small cell of believers until Pentecost. For this they have to remain in a waiting posture (Luke 24:49, Acts 1:4). Second, they are chosen witnesses of what Jesus did and taught, of his passion, of his resurrection appearances, and of his ascension (Acts 1:1–3). Merely being a witness of these events is inadequate to qualify for the role, as the election of Matthias over Joseph Barsabbas shows (vv 23–26). Matthias like the eleven qualifies because he is chosen.[37] 10:41 shows that the authenticity of the apostolic witness is a Lucan theme. Luke specifies that God did not make the risen Jesus manifest to all the people, but only to those who were chosen by God. The apostles are essentially eyewitnesses to Jesus' works, teachings, death, and resurrection who guarantee the authenticity and continuity of the Christian proclamation. To them Luke also traces his own work (Luke 1:2).[38]

Paul is a second generation witness who like Luke derives the authenticity of his proclamation from "those who from the beginning were eyewitnesses and ministers of the word" (Luke 1:2). Like the company of the eleven, he plays a crucial role as a specific example of the comprehensive commission in 24:47. Like the apostles, he qualifies by virtue of divine choice. All three accounts of Paul's call emphasize his election as a witness. In Acts 9:15 the Lord reveals to Ananias that Paul is God's chosen instrument. 22:14 reports the words of Ananias to Paul that God has appointed him in order that he might be a witness. In 26:16 Ananias falls out of the picture, and Paul relates an audition from the risen Jesus who appoints him to bear witness. In addition, like the apostles Paul qualifies by virtue of receiving the power of the Holy Spirit (9:17).

In brief, according to Luke the risen Jesus grounds a comprehensive commission in Scripture and then makes the apostles particular witnesses who guarantee the authenticity and continuity of the proclamation. Paul does not qualify as an apostolic witness since he is not an eyewitness. But he does come under the umbrella of the comprehensive commission in Luke 24, and he stands in a derivative relationship to the commission to the apostles in Acts 1. In this way, although Paul does not qualify as an apostle, he joins with them in the comprehensive mission endorsed by the risen Jesus and grounded in Scripture.

Acts 1:8 and Paul's Mission to Gentiles

Luke's concern with Paul spans his second volume and constitutes the major interest of the last half of Acts. He lays aside the stories of Peter, Philip, Barnabas, and Apollos and turns his attention single-mindedly to Paul. At the climax of the story, Paul is under arrest, repeatedly defending himself.

Paul's apologies are stereotyped and curiously do not adequately respond to accusations in their settings. For example, how does Paul's account of his education under Gamaliel and of his conversion near Damascus (Acts 22:3–16) answer the charge that he brought gentiles into the temple (21:28–29)? Or how does Paul's appeal that he went to the temple as a legitimate worshiper (24:10–21) respond to the charge of Tertullus that he instigates uprisings among all the Jews of the whole world (24:5)? But the discrepancy between the defenses and their settings highlights all the more Luke's purposes. The apologies may not answer the charges of their immediate settings, but Luke does signal the complaints to which they do respond.

James expresses the protest of Jewish Christians that Paul teaches apostasy from Judaism (Acts 21:21). That coincides with the accusation of Jews from Asia: "This is the man who is teaching everyone everywhere against the people and the law and [the temple]" (21:28). The context combines this allegation that Paul is anti-Jewish with opposition to Paul's mission to gentiles. The aroused crowd in Jerusalem listens to Paul until he claims that the Lord sent him to the gentiles (22:21–22). Paul recounts this same event before Agrippa in 26:19–23 and, given the context, indicates that Jews oppose his proclamation to gentiles.[39]

In short, Luke designs a portrait that legitimates Paul before readers who regard him with suspicion.[40] Specifically, Luke explains how Paul executes God's plan without forsaking Judaism. When Paul turns to gentiles, he does not abandon Judaism but affirms and fulfills it.

---

[39] Weiss, *Über der Absicht*, 55; Jervell, *Luke*, 163–66.

[40] Schubert ("Final Cycle," 14) claims that Ananias in Acts 9:10–18 expresses the suspicions of non-Pauline Christians. This proves to be erroneous since Ananias voices fear of Paul as a pesecutor only.

In retrospect, Luke bathes Paul's entire story in the light of Paul's climactic apologies. As a consequence, Luke sets Paul free from responsibility for the course of his ministry. Divine intervention directs Paul's destiny, and, ironically, Jewish opposition to Paul merely serves God's purposes of directing Paul into a ministry to gentiles. Luke's readers who look askance at Paul's mission to gentiles should blame only God and Paul's recalcitrant opponents. Meanwhile, Paul stands as a legitimate heir to the hope of the patriarchs, Moses, and the prophets (Acts 26:6, 22).

The motif of legitimation permeates the Lucan presentation of Paul from beginning to end. At the conversion of Paul in Acts 9, Luke heaps up signs of God's intervention:[41] the light, the voice, the temporary blindness, the interrelated visions of Ananias and Paul, and the immediate cure of the blindness. At the end of Acts, Luke's story closes with Paul's appeal for the legitimacy of his relation to Jews as well as to gentiles (28:17–29).

In fact, Luke's emphasis on Paul's relation to both Jews and gentiles is a key factor to which scholars have paid scant attention. *Luke uses Paul's relation to Jews to legitimate his relation to gentiles.* Luke actually knows nothing of an independent gentile mission or of a Pauline gentile mission as such. The only extension of God's salvation he describes is a mission to both Jews and gentiles. Paul is no missionary to the gentiles. Rather, he pursues a mission to the Jewish diaspora that includes gentiles. Luke thus portrays Paul's relation to gentiles as a thoroughly Jewish commitment to the divine promises.

Conclusion

In view of the thematic development of Acts, Jesus' promise in Acts 1:8 functions as a part of Paul's legitimation. The risen Jesus predicts the baptism with the Holy Spirit and the witness to the end of the earth (1:4–8). When these events materialize, they not only confirm the promises of Jesus but also receive his sanction. Peter overtly defends the abnormal behavior on Pentecost, but Jesus' predictions in 1:4–5, 8 vindicate those same events. Peter legitimates the gentile believers in Cornelius' household by appealing to Jesus' promise of the Spirit, originally addressed to the apostles in 1:5, 8 (11:16–17). The baptism of the twelve Ephesians and the coming of the Spirit upon them also flash back to 1:5, 8. Luke employs prophetic prediction as a literary device to sanction its fulfillment. In this way, the words of the risen Jesus certify the

---

[41] See G. Lohfink, *The Conversion of St. Paul: Narrative and History in Acts* (Chicago: Franciscan Herald, 1976) 75–76.

events on Pentecost, the conversion of Jews in Jerusalem and Judea, the conversion of Samaritans, the conversion of Cornelius, the decision of the Jerusalem Council, and ultimately Paul's ministry to gentiles. Acts 1:8 spreads a canopy of legitimation over the entire book. But in case a reader were to miss Paul's relation to Luke 24:46–47 and to Acts 1:8, Luke makes the authorization specific for Paul with another divine prediction in close parallel. The risen Jesus declares to the company of the eleven in Luke 24:48: ὑμεῖς μάρτυρες τούτων. In Acts 1:8 the risen Jesus foretells: ἔσεσθε μάρτυρες. In the name of God Ananias makes the same kind of prediction for Paul: ἔση μάρτυς (22:15), and Paul himself cites his mandate from the risen Jesus that appoints him μάρτυς (26:16).

CHAPTER FOUR
LEGITIMATING TECHNIQUES IN ACTS

To complete the picture of Luke's legitimation of Paul, we must add to the device of prophetic prediction a host of other Hellenistic literary techniques. To place Luke-Acts within the stream of Hellenistic rhetorical art at all points obviously to literary characteristics that it shares in common with the genus. Any concept of Hellenistic literature is necessarily assembled out of a vast array of exemplars. Variables of time, place, social status, education, and religion provide for such diversity as to threaten any kind of unified vision of the phenomena. Nevertheless, for all the plurality, Hellenistic authors do occupy common ground. This chapter attempts to map some of that common ground with respect to legitimating devices. What techniques communicated authenticity? What methods could an author assume would verify the deeds and claims of protagonists?

By a broad definition of Hellenistic literature, this study ranges over evidence from inscriptions to papyri, from religious materials (pagan, Jewish, and Christian) to philosophical treatises. The time spectrum runs from as early as Plato to as late as the third century C.E. The sources run from anonymous commoners to educated aristocrats of renown. There is no effort to demonstrate direct literary borrowing or derivation of one literary product from another. Rather, the task is to categorize devices with such wide distribution as to assure their commonly accepted function.

If Luke legitimates Paul both by portraying him as faithful to the hopes of Israel and by outfitting him with evidence of authenticity in Hellenistic literary terms, then we possess clues that inform us about the type of Judaism toward which Luke accommodates Paul and about the environment in which Luke writes. The days are over when Hellenistic and Jewish cultures could be viewed as mutually exclusive. Even ardent opponents of Hellenization in Palestine, such as the early Maccabean rulers, accommodated subtly to Hellenism. In spite of attempts among Hellenistic Jews to maintain separate identity, they nevertheless acculturated and blended traits of Hellenism into their patterns of thinking and living.[1] Luke establishes strong continuity with Judaism, but that is not incompatible with the utilization of Hellenistic literary devices. In fact, this chapter suggests that Luke links Hellenistic legitimating devices with his defense of Paul as an authentic Jew. Whereas one dimension of Luke's thought depends heavily on the LXX and continuity with Judaism, Hellenistic storytelling comprises another prominent dimension.

Nevertheless, Luke's combination of literary devices from the larger culture with his defense of Paul as a genuine Jew raises the question of what kind of religion Luke envisions as authentic Judaism. For one thing, Luke's affinity with broader Hellenistic culture demonstrates that he cannot perceive of Judaism as culturally exclusivistic. Further, his candid advocacy of the admission of gentiles as such into the people of God indicates that Luke expects genuine Judaism to surmount ethnic isolationism. Beyond that chapters 6, 7, and 8 below show that Luke can differentiate among Jews. In particular Luke evaluates chief priests, Sadducees, and those who do not believe in the general resurrection as less than worthy of inclusion in Judaism. On the other hand, he holds Pharisees in rather high regard and appeals to their belief in the general resurrection as already embracing in principle the resurrection of Jesus. The kind of Judaism to which Luke ties Paul is that Judaism which is open to this specific case of resurrection, but also open to intimate relationships with gentiles, and discriminatingly open to the broader Hellenistic culture. Therefore, Luke's use of Hellenistic legitimating devices on behalf of Paul is both compatible with and a part of his defense of Paul as thoroughly Jewish. Paul emerges as thoroughly Jewish because as a cosmopolitan Jew he embodies the genuine hopes of Israel as Luke perceives them.

In rejoinder to claims that Luke rehabilitates Paul, a formidable segment of scholarship disputes the legitmation of Paul. One of

---

[1] M. Hengel, *Judaism and Hellenism: Studies in Their Encounter in Palestine during the Early Hellenistic Period* (Philadelphia: Fortress, 1974) esp. 1.58–106; idem, *Jews, Greeks, and Barbarians: Aspects of the Hellenization of Judaism in the pre-Christian period* (Philadelphia: Fortress, 1980). L. Feldman ("Hengel's *Judaism and Hellenism* in Retrospect," *JBL* 96 [1977] 371–82) takes Hengel to task on dating the inroads of Hellenism into Palestinian Judaism to a century prior to the Maccabean revolt. J. Goldstein ("Jewish Acceptance and Rejection of Hellenism," *Jewish and Christian Self-Definition: Volume Two, Aspects of Judaism in the Greco-Roman Period* [ed. E. P. Sanders; Philadelphia: Fortress, 1981] 64–87) argues on the one hand that Hengel overstates opposition to Hellenization in the period prior to the high priesthood of Jason, but on the other hand that Hellenistic immigration into Palestine was less than Hengel proposes.

the leading exponents of the latter view, Karl Löning, for example, contends that, rather than defending Paul, Luke simply allows him to speak as an established figure in the Christian community.[2] This chapter offers part of the evidence for a rebuttal. Luke's use of literary techniques of legitimation is a sign that he consciously composed his story to justify Paul.

Luke punctuates significant junctures in his narrative with prodigious events. Strange signs accompany the inauguration of the Christian mission on the day of Pentecost (Acts 2). Peter extends the mission to a gentile God-fearer because his own heavenly vision coincides with Cornelius's vision of an angel (Acts 10). Saul the persecutor stops devastating the saints and becomes a Christian missionary when a heavenly light and the voice of the risen Jesus confront him (Acts 9, 22, 26). In a larger context such signs provide divine sanction for the course of *Heilsgeschichte*. Legitimation is thus a key to the entire structure of Acts. But in a more particular way portentous signs also explain Paul's motivations and legitimate his activities.

The conspicuous correspondence between Acts and a wide range of literature from antiquity makes it certain that Luke accommodates to Hellenistic literary devices and adapts them for his purposes.[3] Among those literary devices are conventional methods of legitimation which Luke uses to project his portrait of Paul.

When Paul performs miracles, has visions, receives oracles from God, and survives mortal dangers, that is enough for many commentators to conclude that Luke attempts to depict Paul as a Hellenistic "divine man." In Acts 14:11 the crowds at Lystra call Paul and Barnabas divine. In 28:6 Maltese natives say that Paul is a god. Paul and Barnabas reject the divine appellations at Lystra, but Paul makes no disclaimer in Malta. Accordingly, Hans Conzelmann and Ernst Haenchen read 28:6 as a consistent part of a divine-man motif in Acts.[4] Although the concept of the divine man may help to demonstrate parallels between Luke's Paul and

[2] K. Löning, *Die Saulustradition in der Apostelgeschichte* (Münster: Aschendorf, 1973) 185, 193, 204.

[3] M. Dibelius (*Studies in the Acts of the Apostles* [London: SCM, 1956] 138–91) notes literary parallels in the speeches of Acts. H. Cadbury (*The Making of Luke-Acts* [New York: Macmillan, 1927] 140–209) documents parallels elsewhere in Acts. Numerous scholars have followed them. See esp. E. Plümacher, *Lukas als hellenistischer Schriftsteller: Studien zur Apostelgeschichte* (Göttingen: Vandenhoeck & Ruprecht, 1972).

[4] H. Conzelmann, *Die Apostelgeschichte erklärt* (Tübingen: Mohr [Siebeck], 1972) 147; E. Haenchen, *The Acts of the Apostles: A Commentary* (Philadelphia: Westminster, 1971) 716.

other heroes from antiquity, it may also obscure the function of the miraculous in the Lucan portrait of Paul. It is not as if Luke is obligated to fit Paul to a stereotype of the divine man, but that he uses conventional techniques to enhance the status of Paul.[5]

David Tiede traces two distinct lines of tradition which authenticate heroes—the wise man and the miracle worker.[6] The two traditions incline toward mutual exclusion. Cultured authors in the wise-man tradition tend to reject the miraculous. Luke-Acts synthesizes the two traditions so that the miraculous stands in close proximity to appeals to the cultured.

The competition between the two traditions may explain why Luke takes pains to distinguish between Christian and non-Christian miracles. The genuine gift of God to the Samaritans stands over against the efforts of Simon to purchase the power of conferring the Holy Spirit (Acts 8:18-24). Because Paul is filled with the Holy Spirit, he can vanquish the inauthentic magician Elymas (13:8-11). The sons of Sceva invoke the names of Jesus and Paul in vain, whereas Paul performs extraordinary miracles (19:11-19). Luke thus attempts to make the miraculous tradition more palatable to some of his readers who may be cultured and to protect Christian miracles from charges of charlatanry.

But on the larger question of Luke's use of legitimating techniques, the synthesis of the two traditions means that Luke increases the range of authenticating factors. Luke takes such pains to justify Paul that he even uses competing methods. Such a wide range of devices forces us to expand the standard divine-man category and even to move beyond it. No one category is sufficient to encompass Luke's efforts to authenticate Paul. Luke simply uses whatever means he considers appropriate.

The criteria of Luke's intended audience, however, apparently determine the appropriateness of the legitimating techniques. That is, Luke so paints the portrait of Paul that he fits a popular scale of values for judging authenticity.[7] This is to say that Luke writes in an environment where he can expect to advance the

[5] See Carl Holladay, *Theios Aner in Hellenistic Judaism: A Critique of the Use of the Category in New Testament Christology* (Missoula: Scholars, 1977); D. Adams, "The Suffering of Paul and the Dynamics of Luke-Acts" (Ph.D. diss., Yale University, 1979) 81–83.

[6] D. Tiede, *The Charismatic Figure as Miracle Worker* (Missoula: Scholars, 1972) 5, 26, 59–61, 99, 207–37, 254, 285–87.

[7] D. Georgi, *Die Gegner des Paulus im 2 Korintherbrief: Studien zur religiösen Propaganda in der Spätantike* (Neukirchen: Neukirchener, 1964) 191; ET, *The Opponents of Paul in 2 Corinthians: A Study of Religious Propaganda in Late Antiquity* (Philadelphia: Fortress, 1985); idem, "Forms of Religious Propaganda," *Jesus in His Time* (ed. H. Schultz; Philadelphia: Fortress, 1971) 125.

legitimacy of Paul as faithful to his perception of Judaism by using techniques that were widely accepted. The counterparts to Luke's devices of authentication in Hellenistic literature demonstrate that Luke employs conventional devices to authenticate Paul.

Categorizing is subjective and arbitrary. Yet superimposing some structure is also necessary for understanding. With that in mind, the following classification makes no claim to be exhaustive or absolute. It can, however, render good service as a heuristic stimulus. Luke uses at least six major categories of legitimating techniques, all of which have remarkable parallels in Hellenistic literature: (1) divine approval, (2) access to divine power, (3) high motivation, (4) benefiting others, (5) possessing a high level of culture, and (6) adhering to an ancient tradition.

(1) For exposing how Luke confers divine approval, the three accounts of Paul's call provide the best glimpse into his methodology. They constitute an intricate system of techniques that conveys the sense of divine approval and demonstrates high motivation (3). The complexity arises from Luke's use of secondary legitimating factors within the major device of a christophany. Paul's blindness substantiates the christophany; Ananias's vision provides its meaning. The divine message indicates overtly that Paul is chosen by God and his mission divinely ordained (Acts 9:15). But the christophany and the vision of Ananias are themselves legitimating techniques that communicate divine sanction quite apart from the explicit message.

Euripides employs a strikingly similar technique. In the *Bacchanals* (469) Dionysus defends his mission to bring a new religion to Greece by claiming that it was based on a theophany of Zeus.[8] In the context Pentheus questions the status of Dionysus as well as the basis for spreading his mysteries in Hellas. Thus, the theophany plays a role analogous to Paul's christophany. It both vindicates Dionysus and provides divine motivation for his mission.

Paul's survival of opposition and danger also clearly communicates God's approval. In Lystra hostile Jews from Antioch and Iconium foment a near-fatal attack on Paul. But miraculously Paul gets up, reenters Lystra, and continues his journey the very next day (Acts 14:19-20). Ernst Haenchen's inability to see divine activity in Paul's recovery at Lystra[9] hinges on his failure to regard the context adequately. Granted, Luke does not mention God in vv

---

[8] A. Nock, *Conversion: The Old and New in Religion from Alexander the Great to Augustine of Hippo* (Oxford: Oxford University Press, 1961) 154.

[9] Haenchen, *Acts*, 434.

19-20. But the commissioning in Antioch (13:2-3) and the return to Antioch (14:26-27) bracket the entire section, so that everything that happens to Paul and Barnabas is to be interpreted as what God has done with them.[10]

A similar theme emerges in Paul's escape from a shipwreck (Acts 27:13-44) and his survival of a snakebite (28:3-6). Shipwreck and snakebite form one continuous episode in a remarkable parallel in an epitaph recorded by Statyllius Flaccus. The epitaph relates that a man who escaped shipwreck was killed by a viper on the shores of Libya (*Anthologia Palatina* 7.290). Both events reflect conventional ideas in antiquity that calamity metes out divine justice upon evildoers.[11] But Luke looks at those ideas from the opposite side so that survival reveals God's approbation. The unflappable Paul prophesies disaster for the sea voyage in Acts 27:10 and then by means of a message from an angel of God describes the outcome of the shipwreck ahead of time. Once again Luke constructs a complex system of devices. First, Paul's calm demeanor indicates his authenticity. Lucian shows us the other side of the coin when he criticizes Peregrinus's fear in the face of a storm at sea as proof that he is a charlatan (*Peregrinus* 42-44). Second, when things turn out as Paul predicts, his relationship to God is vindicated. If that were not enough, all 276 passengers on board the ship escape with their lives because God wishes to save Paul (Acts 27:24; cf. vv 42-43). Moreover, Paul remains unscathed in spite of a viper's bite. To survive both shipwreck and snakebite reverses the expectations of the Maltese and so astounds them that they consider Paul divine (28:6).

The belief that shipwreck is divine punishment comes to light repeatedly in antiquity. The mariners on Jonah's ship presuppose that divine powers enrage the sea against an evildoer (Jonah 1:4-8). In *b. B. Meṣ.* 59b R. Gamaliel, the Nasi and principal leader in banning R. Eliezer b. Hyrcanus, is traveling in a ship. When a huge wave threatens him, he deduces that it is divine judgment on account of the excommunication, and he cries out, "Sovereign of the Universe! Thou knowest full well that I have acted not for my honour, nor for the honour of my paternal house, but for thine, so that strife may not multiply in Israel!" Then the sea subsided.

In another example of the belief that maritime disaster represents divine retribution, Antiphon (*On the Murder of Herodes* 82-84) presents a defense at the trial of Helos who has been

---

[10] Adams, "Suffering of Paul," 55–56.

[11] G. Miles and G. Trompf, "Luke and Antiphon: The Theology of Acts 27–28 in the Light of Pagan Beliefs about Divine Retribution, Pollution, and Shipwreck," *HTR* 69 (1976) 260–61.

implicated in the death of Herodes during a journey by ship. Helos declares that the murder took place on land while the ship was in harbor. He then argues that the fact that the voyage continued without difficulty proves that the malefactor was not on board. That is, Helos assumes that his jury shares his own belief that if he were guilty, divine retribution would have brought disaster upon the subsequent voyage.[12]

When Paul's voyage resumes, Luke notes that he travels in a ship with the Twin Brothers (Castor and Pollux) as figurehead. Ancients considered Castor and Pollux defenders of truth and chastisers of falsehood. Luke's allusion to the Twin Brothers would likely communicate to a Hellenistic audience the validity of Paul's claims.[13]

There is also wide circulation in antiquity of the view that serpents dispatch divine justice. When the Israelites grumble against God and against Moses in the wilderness, God sends fiery serpents to bite them, and many of them die (Num 21:5-6). In *t. Sanh.* 8:3 Simeon b. Shatah follows a man who has a knife and who chases another man into a deserted building. Inside Simeon discovers the pursuer, with the knife dripping blood, standing over the dead body of the other man. Since the law requires two witnesses, his testimony against the murderer is inadequate. " 'But he who knows the thoughts of man will exact punishment from that man.' He did not move from the spot before a snake bit him and he died." In another case, a papyrus fragment tells about a son who has murdered his father. He attempts to escape into the desert, but a lion pursues him. When he climbs a tree to elude the lion, he encounters a snake.[14]

In a reversal of expectation, however, Paul's survival of the viper's bite reflects divine approval. The question is whether Paul is innocent or guilty, and miraculous survival renders the verdict.[15] This idea also surfaces elsewhere. *B. Šabb.* 156b relates that Ablat predicts that a man will be bitten by a snake and will die. Samuel counters that if the man is an Israelite, he will not die. The man has performed a good deed and so survives what should have been his fate. In the longer ending of Mark, mastery over snakes and poison

---

[12] Ibid., 262–64. D. Ladouceur ("Hellenistic Preconceptions of Shipwreck and Pollution as a Context for Acts 27–28," *HTR* 73 [1980] 436–39) cites evidence that malefactors could have calm voyages and survive shipwreck.

[13] Ladouceur, "Hellenistic Preconceptions," 443–47.

[14] B. Grenfell and A. Hunt (eds.), *New Classical Fragments and Other Greek and Latin Papyri* (Oxford: Clarendon, 1897) 133–34.

[15] G. Theissen, *The Miracle Stories of the Early Christian Tradition* (Philadelphia: Fortress, 1983) 108.

legitimates the gospel message and indirectly its proponents (Mark 16:18-20). Moreover, the tendency to embellish the status of heroes is so strong that in some instances it is the serpent that dies. *B. Ber.* 33a relates an incident about a poisonous reptile that has been injuring people. When R. Hanina b. Dosa hears, he puts his heel over the reptile's hole. The reptile bites him and it dies. Similarly, in *Acts of Thomas* 30-33 a jealous serpent kills the suitor of a beautiful woman it loves. Thomas commands the snake to suck the poison back out of the corpse. The man revives, and the serpent swells, bursts, and dies.

Evidence of divine sanction stands behind miraculous release from prison and fetters. After Paul and Silas have been unjustly accused and imprisoned in Philippi, a great earthquake opens the prison doors and the fetters (Acts 16:19-26). The jailer exhibits a typical interpretation of such an incident. When he prostrates himself before Paul and Silas, trembling with fear, and pleads for his salvation, he testifies that God vindicates his messengers.

Comparable marvels validate Dionysus. Pentheus commands his servents to fetter and imprison Dionysus. He yields willingly, but the fetters fall from his feet of their own accord, and the doors unbar themselves without the aid of human hands (Euripides *Bacchanals* 433-50; Ovid *Metamorphoses* 3.692-700). In another case, when Apollonius's companion Damis is distressed because his master is in prison, Apollonius takes his leg out of the fetters and inserts it once again in order to demonstrate his liberty. The narrator indicates the legitimating force of the incident by remarking that when Damis observed the wonder, he realized for the first time that Apollonius was divine and superhuman (Philostratus *Life of Apollonius* 7.38).

(2) In addition to demonstrating God's approval, another way in which Luke attempts to authenticate Paul is to show that Paul has access to divine power.[16] When Paul exorcises a spirit of divination in Acts 16:16-18, the immediate effect of calling upon the name of Jesus Christ shows his access to divine power. Or when Paul heals a man crippled from birth, he and Barnabas refuse to be identified as divine but use the incident to point to the divine source of the healing (14:8-18). In Acts 28 healing miracles follow Paul's survival of the viper's bite. The healings result in the enhanced status of Paul among the Maltese so that they shower him with gifts (vv 7-10). In 20:7-12 Luke somewhat cryptically relates the raising of Eutychus from the dead. Admittedly, Luke

[16] On charismatic miracles as a source of legitimation in social conflicts see ibid., 258.

makes no mention of the manifestation of the power of God in either of these cases. But his programmatic summary in 19:11 sets the stage for inferring such a manifestation: "And God did extraordinary miracles by the hands of Paul."[17]

Parallels from a wide variety of sources show once again that Luke is using popular devices. Josephus tells about a certain Eleazar who performs exorcisms through means that go back to Solomon who received knowledge of the art from God (*Ant.* 8.2.5 §45-48). Apollonius of Tyana performs a notable exorcism in Athens that is verified when the expelled demon throws down a statue (Philostratus *Apollonius* 4.20). In *Acts of Peter* 31.2, Peter heals the sick in contrast to Simon the magician, who only appears to do so. Simon is discredited, but Peter's miracles reveal his faith in the true God. The raising of Eutychus carries overtones of similar actions of Elijah (1 Kgs 17:17-24) and Elisha (2 Kgs 4:32-37). Another miraculous raising of the dead occurs when Apollonius touches a young woman who died on her wedding day and whispers a secret spell to her (Philostratus, *Life of Apollonius* 4.45). The restoration to life enhances the status of each miracle worker, but the authentication is nowhere more clear than in the words of the widow of Zarephath to Elijah: "Now I know that you are a man of God, and that the word of the Lord in your mouth is truth" (1 Kgs 17:24).

(3) Besides showing that Paul's mission is divinely motivated from the beginning, Luke presents Paul's subsequent behavior as based on high motives. Paul obeys the guidance of visions and of the Spirit (Acts 16:9, 18:9-10, 19:21, 22:18-21, 26:19). Actually, the vision that directs Ananias to Paul is a double vision. Ananias and Paul have simultaneous visions, and each vision contains the other. The Lord informs Ananias within his vision that Paul is praying and that he also is having a vision in which Ananias comes to minister unto him. If following a vision communicates legitimacy, a double vision compounds the effect.

Alfred Wikenhauser gives descriptions of nineteen similar cases of double visions.[18] In one case, Livy (*From the Founding of the City* VIII. 6.8-16) relates that Titus Manlius and Decius lead Roman troops against the Latins. Both have a nocturnal apparition that the commander of one side and the army of the other would be sacrificed to the spirits of the underworld and to Mother Earth. They determine that one of them must offer his life so that the

---

[17] On Acts 19:11–12 as an editorial summary see K. Lake and H. Cadbury, *The Beginnings of Christianity* (London: Macmillan, 1933) 4.239 and a related note p. 54.

[18] A. Wikenhauser, "Doppelträume," *Bib* 29 (1948) 100–111.

Latin army would then be sacrificed. Decius does this and the Romans win. The event redounds to the honor of Decius.

In another case Dionysius of Halicarnassus (*The Roman Antiquities* 1.55-59) tells about the founding of the Trojan city Lavinium in Italy. At Laurentum the Trojans receive an oracle that they must follow a four-footed beast until the animal wearies and there found a city. Aeneas prepares a sacrifice, but the victim, a sow, breaks loose. Aeneas takes this as the referent of the oracle and follows until she tires. But Latinus, the opposing king, is preparing for war against the Trojans. That night both Aeneas and Latinus have visions of divinities like the gods of the Trojans. The next morning, each sends envoys to the other, and they enter a treaty for amicable coexistence. The double vision confirms the validity of the Trojan city.

Paul's high motivation is also apparent in his willingness to expose himself to danger. He explicitly declares that he risks his life to fulfill the commission from Jesus Christ (Acts 20:24, 21:13-14) and that he seeks no personal gain (20:33).

Demonstrating the laudable motives of a hero such as Paul was a virtual imperative because of frequent charges of charlatanry against philosophers and orators in antiquity. When Euphrates wishes to discredit Apollonius, he ascribes selfish and egotistical motives to him, even though he only succeeds in discrediting himself (Philostratus *Apollonius* 6.7). To attribute behavior to dreams and oracles is a prominent means of justifying motives in antiquity. Socrates feels commanded by God through oracles and dreams (Plato *Apology* 33C). Apollonius detours on a trip to Rome because he has a dream that compels him to go to Crete (Philostratus *Life of Apollonius* 4.34). Although Lucian views Alexander of Abonoteichus as a fraud, he reports that the impostor attempted to legitimate himself and to enhance the reputation of a new temple by oracles (*Alexander* 22-24). Josephus notes that some of the Greeks attribute their laws to oracles, hoping in such fashion to facilitate their acceptance (*Ag. Ap.* 2.16 §161-62).

Disregard of hardship and death also legitimates heroes. Socrates willingly accepts hardship and faces death most nobly.[19] Demosthenes' suicide by poison to avoid capture by the Macedonians reveals his invincible soul and brave spirit (Lucian *Demosthenes* 43-50). Diogenes is a model for a young scout to emulate, because he disdained death and hardship (Epictetus *Discourses* 1.24.3-10).

A closely related authenticating characteristic is the willing-

---

[19] Xenophon *Memorabilia* 1.2.1; 4.8.2; *Apology* 33–34; Plato *Apology* 40 C–E.

ness to disregard personal gain. Part of Socrates' defense is that he does not profit from his philosophy (Plato *Apology* 19D-E), and he denounces those who do (Xenophon *Memorabilia* 1.2.6-7). Philo notes that some people travel for pleasure or financial advantage, but he portrays Abraham in contrast as one who migrates in obedience to God and gives no thought to personal gain (*On Abraham* 62-67). Josephus charges that his colleagues accept bribes to allow John of Gischala access to imperial grain, but he defends himself as unswayed by monetary enticements (*Life* 13 §70-73).

(4) The other side of disregard for personal gain is concern for the benefit of others. Throughout his mission in Acts, Paul exemplifies the saying of Jesus, "It is more blessed to give than to receive" (Acts 20:35). But the behavior of Paul and Silas when the Philippian jail is opened aptly illustrates the extent to which others receive benefit. After saving the jailer from suicide, Paul imparts to him and his household yet another salvation (16:25-34). Moreover, if the goodness of God has already been manifested prior to the advent of the gospel (14:17), how much more the benefit now that Paul calls his hearers to God.[20]

Laudable action on behalf of others redounds to the honor of many of the ancients. Socrates claims that he merits no punishment, since he has been the benefactor of Athens (Plato *Apology* 36 A-D). Demosthenes defends himself as worthy of a golden crown, awarded to him by Ctesiphon, because he has acted for the genuine benefit of the city (*De Corona* passim). Josephus claims that the Galileans in Gabaroth rally to him and proclaim him benefactor and savior (*Life* 47 §244).

(5) When Luke presents Paul as cultured and educated, he relies on a stock method of claiming authenticity. The clearest examples of Paul's social standing are his claims to Roman citizenship (Acts 16:37, 21:39, 22:25-28) and his account of his education under Gamaliel (22:3). But elsewhere in Acts, Paul more subtly exhibits his culture. In the Areopagus scene Luke uses motifs reminiscent of Socrates (17:16-31),[21] and a sophisticated Paul quotes poets who express Stoic themes.[22] Moreover, Luke spatters Paul's speech before Agrippa with cultivated language (26:2-23)[23] and has Paul claim a heavenly message addressed to him in

[20] F. Danker, "The Endangered Benefactor in Luke-Acts," SBLSP (ed. K. Richards; Chico, CA: Scholars, 1981) 48.
[21] Haenchen, *Acts*, 527.
[22] Dibelius, *Studies*, 47–54.
[23] Literary language accounts for the superlative νεότητος and the Attic ἴσασι (Acts 26:4). See *BDF*, 2, n. 4, §60(1).

Hebrew (Aramaic?) that has Greek literary antecedents: "It is hard for you to kick against the goads" (v 14).[24]

In antiquity education and culture appear repeatedly as important factors in establishing status.[25] Demosthenes expresses the negative side of the value of culture by arguing that his opponent Aeschines was reared in proverty as a servant rather than as a freeborn son (*De Corona* 258). Josephus extolls his own illustrious genealogy and boasts his education (*Life* 2 §8-9). When Cicero wishes to place himself among the orators, he details his education and emphasizes that much of it took place among distinguished teachers in Greece and Asia Minor (*Brutus* 306-21).

(6) Cicero prizes the location of his education, because many ancients were infatuated with long-standing traditions from the East.[26] Luke betrays his own distrust of novelty by describing the curiosity of the Athenians (Acts 17:21) and then having Paul allude to their disposition as the "times of ignorance" (v 30). Although the Athenians label the resurrection a "new teaching" (v 19), Paul traces God's activity back to creation (v 24). Elsewhere, Luke shows that Paul's proclamation of the resurrection represents ancient Jewish tradition attested by written prophecies (24:14; 26:6, 22). Thus, for all the novelty of the specific resurrection of Jesus, Paul's message is nothing other than the venerable Jewish tradition.

Parallels in other literature from antiquity verify the veneration of tradition. Demosthenes repeatedly defends his actions as being in accord with the forefathers (*De Corona* 199, 204, 210). Although Apollonius has supernatural knowledge, he still associates with the sages of the East and claims that the wise men of India are the true fathers of philosphy (Philostratus *Life of Apollonius* 1.18, 3.13, 6.6-11). Josephus acknowledges a tendency of virtually every nation to trace its law back to early dates to create the impression that it set the example for its neighbors. Then Josephus asserts that Moses is the most ancient of all legislators (*Ag. Ap.* 1.4 §20-21, 1.20 §151-56). Tertullian takes advantage of the common acceptance of the value of high antiquity to argue that Christianity is supported by Jewish scriptures, ". . . the oldest which exist" (*Apology* 19-21).

The upshot of this documentation of parallels in the literature of antiquity is that Luke employs conventional literary techniques to project his image of Paul. Because those devices are so wide-

---

[24] W. Nestle, "Anklänge an Euripides in der Apostelgeschichte," *Philologus, Zeitschrift für das classische Altertum* 59 (1900) 48–51.

[25] H. D. Betz, *Lukian von Samosata und das Neue Testament: Religionsgeschichtliche und paränetische Parallelen* (Berlin: Akademie, 1961) 107.

[26] Ibid., 107–108.

spread, the evidence stops short of demonstrating direct literary appropriation. Rather, the techniques belong to the public domain. Moreover, the extensive distribution of the devices makes it unnecessary to trace genealogical relationships. The vast diffusion of similar methods testifies to their far-reaching effectiveness whether the authors predate or postdate Luke. What is noteworthy is that on a large number of counts Luke uses popular methods to explain Paul's motivation and to legitimate his activities. These techniques serve as a clue to Paul's particular character. Luke expends considerable energy to justify Paul as an emissary of the divine.

Legitimating Techniques and the Protagonists in Luke-Acts

Any sensitive reader of Luke-Acts will likely be aware, to balance the evidence, that Luke utilizes many of these same devices in his portraits of Jesus and Peter. The voice from heaven at the baptism of Jesus and on the Mount of Transfiguration confers divine approval upon Jesus. Jesus' survival of the hostile attack in Nazareth corresponds to Paul's survival of stoning at Lystra. The appeal to prophetic prediction both from the OT and from Jesus himself reverses the scandal of the cross. Jesus' miracles illustrate his access to divine power, and that is especially apparent in the Q saying where Jesus claims that his exorcisms are ". . . by the finger of God" (Luke 11:20). The temptations demonstrate that Jesus is motivated by the Holy Spirit rather than by the satanic. Indeed, the whole course of Jesus to Jerusalem shows his submission to God's plan, especially his willingness to suffer hardship and death unjustly. Peter's summary of Jesus' ministry in Acts 10:38 portrays Jesus as a benefactor to others. The astounding performance of the twelve-year-old Jesus among the teachers in the temple stands in place of an elaborate education.[27] Luke brackets the life of Jesus with signs of his adherence to Judaism. The infant Jesus begins his life in compliance with the law of Moses and is presented in the temple. At the end of his life, he drives usurpers out of the temple and makes his own claim upon it. This manifests, along with Jesus' fulfillment of prophecy, his standing in an ancient tradition.

Peter mirrors virtually the same catalogue of devices as does Paul. Peter's discourse at Pentecost interprets the gift of the Holy Spirit as divine sanction for all who receive it, including himself. Peter survives hostile opposition and especially Herod Agrippa's

---

[27] Evidence is lacking to show the existence of a synagogue within the temple precincts to account for Jesus' discussion with teachers. H. de Jonge, "Sonship, Widsom, Infancy: Luke II.41– 51a," NTS 24 (1977–78) 327–29.

attempt to kill him. In fact, his escape from Herod constitues his second miraculous release from prison. Peter's access to divine power is such that the sick seek even his shadow to fall upon them. Peter and John tell the Sanhedrin in Acts 4:19-20 that their motivation comes from God rather than men. They confirm this by their willingness to suffer dishonor for the name. Divine providence sends Peter to Cornelius by means of a vision, to be precise, a double vision of both Peter and Cornelius. Peter's proclamation of the promises of God, his healing miracles, and the raising of Tabitha from the dead all portray him as a benefactor to others, in spite of the fear that the deaths of Ananias and Sapphira before him evoke. In contrast to Paul's education, Luke specifies that Peter is an uneducated commoner. But what is remarkable is that because he has been with Jesus, he does not behave like an uneducated commoner. Justin makes precisely the same point with respect to all the apostles. Although they were unlearned, the power of God made them the very ones who were to *teach* everyone (*Apology* I.39.3; cf. I.60.11). Finally, by his appeals to Moses, David, and the prophets, Peter certainly evidences his adherence to the ancient Jewish tradition.

If Luke uses legitimating techniques to rehabilitate Paul, do the same devices in the hands of the same author also imply the rehabilitation of Jesus and Peter? The ultimate answer, of course, is no. Both Jesus and Peter are established figures who speak with authority. But in a penultimate sense it is also yes. In the first place, Luke writes with a general intent of furthering his cause.[28] Luke wants his work to win popular approval. These methods of authentication facilitate the acceptance of Luke's program among curious Hellenistic audiences. In the second place, there is also a more specific purpose. Luke views the ignominious death of Jesus as a problem that must be explained. He does so by portraying it both as the martyrdom of an innocent and as a divine necessity. In the Hellenistic world, a wide range of examples demonstrates that martyrdom validates the claims of the victim.[29] This likely is one of the reasons Luke goes to greater pains than his fellow evangelists to depict the innocence of Jesus in his passion.

Similarly, Luke finds the social status of the earliest Christians a slight embarrassment. He particularly notes that Peter and John

---

[28] For some time scholars have recognized a general propagandistic intent behind the use of legitimating devices. So Nock, *Conversion*, passim; Georgi, *Gegner des Paulus*, 187–201.

[29] C. Talbert (unpublished lectures, Stetson Universtiy, ca. 1981); idem, *Reading Luke: A Literary and Theological Commentary on the Third Gospel* (New York: Crossroad, 1982) 221–24.

are uneducated lay people (Acts 4:13). And yet the Sanhedrin, specialists in deciding disputes, is unable to say anything in opposition. That is, Luke notes the common and ordinary standing of Peter and John in order to give the impression of the exact opposite. Luke is here repeating a pattern he has used with Jesus (Luke 20:26, 40) and that he also uses in describing Stephen (Acts 6:10) and Paul (9:22). This raising of Peter's status corresponds to Luke's presentation of his whole story as a significant part of world history. He starts his account with an elaborate synchronization in Luke 3:1-2 to avoid the impression that it is merely a local Galilean phenomenon. Close to the end, he has Paul surmise that Agrippa ". . . knows about these things . . . for I am persuaded that none of these things has escaped his notice, for this was not done in a corner" (Acts 26:26).

But enough of the penultimate. Luke flatters Jesus and Peter, but in the last analysis fights no major battles on behalf of their character. A major battle, however, is precisely what he does wage for Paul. When Jesus is accused at his trials, he gives some cryptic responses, but sees little need to defend himself. Indeed, before Herod Antipas, Jesus makes no answer. The Pentecost discourse vindicates all who have received the Holy Spirit from the charge of intoxication, but makes no particular defense of Peter. In face of the demand of the Sanhedrin to know the authority for the actions of Peter and John, Peter vindicates Jesus from the scandal of the crucifixion (Acts 4:11). He attempts to vindicate Jesus again in his second appearance before the Sanhedrin (5:30-31). In response to the complaint of the circumcision party about his social intercourse with gentiles (11:3), Peter actually exonerates the gentiles more than himself (vv 17-18).

In contrast Luke devotes virtually a quarter of his second volume to Paul's defense. A rather sober Paul quiets an animated crowd that has just attempted to lynch him. He specifically requests that they listen to his defense (μου ἀπολογία, Acts 22:1). In Acts 23, Paul defends himself by proposing that the resurrection is the genuine reason for his problems with the Sanhedrin, even if that also functions as a subterfuge. Again Paul says explicitly that he is defending himself before Felix (τὰ περὶ ἐμαυτοῦ ἀπολογοῦμαι, 24:10). Paul speaks in his defense before Festus (τοῦ Παύλου ἀπολογουμένου, 25:8). Finally, he defends himself before Agrippa (ἀπελογεῖτο, 26:1). In conjunction with these defense speeches, the Miletus address clearly functions as an additional apology. In fact, Paul's declaration of his innocence in 20:26 forms the climactic turning point between two halves of the speech that parallel each other.[30] To complete the picture we must add Paul's declarations to go to the gentiles in 13:46 and 18:6. Both cases vindicate Paul, and in 18:6 he expressly asserts his innocence. Why is the essential figure of Acts so constrained to exonerate himself?

Since function follows form, one of the strongest pieces of evidence is the genre of Luke-Acts. Charles Talbert argues persuasively that Luke-Acts is similar in both content and form to certain Greco-Roman biographies that are followed by narratives about successors, a genre particularly evident in Diogenes Laertius's *Lives of Eminent Philosophers*. Narratives about successors follow the biography of the founder to establish genuine successors and the authentic tradition.[31] In Acts narratives dominated by Peter and Paul follow the biography of Jesus the founder. A Hellenistic audience would have found in the parallels between Jesus and the protagonists in Acts clues to the true successors of the founder and to the legitimate tradition.

But the narrative of successors in Acts is preoccupied with Paul. Not only does Paul dominate the structure of Acts, but Peter, the next in prominence, already plays a prestigious role in Luke. Luke can relate the healing of Simon's mother-in-law (Luke 4:38-39) before introducing Simon in the calling of the first disciples (5:1-11) because he assumes the prominence of Peter. Peter's confession of Jesus as the Christ and his place in the transfiguration enhance his image. The enigmatic reference to the appearance of the risen Jesus to Simon (24:34) rehabilitates him from the temporary backslide when he denies Jesus (22:54-62), so that Peter assumes the place of authority in Acts 1:15 without any additional vindication. In Acts Luke presupposes Peter's legitimacy rather than establishes it. It is as an authoritative figure that Peter preaches at Pentecost, speaks before the Sanhedrin, under-

---

[30] H.-J. Michel (*Die Abschiedsrede des Paulus an die Kirche Apg 20, 17–38: Motivgeschichte und theologische Bedeutung* [Munich: Kösel, 1973] 27) shows that Paul's announcement of his death and his declaration of innocence in Acts 20:25–27 are the high point of the speech. C. Exum and C. Talbert ("The Structure of Paul's Speech to the Ephesian Elders [Acts 20:18–35]," *CBQ* 29 [1967] 233–36) see the death of Paul alone as the turning point. Cf. T. Budesheim, "Paul's *Abschiedsrede* in the Acts of the Apostles," *HTR* 69 (1976) 9–30.

[31] C. Talbert, *Literary Patterns, Theological Themes, and the Genre of Luke-Acts* (Missoula: Scholars, 1974) esp. 125–35; idem, *What Is a Gospel? The Genre of the Canonical Gospels* (Philadelphia: Fortress, 1977) 95, 107–108, 134. On the debate about the genre of Luke, see also M. Smith, "Prolegomena to a Discussion of Aretalogies, Divine Men, the Gospels, and Jesus," *JBL* 90 (1971) 174–99; D. Barr and J. Wentling, "The Conventions of Classical Biography and the Genre of Luke-Acts: A Preliminary Study," *Luke-Acts: New Perspectives from the Society of Biblical Literature Seminar* (ed. C. Talbert; New York: Crossroads, 1984) 63–80.

takes the evangelization of Cornelius, and proposes a solution to the Jerusalem Council.

In contrast, Paul comes onto the stage as an adversary, persecuting the church (Acts 7:58, 8:3). He becomes a Christian only to continue to arouse opposition from outside the church and suspicion within it (21:20-21). The burden of the succession narratives in Acts is to prove that Paul is a genuine successor. To repeat a point made above, Luke wages a major battle for the defense only of Paul. The parallels between Peter and Paul, therefore, establish Paul's legitimacy on a par with Peter's. Paul is Peter's equal as a successor in the authentic tradition from Jesus.

Luke develops a succession document for Paul out of exigencies of his era still visible beneath the surface of Acts. But to what end does Luke defend Paul by utilizing Hellenistic legitimating devices within the structure of a succession narrative? The following chapter attempts to show that Luke confronts adversaries who oppose Paul's universalism and critics who censure Paul as an apostate from Judaism. Over against them, Luke paints a portrait that accommodates the Paul of the Epistles toward Judaism as Luke presents it and explains Paul's mission among gentiles. Paul's venture among the gentiles is simultaneously ordained by God and motivated by the unbelief of some Jews. But Paul's entire enterprise never goes beyond the aspirations of Judaism as Luke understands it.

CHAPTER FIVE

PAUL IN ACTS

The problem of the Lucan Paul in its briefest form is that the Paul of the Epistles is a different personage. In the sequences of Paul's activities, garnished with portentous exploits and crowned with defense speeches, Luke leaves the imprint of his own themes. Specifically, Paul so exonerates himself as a faithful Jew that Luke has accommodated the Paul of the Epistles toward Judaism as Luke portrays it. How is this evidence to be handled? Nineteenth-century *Tendenz* criticism offered answers ranging from views that Acts is an apology against Jewish detractors of Christianity to appraisals that it is an irenic attempt to reconcile conflicts between Jewish and gentile Christianity.[1] These solutions are lightly regarded today because of the dominant opinion that Luke so definitively rejects the Jews that he could not have addressed them or their sympathizers. According to the vast majority of scholars, by the time of Luke's composition, a predominantly gentile church had evolved beyond Jewish and Jewish Christian debates. If Luke gives up on the Jews, then his interest in Jewish-Christian relationships can be attributed to his desire to trace continuity between Christianity and Judaism.

This chapter checks the accuracy of this modern consensus against the function of Paul's alleged repudiation of the Jews in Acts 13:46, 18:6, and 28:28. This chapter is also an avowed revisionist attempt to reclaim some of the seminal features of the dormant concepts of *Tendenz* criticism. The thesis is that Luke textures his portrait of Paul to counter anti-Paulinism from both

[1] M. Schneckenburger (*Apostelgeschichte: Zugleich eine Ergänzung der neueren Commentare* [Bern: Fischer, 1841] 52–58, 92, 221–22) suggests that Acts is an apology against anti-Pauline Judaists. F. C. Baur (*Paulus, der Apostel Jesu Christi: Sein Leben und Wirken, seine Briefe und seine Lehre* [Stuttgart: Becher & Müller, 1845] 5–12) argues against Schneckenburger that Acts is an attempt to reconcile opposing parties rather than to defend one against the other. J. Weiss (*Über die Absicht und den literarischen Character der Apostelgeschichte* [Göttingen: Vandenhoeck & Ruprecht, 1897] 55–56) proposes that Acts is an apology for gentiles in response to criticism from Jews.

Jewish and Christian sectors, that is, against both external and internal opponents. It hinges on the fundamental importance of the course of Paul's ministry. Luke focuses on Paul's mission rather than on the general spread of God's salvation in the Roman Empire. The salient features of Paul's operations dominate the narrative more than the story of the extension of the gospel as such. The thesis also hangs on the proposal that Paul's defense speeches vindicate him and him alone. The approach to the problem that follows is (1) to demonstrate that Luke does not repudiate the Jews but uses them as a part of his explanation of why Paul turns to gentiles and (2) to describe Luke's anti-Pauline opponents from traces he leaves in the text.

Luke and the Jews

According to F. C. Baur, Acts attempts to explain Paul's mission as a result of the rejection of the gospel by Jews. Again according to Baur, such an explanation presupposes a party that opposes Pauline universalism.[2] To reconsider this basic idea of Jewish or Jewish Christian opposition to Pauline Christianity is to enter notoriously disputed territory. Baur's inclination to date the struggle well into the second century certainly must yield to a more sober date toward the end of the first. But the problem of dating aside, Baur's thesis arouses strong resistance on other grounds. The historical judgment that gentiles had become overwhelmingly dominant in the church by the end of the first century has seemed to militate against the notion that Luke addresses Jewish opposition to Paul. If Acts attributes the development of gentile Christianity to stubborn unbelief of Jews and portrays them as hardhearted, that would appear inconsistent with an address to an audience that would sympathize with Jews.

Martin Dibelius sets the stage for the predominant interpretation of Luke's view of the Jews among modern scholars. Dibelius detects a design whereby Luke intentionally rejects Jews in Asia Minor (Acts 13:46), Greece (18:6), and Rome (28:28). On this point Hans Conzelmann and Ernst Haenchen follow him—an imposing triumvirate wielding weighty influence on Lucan scholarship. When Luke repeats the rejection of the Jews for the third time, Christianity severs itself from Judaism once and for all.[3] According

[2] F. C. Baur, "Über Zweck und Veranlassung des Römerbriefs und die damit zusammenhangenden Verhältnisse der römischen Gemeinde," *Tübinger Zeitschrift für Theologie* (1836) 59–178, esp. 113–14.
[3] M. Dibelius, *Studies in the Acts of the Apostles* (London: SCM, 1956) 149–50; H. Conzelmann, *Die Apostelgeschichte erklärt* (Tübingen: Mohr [Siebeck], 1972)

to this view, the repudiation of the Jews retaliates for their initial rejection of the gospel. When the Jews refuse to believe, the gospel passes from them to the gentiles.

In contrast, Jacob Jervell argues strongly that it is only when Jews accept the gospel, rather than reject it, that the mission can turn to gentiles.[4] According to Acts 2:41, 47; 4:4; and 5:14, the church expands by a progressive increase of Jewish converts. By 21:20 many myriads of Jews have believed. To a considerable extent the Jewish mission is a success. Thus Jervell thinks that Jewish conversion means that Israel's role is to mediate the gospel to gentiles. For Jervell, therefore, Jewish unbelief has no causal relationship to the gentile mission. Rather, the mission is the result of God's plan alone.

Jervell, however, fails to consider adequately the relationship between Jewish unbelief and the orientation of the mission in the second half of Acts. He contends that when Paul and Barnabas declare that the Lord has commanded them, ". . . to be a light for the Gentiles" (Acts 13:47), they are claiming to be gentile missionaries in the first instance. It is, therefore, only as gentile missionaries that they acquiesce to preach to Jews.[5] But against Jervell, v 47 in its context obviously explains why Paul and Barnabas turn to the gentiles (see v 46). Moreover, for Luke to justify the mission of Paul and Barnabas by the command of God does not prevent Jewish obduracy from coinciding with the divine impetus.

Jervell actually provides the key to unlock a better understanding of the connection between Jewish unbelief and the direction of the Christian mission, albeit unwittingly. Paul's defense speeches in Acts 22-26 are biographical, appropriate for Paul and Paul alone.[6] Paul's birth in Tarsus, education under Gamaliel, standing as a Pharisee, faithfulness as a Jew, and obedience to God as a missionary to Jews and gentiles apply only to him rather than to Christianity at large. What Jervell fails to perceive is that Luke's peculiar concern for Paul extends to his mission among gentiles as

---

85–86, 115, 159–60; E. Haenchen, *The Acts of the Apostles: A Commentary* (Philadelphia: Westminster, 1971) 101, 414, 417–18, 535, 724, 729–30. Cf. K. Lake and H. Cadbury, *The Beginnings of Christianity* (London: Macmillan, 1933) 4.348; S. Wilson, *The Gentiles and the Gentile Mission in Luke-Acts* (Cambridge: Cambridge University Press, 1973) 138, 222–23, 232.

[4] J. Jervell, *Luke and the People of God* (Minneapolis: Augsburg, 1972) 41–74, esp. 74, n. 101.

[5] Ibid., 58–61.

[6] Ibid., 153–83. Surprisingly, J. Jervell ("Paulus in der Apostelgeschichte und die Geschichte der Urchristentums," *NTS* 32 [1986] 383) has recently presented Paul as a symbol of the church, particularly on the basis of the Miletus address.

well. That is, Luke is preoccupied with Paul's work among gentiles rather than with the gentile mission as such.

Both the standard theory of reciprocal rejection and Jervell's theory of Israel as a mediator for the gentiles place far too much emphasis on the gentile mission in its broader scope. Luke exhibits less interest in the extension of the gospel beyond Israel than do most of his commentators. For example, Adolf Harnack makes Luke's desire to explain and justify the gentile mission the controlling idea and determining principle for the entire book of Acts.[7] But in truth Luke concentrates more on Paul's story.

To be sure, Luke has a stake in the larger gentile mission. He validates the accession of gentiles to the church in his accounts of the conversion of Cornelius and the Jerusalem Council. But he has no interest in following Peter or Philip beyond Caesarea. After Barnabas and Mark separate from Paul, Luke provides only the barest summary of their activities (Acts 15:39). Apollos appears on the scene suddenly in 18:24, then disappears just as suddenly. Paul's associates Silas, Timothy, and Erastus play subsidiary roles for Luke. Luke focuses single-mindedly on Paul's mission.

Certain elements of the rejection of the Jews in Acts 13:46, 18:6, and 28:28 actually bring Luke's emphasis on the Pauline ministry into greater clarity. Obviously, Paul declares in each case a reorientation of his mission. The question is how those declarations function. Do they depict a new direction for Christianity in its entirety? In Antioch of Pisidia the opposition of Jews to Paul and Barnabas leads the missionaries to resolve, "We turn to the gentiles" (13:46). The explicit reference to Paul and Barnabas in the first person plural means that these two (and these alone) now turn to the gentiles. On a second occasion, Jewish opposition to Paul leads to Paul's personal declaration to go the gentiles: "I am innocent. From now on I will go to the gentiles" (18:6). Against Jervell, in Acts Jewish antagonism is connected causally with the reorientation of mission. But against the standard theory of reciprocal rejection, it is connected with the gentile mission only when Paul is involved.

The failure of Jews to accept the gospel has little to do with the overall fact that God's salvation extends to gentiles. Acts provides for the inclusion of gentiles solely at divine initiative. In fact, Jews raise opposition to gentiles only *after* Peter baptizes Cornelius. But the refusal of Jews to believe has much to do with reorienting Paul's mission to the gentiles. Jewish unbelief forms half of a double-edge explanation for why Paul himself moves beyond the

---

[7] A. Harnack, *The Acts of the Apostles* (New York: Putnam's Sons, 1909) xxi.

Jews. On the one hand, the course of Paul's ministry is controlled supernaturally. On the other hand, it has an empirical cause. From the time of Paul's conversion, Acts testifies that his gentile mission proceeds from God's plan. His experience on the road near Damascus destines him to be God's envoy to the gentiles as well as to the Jews (9:15, 22:21, 26:17). His selection along with Barnabas for a mission beyond Antioch is made in response to the word of the Holy Spirit (13:2). Paul and Barnabas claim God's command as the basis for their turning toward the gentiles (v 47). Thus, God clearly controls the direction of Paul's mission. But on an experiential level the opposition of unbelieving Jews coincides with the supernatural impetus for Paul's departure to the gentiles. God's design for Paul's mission to the gentiles moves toward its fulfillment, at least in part, because some Jews refuse Paul's preaching.[8]

But at no place are the Jews definitively rejected. After resolving to turn to the gentiles, Paul himself continues to go to the synagogue. The excursion into the Jewish synagogue in Iconium is Paul's first reported activity after he declares his intention to go to the gentiles (Acts 14:1). Similar scenes occur at 16:13; 17:1, 10, 17; 18:4. Likewise, after Paul's second announcement of his decision to go to the Gentiles (18:6), he continues to frequent the synagogue (v 19; 19:8). Furthermore, Paul's interest in reflecting a positive image to Jews leads to his purification in the temple (21:20-26). In his apologetic speeches he consistently claims solidarity with Judaism. Before an antagonistic crowd in Jerusalem, he repeats that he is a Jew, and he claims a thoroughly Jewish education and illustrates his zeal as a Jew even to the point of persecuting Christians (22:39-23:5). Before Felix, Paul contends that his activity conforms to the ancient Jewish hope (24:14-15; cf. 25:8). In his defense before Agrippa, he claims that his activities all his life have been consistent with Judaism (26:4-8, 22). Three days after arriving in Rome, Paul summons Jewish leaders to tell them that his imprisonment is the result of his commitment to the hope of Israel (28:17-20). His ministry in Rome indicates that in spite of his declarations to go to the gentiles, the Jews continue to occupy a strategic place in his mission (v 23).

Although Paul meets Jewish obduracy with severe warnings, he never gives up on the Jews as such. In Acts 13:46 Paul holds impenitent Jews responsible for renouncing the word of God and

---

[8] Wilson (*Gentiles and the Gentile Mission*, 135, 166, 169) recognizes Jewish rejection and the command of God as dual causes for the direction of mission, but he focuses on the gentile mission at large rather than on the Pauline gentile mission.

thereby judging themselves unworthy of eternal life. His emphasis there is on the personal accountability of Jews who have heard the word of God rather than on some implicit resolve to forsake all Jews. The responsibility of the Jews who have heard Paul's testimony is once again the issue in 18:6. Here Paul alludes to Ezek 3:18, 20. For Ezekiel, God's representative is charged with responsibility for the destiny of the guilty. But Paul reverses the argument. The representative disclaims his own liability and places the burden of responsibility on the unbelieving Jews.

Two symbolic gestures accompany Paul's diversion to the gentiles. In Antioch of Pisidia, Paul and Barnabas shake the dust off their feet against their Jewish persecutors (Acts 13:51). In Corinth Paul associates a similar sign with his declaration to go to the gentiles. He shakes out his clothing (18:6). Shaking dust from the feet complies with the instructions of Jesus to the twelve and to the seventy(-two) (Luke 9:5, 10:11), but otherwise is rare in ancient literature. Strack and Billerbeck (Str-B 1.571) claim that Jewish disdain for the impure soil of foreign lands is the basis for the gesture and conclude that it implies that the recipients are regarded as heathen. That conclusion likely exaggerates by the error of definition by derivation. Jesus' words in Luke 9:5, 10:11 and Paul's explanation of the analogous sign in Acts 18:6 give clues for a far more probable interpretation, at least from Luke's perspective. Paul's words parallel his gesture in 18:6 and interpret it: "Your blood be upon your heads! I am innocent." This sign admonishes Paul's opponents with respect to their liability and releases Paul from obligation. Jesus' instructions in Luke 9:5, 10:11 provide another limitation on the meaning of shaking dust off the feet. In comparison with parallels in Mark and Matthew, Luke emphasizes the gesture as a sign against an entire town. Shaking dust off the feet is appropriate only when the disciple abandons the town. This is precisely what Paul and Barnabas do. After shaking the dust off their feet they leave Antioch for Iconium. Although shaking out clothing is obviously a close parallel, it does not necessitate abandoning the town. And so after shaking out his garments Paul abandons only the synagogue in Corinth merely to move next door. The two signs have some particular individuality, but their fundamental referent is the same. They warn the Jews of their responsibility and absolve Paul of his.[9]

Under the assumption that shaking dust off the feet implies a final repudiation, Gottfried Schille argues that since Paul and

[9] See H. Cadbury, "Dust and Garments," *The Beginnings of Christianity*, 5.269–77.

Barnabas return to visit the Christian community in Antioch (Acts 14:21), the gesture is restricted to the Jews.[10] But the argument makes more sense precisely the other way around. The return of Paul and Barnabas to Antioch means that the warning is not a final repudiation. Again the parallel in 18:6 also shows that the latter interpretation is far more likely. Immediately after Paul shakes out his clothing, he converts Crispus, the ruler of the synagogue, and his entire household (18:8). Moreover, after Paul and Barnabas leave Antioch of Pisidia, they go to the synagogue in Iconium where many Jews believe along with many Greeks (14:1). Using the two gestures, Paul certainly counters Jewish opposition with stringent warnings, but the alleged reciprocal rejection does not materialize in 13:46 or 18:6.

The pattern of Acts 13:46 and 18:6 sheds light on the third member of the parallel. 28:28 repeats the pattern. The incredulity of some of Paul's Jewish visitors in Rome merits the insulting characterizations of Isa 6:9-10:

> This people's heart has grown dull,
> and their ears are heavy of hearing
> and their eyes they have closed;
> lest they should perceive with their eyes,
> and hear with their ears,
> and understand with their heart,
> and turn for me to heal them (Acts 28:27).

But once again the alleged reciprocal rejection does not develop. The unbelief of some of the Roman Jews occasions Paul's advocacy of the gentiles, but there is no anathema against Jews as such. The failure of some of the Jews in Rome to believe finds an explanation in the harsh prophecy of Isaiah 6. But Isaiah 6 applies to the hardening of Jews who have already been addressed instead of those yet to be addressed in the future.[11] Paul censures Jews who have heard the gospel and compares them unfavorably with gentiles who will listen. In order to add force to Israel's responsibility, Luke turns to a prophetic reproof. In the prophetic tradition reproofs impress responsibility upon froward people without conveying literally final rejection.[12] In line with 13:46 and 18:6, 28:28 uses the behavior of the Jews as a partial explanation of Paul's mission among gentiles.

[10] G. Schille, *Die Apostelgeschichte des Lukas* (Berlin: Evangelische, 1983) 298.
[11] V. Stolle, *Der Zeuge als Angeklagter: Untersuchungen zum Paulusbild des Lukas* (Stuttgart: Kohlhammer, 1973) 85.
[12] D. Tiede, *Prophecy and History in Luke-Acts* (Philadelphia: Fortress, 1980) 121–22.

Paul in Acts 75

In an otherwise admirable study on the use of Isa 6:9-10 in Acts 28, Joachim Gnilka falls prey to the fallacy of considering Acts an account of the expansion of the gospel to gentiles in general. He quite correctly concludes that at the end of Acts, Isa 6:9-10 shows that the hardening of unbelieving Jews was foreseen by God and predicted by Isaiah. But he incorrectly infers that the hardening results in the definitive transition of the gospel from Jews to gentiles and, therefore, that Luke rejects the Judaism of his own time.[13] In Acts 28:28 gentiles hold no exclusive proprietorship over the gospel. In fact, v 30 makes it clear that even Paul's mission is still open to "all" (πάντες).[14] The second half of Acts, rather than describing in general the accession of the gentiles to the gospel and their assumption of a place of preference over the Jews, chronicles the development of Paul's mission in the diaspora and demonstrates why he turns to gentiles without reservation.

The way Isa 6:9-10 functions elsewhere supports the conclusion that Acts 28 does not write off the Jews, but explains their unbelief. In the original setting in the concrete circumstances of the Syro-Israelite war, Isaiah proclaims what he has heard as an observer of a heavenly council, namely, that God's judgment upon Judah has been predestined. So strongly has Judah's destruction been determined that it is the task of the prophet to keep the people unaware of the inevitable judgment: "Make the heart of this people fat, and their ears heavy, and shut their eyes" (v 9).[15] Nevertheless, Isaiah pursues the salvation of the people of Judah rather than their rejection. In 7:3 the prophet goes to meet King Ahaz to persuade him to cast himself in dependence upon God rather than upon the Syro-Israelite alliance. In spite of the threats of Assyria, Isaiah proclaims, "God is with us" (8:8, 10). In the face of all these political machinations, Isaiah calls for reliance upon "the Lord of hosts" (vv 12-15).

NT allusions to Isa 6:9-10, following the LXX, give up the idea that the hardening of the people is a part of the prophet's task. Rather, the failure to understand has become characteristic of the people from the start. In the synoptic Gospels, Isa 6:9-10 explains

[13] J. Gnilka, *Die Verstockung Israels: Isaias 6, 9–10 in der Theologie der Synoptiker* (Munich: Kösel, 1961) 17, 130–54.
[14] For brief discussions on πάντες as an inclusive term see Stolle, *Zeuge*, 86–87; and H. Hauser, *Strukturen der Abschlusserzählung der Apostelgeschichte (Apg 28,16–31)* (Rome: Biblical Institute, 1979) 46, 107–10, 228.
[15] O. Steck ("Bemerkungen zu Jesaha 6," *BZ* nf 16 [1972] 188–206) has shown that Isaiah 6 is a report of the proceedings of a heavenly council rather than a call. The reference to the death of Uzziah provides a retrospective glance to explain the failure of Isaiah's advice to catch the ear of the people.

the failure of the crowds to understand the parables of Jesus. In Mark it emphasizes the distinction between the crowds and the disciples of Jesus. To the disciples it is given to know the mystery of the kingdom of God. Matthew 13 agrees with Mark's idea of special instruction to the disciples. But in Matthew, Jesus speaks in parables because (ὅτι) the people are hardened rather than in order to (ἵνα) harden them. Thus, in Matthew hardening is the basis for speaking in parables; in Mark it is the purpose of speaking in parables. Like Matthew, Luke agrees with Mark's theme that Jesus wishes to impart special teaching about the Kingdom of God to his disciples. But Luke 8:9 has substituted the singular "parable" for Mark's reference to "parables" (Mark 4:10), so that Isa 6:9-10 has to do only with the parable of the sower rather than with parables in general. John 12:40 refers to Isa 6:10 at the conclusion of Jesus' public ministry in order to explain the unbelief of the Jews in the face of Jesus' entire ministry.

A similar tendency to explain a refusal to believe appears in Justin Martyr's use of Isa 6:10. Although there is only slight literal correspondence between Justin's vocabulary and that of the LXX, and although in one instance Justin claims to refer to Jeremiah, he likely has Isa 6:10 in mind in at least three places in the *Dialogue with Trypho*. In chaps. 12 and 33 he chides Jews for their refusal to repent. In chap. 69 he speaks of gentiles who did not believe before their access to the gospel. Thus, although Justin polemizes against the Jews, he uses Isa 6:9-10 to explain unbelief rather than to express rejection.

Barnabas Lindars correctly concludes that the early church used Isa 6:10 to justify the failure of the mission to Jews and to explain their unbelief.[16] But he is off the mark when he says,

> . . . Luke has been saving up this quotation as the climax to the repeated theme that Paul was opposed by the Jews, but found a better hearing among the gentiles. He has saved *this* text for the purpose, because it is now the classic passage for the rejection of the Jews.

The function of Isa 6:9-10 outside Acts 28 shows rather that it is the classic passage for explaining unbelief.

Explaining unbelief is also its fundamental function at the end

---

[16] B. Lindars, *New Testament Apologetic: The Doctrinal Significance of the Old Testament Quotations* (London: SCM, 1961) 159–67. Isa 6:9–10 is not quoted in QL. See Gnilka, *Verstockung*, 155–85. Rabbinic literature rarely alludes to Isa 6:9–10. According to Str-B (1.663) the allusions that do occur show that the synagogue did not understand it as God's judgment with the purpose of hardening Israel.

of Acts. It accounts for the rejection of the gospel by Jews, but not for the rejection of the Jews for the gospel. Luke obviates the scandal of the refusal of some Jews to accept God's salvation by a proof from prophecy, just as proof from prophecy obviates the scandal of Jesus' crucifixion at the end of Luke. Acts 28:26-27 carries no more evidence of a final abandonment of the Jews than 13:46 or 18:6. Granted, Paul's citation of Isa 6:9-10 rounds off a threefold schema of announcing the reorientation of Paul's mission, but not at the cost of abandoning the Jews.

To be sure, Luke underscores the first and last of these three scenes by making them the culmination of dramatic incidents. Moreover, as the climax of the beginning and end of Paul's ministry after he is set apart by the church at Antioch, these episodes bracket Paul's mission from Antioch to Rome. Luke thus depicts a serious flaw of character in Paul's Jewish audiences. Hardened Jews spurn the word of God and judge themselves unworthy of eternal life.

Nevertheless, the narrator attributes the defect in character only to a part of Paul's Jewish audiences. Belief among the Jewish populace also brackets Paul's mission. And so to complete the symmetry between Paul's encounters with Jews in Rome and in Antioch and Corinth, the end of Acts must be read as anticipating additional ministry to Jews. In fact, on the basis of the pattern of turning to Jews after the declarations in Acts 13:46 and 18:6, there is every reason to interpret the reference to Paul's welcome to "all" (πάντες) in 28:30 as including the Jews. Paul is still engaged in a mission to Jews after v 28.

Luke gives high visibility to the theme of Paul's mission to all. In the vision of Ananias, the Lord designates Paul ". . . a chosen instrument to carry my name before the gentiles and kings and the sons of Israel" (Acts 9:15). The second account of Paul's conversion reiterates his calling to be a witness for the Just One "to all" (22:15). Paul's preaching consistently bears fruit among both Jews and gentiles (13:43, 48; 14:1; 17:4, 11-12; 18:4; 19:10). In the Miletus address, Paul summarizes his ministry as testifying both to Jews and to Greeks (20:21). Before King Agrippa, Paul recalls that Jesus commissions him to go both to the people and to the gentiles (26:17) and reflects over the course of his ministry as including both (vv 20, 22-23). At the end of Acts, Paul is receiving all, preaching and teaching openly and unhindered (28:31). Luke brackets Paul's entire career with references to its inclusive nature (9:15, 28:30-31) and thus protects it from being construed as exclusive.

Since Paul never confines his mission solely to the gentiles and never establishes a single congregation that is exclusively gentile, it is incongruous to insist that through him Luke abandons the Jews. Luke actually goes to great pains to vindicate Paul from the charge that he forsakes Judaism. The accusation of Jewish Christians in Jerusalem implies that Paul himself has rejected Judaism (Acts 21:21). That is why both James and Paul agree that the way to disabuse them of their error is for Paul to demonstrate that he lives in observance of the law (vv 24-26). He not only attempts to act out his fidelity to Judaism, but repeatedly declares it directly in his defense speeches. Can this Paul be Luke's symbol for the renunciation of Israel? Impossible!

But beyond accounting for the refusal of Jews to believe, the ending of Acts also continues to clarify why Paul turns to the gentiles. One reason Paul reorients his mission is that the poverty of response among some Jews motivates him to turn to the gentiles.

Luke does not leave us in the dark about why he wishes to account for the course of Paul's ministry (and here we return to the theme of legitimation). In Acts 22:21 the mob in Jerusalem tolerates Paul's defense until he claims that the risen Christ commanded him to go to the gentiles. At that point they cry out against him (vv 21-22). According to 26:21, 23 Jewish opponents protest when Paul extends the gospel to gentiles. It is against such objections to Pauline universalism that Luke takes up the challenge of defending Paul's mission among gentiles.

The threefold announcement of Paul's mission to the gentiles, occurring strategically in Asia Minor, Greece, and Rome, is designed to serve as part of Luke's response to the question, Why does Paul go to the gentiles? Luke provides two basic answers. First, God determines the direction of Paul's mission. Second, the unbelief of some Jews is the occasion for Paul to turn to gentiles. In a sense Luke also has a third answer. Paul does not simply ignore the Jews in order to embrace the gentiles. Rather, he consistently proclaims the gospel to both.

Luke's Opponents

What purpose does Luke's legitimation of Paul's diversion to the gentiles fulfill? Some of the most compelling evidence for the function of the vindication of Paul lies imbedded in Luke's combat against perspectives he wishes to discredit, that is, by the way he deals with opponents.

The attempt to characterize Luke's opponents calls for a methodological caveat. The internal evidence in Acts takes precedence over external history. For example, S. G. F. Brandon identifies Luke's opponents as Alexandrian Jewish Christians, a patently speculative construct from external history.[17] When external history claims priority over the evidence in Acts, it tends to prescribe the identity of opponents rather than to describe it. To take another case in point, Charles Talbert excludes Jewish Christians from consideration as Luke's opponents by arguing from external history that nomistic Jewish Christianity had little effect outside Palestine and ceased to be important after the destruction of Jerusalem in 70 C.E.[18] A more accurate description of Luke's adversaries derives from indications that Luke leaves in the text without criteria presupposed from external history taking precedence.

Paul's speech at Miletus (Acts 20:18-35) is an informative starting point for discovering the identity of the opponents. Here Luke uses a farewell discourse ostensibly to warn against future heresy; in actuality he polemizes against dangers of his own time. Paul predicts the advent of heretics after his departure (v 29). But Luke conceives of his era so definitively as the time after Paul's departure that he stands in the period of the heretics.[19] In the farewell discourse the problem of the heretics stands behind Paul's attempts to justify himself. Their unspoken charges draw two particular rejoinders: (1) that Paul cannot be responsible for the disintegrating situation in Asia Minor and (2) that his gospel is complete. Because Paul maintains that he has declared the entire counsel of God (vv 20, 27), many interpreters deduce that the heretics are Gnostics who appeal to a secret teaching that they claim comes from Paul.[20] Paul's assertion that he has proclaimed the entire will of God would imply that his message is complete apart from any secret sources and, therefore, rob the heretics of their esoteric Pauline tradition.

Such perceptive exegesis merits esteem if not approval. It runs aground because it fails to give adequate consideration to the larger context. When we scrutinize the entire career of Paul in

---

[17] S. Brandon, *The Fall of Jerusalem and the Christian Church* (London: SPCK, 1975) 23–26, 210–212.

[18] C. Talbert, *Luke and the Gnostics* (New York: Abingdon, 1966) 100–101.

[19] H.-J. Michel, *Die Abschiedsrede des Paulus an die Kirche Apg 20,17–38: Motivgeschichte und theologische Bedeutung* (Munich: Kösel, 1973) 82. G. Kennedy (*New Testament Interpretation through Rhetorical Criticism* [Chapel Hill: University of North Carolina Press, 1984] 133) contends that the speech is not a defense because it is primarily concerned with the future. He has failed to see that Paul's future in this case is Luke's present.

[20] So Haenchen, *Acts*, 591, 596; Conzelmann, *Apostelgeschichte*, 117–18; G. Klein, *Die zwölf Apostel: Ursprung und Gehalt einer Idee* (Göttingen: Vandenhoeck & Ruprecht, 1961) 183, 213–14; Talbert, *Luke and the Gnostics*, 13.

Acts, we discover that it is Jews who consistently raise problems for Paul. Jews plot to kill Paul in Damascus (Acts 9:23). Paul draws the wrath of Jewish Hellenists in Jerusalem (v 29). The Jewish false prophet Bar-Jesus opposes Paul at Paphos on Cyprus (13:6-8). Jealous Jews in Antioch of Pisidia incite persecution against Paul and Barnabas (vv 45, 50). Unbelieving Jews in Iconium stir up gentiles against the Christian missionaries (14:2, 5). Jews from Antioch and Iconium lead a lynch mob against Paul in Lystra (v 19). Jews create an uproar in Thessalonica (17:5) and then hound Paul out of Beroea (v 13). In Corinth, Jews revile and accuse Paul (18:6, 12). In Jerusalem, Jews drag Paul out of the temple, attempt to kill him (21:30-31), and demonstrate against him when he addresses them (22:22-23). More than forty Jews plot to kill Paul in Jerusalem and take the chief priests and elders into their confidence (23:12-14). Tertullus prosecutes Paul before Felix (24:1-8), and Jews at large second his charges (v 9). The chief priests and leaders of the Jews in Jerusalem contrive with Festus against Paul (25:2-3). Later, Jews from Jerusalem go to Caesarea to testify against him (v 7).

There are two exceptions to the Jewish matrix of Paul's problems. In Philippi the owners of a slave girl seize Paul and Silas and drag them before the magistrate (Acts 16:20). In Ephesus, Demetrius the silversmith leads a riot against Paul (19:23-41). A notable coincidence between the two cases holds a clue to the way Luke views these incidents. In both instances the Jewishness of Christianity comes to the fore. The slave owners accuse Paul and Silas of being Jews (16:20). And Alexander inadvertently incites the Ephesian rioters when they recognize that he is Jewish (19:34). These cases show that Luke is aware of pagan opposition to the Jewishness of Christianity, but the repeated instigation of hostility by Jews proves to be the critical problem.

Moreover, in the Miletus address Paul explicitly attributes his difficulties in Ephesus to the plots of the Jews (Acts 20:19). Shortly thereafter in the line of the narrative, Jewish accusations await Paul on his final visit to Jerusalem. Unsettling rumors that Paul teaches Jews of the diaspora to forsake the law have adverse effects on Jewish Christians there (21:21). Paul then devotes his energies to vindicating himself from such a false understanding by purifying himself in the temple (vv 22-26). When that backfires, he spends significant portions of the remainder of the book defending his Jewishness. On two occasions Paul recalls his persecution of Christians as a sign of his commitment to Judaism (22:4-5, 26:9-11). Günter Klein contends that Luke progressively intensifies Paul's persecution in order to emphasize the magnitude of his conversions.[21] But this overlooks that in 22:4-5 and 26:9-11 the persecution has a relatively positive function, namely, to demonstrate how Jewish the Christian Paul is. In four apologetic speeches Paul claims Pharisaic faithfulness to the law and the Scriptures, and he justifies his preaching as true to Jewish tradition. Furthermore, when Paul arrives in Rome, he deems it necessary to explain to the local Jewish leaders that he has not offended against Jewish tradition, even though they have no reports that he has. The Miletus speech, therefore, falls in a larger context where Jews contend against Paul. The nexus of Jewish antagonism and accusations surrounding Paul's farewell discourse militates against identifying the opponents as Gnostics. Rather, the larger perspective demands that Paul's claim to have declared the whole counsel of God (20:27) be understood not as a device to deprive Gnostics of their secret Pauline tradition, but as a response to charges that his gospel is incomplete.

An additional factor that links the Miletus speech to Paul's arrest in the temple corroborates this exegesis. In the farewell discourse Paul describes his encounter with Jews from Asia and warns of dangers from future opponents in Ephesus (Acts 20:29-30). Then in Jerusalem it is precisely Jews from Asia acquainted with Trophimus the Ephesian who incite Paul's arrest (21:27-29). Luke makes a close identification between Asia and Ephesus. For example, when he summarizes Paul's sojourn in Ephesus, Luke says that "all the residents of *Asia* heard the word of the Lord" (19:10; emphasis added). Again, in the Miletus address Paul equates Asia with Ephesus (20:18). And so the warning against future opponents in Ephesus in the Miletus speech could hardly have anticipated more accurately Paul's Asian accusers in Jerusalem.[22] The content of their accusation is that Paul teaches against the people, the law, and the temple. It is this kind of indictment that compels Luke to defend Paul's gospel from its alleged incompleteness.

Although Luke nowhere delineates Paul's gospel, the so-called apostolic decree, Paul's sermons, and his apologetic speeches reveal at least some of its features. The apostolic decree (Acts 15:20-29) validates gentile Christianity without invalidating nomistic Jewish Christianity. It even enjoins gentiles to keep certain prescriptions as a concession to Jews. Luke returns to the apostolic decree in 21:25, where it is actually linked with the remark of James that Paul himself lives in observance of the law (v

[21] Klein, *Zwölf Apostel*, 127–30, 211.
[22] Michel, *Abschiedsrede*, 29.

24). Elsewhere Paul reiterates his claim to be innocent of offenses against the Jewish law (25:8, 28:17). Paul's gospel, therefore, stands in continuity with the law rather than over against it.

Paul's preaching to Jews and his apologetic speeches emphasize the continuity of the gospel with the acts of the God of Israel. At Antioch of Pisidia, Paul argues before Jews that the God of Israel who chose the partriarchs has now raised up a prophet like Moses by raising Jesus from the dead (Acts 13:16-41). In the defense speeches Paul claims that his commission comes from the God of Israel (22:14, 26:22). Before gentiles, Paul proclaims the true God who is creator (14:15, 17:22-27). He calls both Jews and gentiles to repentance and to faith in Jesus Christ (16:31; 17:30; 20:21; 26:18, 20) and offers forgiveness of sins (13:38, 26:18).

In Paul's preaching, the resurrection of Jesus receives major attention before Jews in Antioch of Pisidia (Acts 13:28-37) but surprisingly little emphasis before gentiles in Athens (17:31). In the Aeropagus speech the resurrection merely confirms that the Risen One will judge the world. This unexpected imbalance betrays a Lucan concern, because in the defense speeches Paul describes the resurrection as the pivotal point of his conflict with *Jews*. Before the Sanhedrin he declares that he is on trial with respect to the resurrection of the dead, when the immediate cause is the charge that he has profaned the temple (23:6). Tertullus accuses Paul of agitating among the Jews; Paul responds, "With respect to the resurrection of the dead I am on trial before you this day" (24:21). He claims that the resurrection is the reason for his trial a third time before Agrippa (26:6-8). In these exaggerations of the resurrection as the crucial issue between Paul and the Jews, the interests of Luke meet us.

Paul's acceptance of the apostolic decree and his declarations of faithfulness to the law commit him to a gospel that provides room for Jewish Christians to keep the law as well as for gentile Christians to live free from it, provided they observe the basic prohibitions of the decree. Furthermore, when Paul makes the resurrection the crux of his dispute with the Jews, he specifies that it is the Jewish hope. When these features of Paul's gospel are yoked with the objections of his opponents, a gospel emerges that is complete, specifically with regard to the Jewish law and the resurrection of Jesus. That is to say, in the context of Paul's apologies, Paul's universalism is no rejection of Judaism.

It is noteworthy that throughout Paul's mission in Acts, Jewish opponents stir up both Jews and gentiles. Luke, therefore, is concerned with the impact of the opponents on both groups. James expresses Luke's anxiety about rumors that Paul had encouraged

Jews of the diaspora to forsake the law because of the detrimental effects on Jewish Christians (Acts 21:20-21). But Luke has a similar uneasiness about the consequences of Jewish propaganda on gentiles. Elymas the magician seeks to turn the proconsul Sergius Paulus away from the faith (13:8), and incredulous Jews in Iconium spread anti-Christian propaganda among the gentiles (14:2). This means that Luke probably targets Jewish opponents of his own day who seek to influence both Jews and gentiles by maligning Paul and his message.

But the problem goes beyond Jewish propaganda. The Miletus speech recognizes threats to the congregation both from outside (Acts 20:29) and from inside (v 30).[23] The Jewish critics of Paul correspond to the outsiders, but there is also an internal division over the alleged Pauline gospel. Although it is tempting to identify the internal heretics as Jewish Christians, the evidence is insufficient. They may be gentiles who lean toward the synagogue, come under its influence,[24] and find Pauline universalism inconsistent with Christianity's origins in Judaism. At any rate Luke fights on a double front against Jewish propaganda and schismatic anti-Paulinism.

Conclusion

Luke's portrait of Paul is an attempt to defend and to legitimate Paul and his gospel. Acts presents Paul as completely Jewish and his gospel as complete in Jewish terms over against Jews and Christians who oppose Pauline universalism. The failure among scholars to regard the Lucan Paul in this way can be attributed to three primary misplays. (1) The second half of Acts has been read as an account of the gentile mission *per se* rather than as an account of the Pauline mission in the diaspora that includes gentiles. (2) Acts has been read as a reflection of Luke's repudiation of the Jews. (3) The seminal proposals that Acts is either apologetic or irenic have been taken as mutually exclusive. What has been interpreted as Luke's rejection of Jews is actually part of his explanation of the Pauline mission among gentiles. And the Lucan portrait of Paul is both apologetic and irenic. Against Jewish detractors and their sympathetic Christian heretics alike Luke portrays Paul as innocuous to genuine Judaism as he understands it.

---

[23] Ibid., 82.
[24] N. Dahl (*Jesus in the Memory of the Early Church* [Minneapolis: Augsburg, 1976] 96–97) suggests that God-fearers were Luke's prospective readers. See Haenchen, *Acts*, 414.

CHAPTER SIX

THE PHARISEES IN LUKE-ACTS

Luke manifests a special interest in the Pharisees. He mentions them as often as Matthew, even though Matthew appears to be more concerned with Jewish issues. Luke introduces them into contexts even when his probable sources do not mention them. But in spite of Luke's interest, it is not immediately apparent that he deals with the Pharisees with enough consistency to reflect his view of them at all. On the one hand, he juxtaposes Jesus and Pharisees as if there is a serious fissure between them. Notably, Jesus assails the Pharisees in a series of polemical woes in Luke 11:39-54. On the other hand, Luke alludes to positive relationships between them. Some Pharisees warn Jesus to flee from Herod (13:31) and others invite him to their table on three occasions (7:36, 11:37, 14:1). In Acts, Pharisees and Christians are kindred spirits. Paul confesses his fidelity to Pharisaism (Acts 23:6, 26:5), and the Pharisee Gamaliel adopts an approving attitude toward Christianity (5:34-39).

In addition, in Luke's Gospel the Pharisees are frequently associated with a type of exclusivism that stands over against toll collectors and sinners, whereas in Acts they are capable of advocating both the apostles and Paul before the Sanhedrin. In Luke, Pharisees may take issue with the words and actions of Jesus and his disciples. In Acts they are preeminently Jews who believe in the resurrection. This ambivalent picture of the Pharisees is enough to caution against oversimplification. But this chapter shows that in spite of the ambiguities, the Gospel already tends to present the Pharisees in comparatively favorable light and anticipates their posture in Acts. In the two volumes, Luke presents the Pharisees as possessing serious character flaws, but nevertheless as respected and authoritative representatives of Judaism who can hover close to the edge of Christianity. Moreover, Luke likely expects some of his readers to identify favorably with the Pharisees, and he uses them as a point of contact for such readers.

To distinguish sharply among Jews, Jewish Christians, and

gentile Christians is somewhat anachronistic for Luke. In Acts Jewish authorities consider Christianity to be a sect—a thorn in the flesh perhaps, but nevertheless, a sect, a part of internal Jewish diversity. To be sure, Luke knows of gentile believers, and he distinguishes between Jews who believe in Jesus and those who do not. But believers, both gentile and Jewish, have associated themselves with the most authentic Judaism as Luke understands it.

Lucan Redaction

In Luke Pharisees appear in only four pericopes where they are a part of the main body of the narrative (Luke 7:30, 11:39-52, 12:1, 18:10-11). More than twenty additional allusions betray an editorial perspective. Only five of the references with an editorial perspective have synoptic parallels[1] even though twelve appear in contexts that do. This indicates that Luke devotes conscious attention to the role of the Pharisees.

In comparison with Mark 2:1-3:6, Luke structures his parallel (Luke 5:17-6:11) into a more coherent series of encounters between Jesus and Pharisees. Accordingly, he introduces Pharisees at the very beginning, whereas Mark accounts only for scribes. Luke 5:33 carries over the setting of the call of Levi to the question of fasting and produces an incongruity in that Pharisees refer to themselves in the third person. 6:7 mentions the Pharisees in setting the scene for the healing of the man with the withered hand, whereas Mark refers to them only in the conclusion. By themselves these last two bits of editorial activity seem insignificant. But together with 5:17 they confirm Luke's intent to present the complete block of material as consecutive confrontations between Jesus and Pharisees.

Rudolf Bultmann interprets this data as a tendency on the part of Luke to increase the controversy between Jesus and the Pharisees. He speaks of a specific tendency of the synoptic tradition to introduce Pharisees as typical opponents of Jesus where the original historical setting has been forgotten.[2] In two brief refer-

---

[1] Luke 5:30, 33; 6:2, 11; 11:37–38. there are two references to Pharisees in Luke 5:33. The first reflects the point of view of the narrator. The second does not, but functions nevertheles to establish the setting and is not integral to any of the following parables.

[2] R. Bultmann, *The History of the Synoptic Tradition* (New York: Harper & Row, 1963) 51–54. H.-F. Weiss (*Der Pharisäismus im Lichte der Überlieferung des Neuen Testaments* [Berlin: Akademie, 1965] 102, 111) agrees with Bultmann that there is a tendency in the tradition to make the Pharisees typical opponents. He

ences Paul Winter adopts the view that Luke expands the hostility between Jesus and the Pharisees.[3] James Parkes claims that there is an unmistakable increase in hostility in the three synoptists when they are read in the historical order of their appearance.[4] H. J. Cadbury posits a tendency in Luke to rebuke the Pharisees and sees Jesus' association with toll collectors and sinners as a part of that tendency. "It is not that Luke loves the publicans and sinners more, but the self-righteous Pharisees less."[5]

But these views assess the evidence inaccurately. In comparison with the Marcan parallels, both Luke 5:30 and 6:2 redirect the complaints of the Pharisees against the disciples rather than against Jesus himself. 6:11 also tones down the reaction of the Pharisees to the healing of the man with the withered hand on the sabbath. According to Mark 3:6 the Pharisees plot with the Herodians to kill Jesus, whereas Luke reports general anger and an indefinite discussion of what to do with Jesus. In this manner Luke tempers direct confrontation between Jesus and the Pharisees.[6]

Rather than increasing the controversy, Luke juxtaposes Jesus and the Pharisees so that the sayings and actions of Jesus are transparently superior to theirs. Luke 16:14 provides one of the chief clues to substantiate the thesis that Luke uses the Pharisees to set Jesus off to advantage. Here Luke dubs the Pharisees φιλάργυροι. Φιλάργυρος appears in Greek literature as a convention to characterize the opponents of the philosophers. For example, in Diogenes Laertius 6.56 a φιλάργυρος stands over against the φιλόσοφος as a foil to the latter's superiority. The φιλάργυρος plays a role similar to the sophists in Plato's *Dialogues*. Luke 16:15 fills out the convention with the picture of the Pharisees as those who justify themselves. Luke, therefore, adapts a literary device in order to juxtapose Jesus and the Pharisees. This background sheds light on 5:26 where, if the context is consistent, Pharisees themselves participate in recognizing Jesus' superiority. Vv 17 and 25 together imply that they are included in the "all" who glorify God and are filled with awe.[7]

---

does recognize that Luke is less severe and less schematic than Matthew (104, n. 1, 111).

[3] P. Winter, *On the Trial of Jesus* (Berlin: de Gruyter, 1961) 126–29.

[4] J. Parkes, *The Conflict of the Church and the Synagogue: A Study in the Origins of Antisemitism* (London: Soncino, 1934) 42.

[5] H. Cadbury, *The Making of Luke-Acts* (New York: Macmillan, 1927) 258–59.

[6] J. Ziesler ("Luke and the Pharisees," *NTS* 25 [1978–79] 146–57) documents a similar softening of conflict between the Pharisees and Jesus in Luke.

[7] So T. Zahn, *Das Evangelium des Lucas* (Leipzig: Deichert, 1913) 262. Jack T. Sanders ("The Pharisees in Luke-Acts," *The Living Text; Essays in Honor of*

The reference to the leaven of the Pharisees in Luke 12:1 has a somewhat analogous literary function in that it juxtaposes the woes against the Pharisees to warnings against Christian apostasy. This structure bestows a double nuance on the saying. On the one hand, it interprets Jesus' attack on the Pharisees so that, as strong as the woes are, they oppose Pharisaic hypocrisy rather than Pharisaism as such. On the other hand, as an introduction to the admonition against Christian apostasy, it applies the woes against the Pharisees to Christian readers. The judgment of Jesus against the hypocrisy of the Pharisees serves as a model for judgment against Christian hypocrisy.

The strong verbal relationship in the woes between Luke 11 and Matthew 23 demonstrates that Luke had a source for this material. Luke mentions the Pharisees in this section only where Matthew does also. In all other cases, outside of Marcan parallels, the exact opposite occurs—when Matthew mentions the Pharisees Luke does not; when Luke mentions the Pharisees, Matthew does not. That is, outside of this section and Marcan parallels each evangelist refers to the Pharisees independently. Thus, in the case of the woes, the Pharisees undoubtedly appear in Luke's source.

The larger structure of Luke 11-12 provides a strong clue to how this material functions. In contrast with Mark and Matthew, Luke separates the accusation that Jesus casts out demons by Beelzebul (11:15) from the admonition against blaspheming the Holy Spirit (12:10). Both Mark and Matthew connect blasphemy against the Spirit with the charge of Jesus' opponents that he acts by virtue of the demonic. In Luke, however, blasphemy against the Spirit is related to Christian apostasy. From 11:14 to 12:12 the author is interested in an exhortation to fidelity in face of the danger of apostasy. And so the woes against the Pharisees warn Christian readers against apostasy. Inasmuch as Jesus can level a volley of woes at Pharisees, he can also truculently reprove Christian apostates. Christian readers cannot use Jesus' censure of the Pharisees for their own justification. Rather, Luke transforms it into a model for woes against Christians who abandon their faith.[8]

Ernest W. Saunders [ed. D. Groh and R. Jewett; Lanham, MD: University of America, 1985] 154) suggests that for Luke the Pharisees undergo a transformation in this pericope so that they move from accusing Jesus of blasphemy to amazement.

[8] Cf. H. Flender, *St. Luke: Theologican of Redemptive History* (Philadelphia: Fortress, 1967) 109. D. Juel (*Luke-Acts: The Promise of History* [Atlanta: Knox, 1983] 65) interprets the blasphemy as refusal to accept the testimony of the Spirit-filled apostles. Sanders ("Pharisees in Luke-Acts," 185–86) interprets Pharisaic hypocrisy in Luke 12:1 as self-justification and self-exaltation. But neither

Luke concurs with the synoptic tradition in that he continues to depict antithetical encounters between Jesus and the Pharisees.[9] Pharisees are ranged among those who stand over against God's purpose (Luke 7:29-30). In special Lucan material they can object to Jesus' relations with outcasts (15:1-2). They scoff at Jesus' teaching on wealth (16:14). A Pharisee plays the role of an unsuspecting self-righteous person upon whom the tables are turned in 18:9-14. But they are not merely typical opponents. In spite of conflict with Jesus, they do not have a hostile predisposition. In 17:20 they approach Jesus as honest inquirers. His answer is surprisingly open toward them. In specific situations Luke may not choose to present them in a favorable light, but he is certainly capable of doing so. Thus, they are congenial enough to invite Jesus to dine with them and to warn him of the danger from Herod.[10]

Luke's portrait of the Pharisees is even more flattering in Acts.[11] Luke distinguishes Gamaliel as a Pharisee of particular prestige. Gamaliel gives advice that makes him favorable to Christianity. The hand of the author is evident in the well-known anachronisms in Gamaliel's speech. Judas the Galilean revolted when Coponius was procurator of Judea (6-9 C.E., Josephus J.W. 2.8.1 §117-118), or as Acts 5:37 says, in the time of the census (cf. Luke 2:2). The insurgent Theudas led an uprising under Cuspius Fadus, and Fadus became procurator in 44 C.E. (Josephus Ant. 20.5.1 §97-99; 19.9.2 §363). This creates a double historical problem for Gamaliel's speech. First, Luke reverses the order of appearance and displaces Theudas by some forty years. Second, Fadus became procurator at least a decade after the incident with Gamaliel supposedly took place. Furthermore, Gamaliel's argu-

---

Juel nor Sanders has noted the larger context of Luke 12:8–12 where the problem is Christian apostasy.

[9] M. Salmon ("Hypotheses about First-Century Judaism and the Study of Luke-Acts" [Ph.D. diss., Hebrew Union College, 1985] 127) thinks that Jesus' harsh criticism of the Pharisees can be accounted for by internecine feuds within the larger confines of Judaism. By means of harsh criticism of the Pharisees, Luke confronts his opponents as if in a family quarrel.

[10] As Sanders notes ("Pharisees in Luke-Acts," 145–46) repeated invitations to table fellowship are not signs of hostility. Ziesler ("Luke and the Pharisees," 149–50, 52–53) suggests that Luke 13:31 is relatively positive toward the Pharisees since in Mark 12:13 Pharisees align with Herodians against Jesus.

[11] M. Dibelius (Studies in the Acts of the Apostles [London: SCM, 1956] 1–25) does not claim to have decided the issue of composition and tradition for every verse in Acts. But he does think that he has identified the units that can be categorized as tradition by an examination of their style. None of the pericopes in which the Pharisees appear is classed among the units of tradition.

ment hinges on the demise of the revolutionaries and bears additional weight when viewed from the pespective after the war with Rome when the defeat of the Jews had discredited the revolutionary impulse.[12]

Gamaliel couches his counsel in a grammatical structure that makes the position of Christianity favorable. The form of Gamaliel's advice gives a higher degree of probability to the possibility that the activity of the apostles may be from God than to the possibility that it may have a human origin. True, it is possible to understand the second conditional clause as a paraphrase of the claim of the apostles that their activity has a divine basis. The grammar may be construed to mean, "if (hypothetically) this movement has a human foundation, it will fail; but if (as the apostles attest) it really is from God, you (the Sanhedrin) will not be able to overthrow them."[13] But to understand the sentence in this fashion is to fail to note that opposing groups make contradictory claims. If the second conditional clause expresses the claim of the apostles, the first should reflect the claim of the opponents. Furthermore, since Gamaliel presumably would have spoken in Aramaic, this grammatical form certainly indicates Luke's preference for Christianity rather than his.

The cases of Theudas and Judas are capable of two distinct meanings, depending on the point of view. From an authentic viewpoint of Gamaliel, the activity of the apostles would be analogous to the movements led by the two insurgents. And so scholars who emphasize the historicity of Gamaliel's speech tend to focus on the parallels of the three dead leaders, Theudas, Judas, and Jesus. But from the perspective of the author and audience of Acts, the movements led by Theudas and Judas stand in contradistinction to Christianity. And so when the viewpoint shifts to the end of the first century, Gamaliel's speech becomes a confirmation of Christianity. By the time of Luke, not only the failure of Theudas and the dispersion of the followers of Judas, but also the collapse of the Jewish revolt against Rome would have demonstrated the human origin of their movements. From the perspec-

---

[12] F. Overbeck, *Kurze Erklärung der Apostelgeschichte* (Leipzig: Hirzel, 1870) 79. F. F. Bruce (*The Acts of the Apostles* [London: Tyndale, 1951] 147) argues that Luke refers to another Theudas who rebelled before the one mentioned by Josephus. A. Wikenhauser (*Die Apostelgeschichte: Übersetzt und erklärt* [Regensburg: Pustet, 1961] 76) raises the same possibility without making a decision. P. Winter ("Miszellen zur Apostelgeschichte," *EvT* 17 [1957] 398–99) argues convincingly that two such rebels with the same name is unlikely.
[13] *BDF*, §372 (1).

tive of Luke and his readers, then, the success of Christianity makes Gamaliel's advice a verification of Christianity. The defense of Paul by the Pharisees in Acts 23:1-10 is a striking parallel to the defense of the apostles by Gamaliel in 5:33-39. The Pharisees exhibit extraordinary openness to Paul as does Gamaliel to the apostles. The Pharisees oppose the high priest and the Sadducees in a fashion similar to Gamaliel's restraint of the high priest and the Sadducees (cf. 5:17). The Pharisees actually take the side of Paul, just as Gamaliel takes the side of the apostles.

The Pharisees' support of Paul is disarmingly emphatic. First, the Pharisees explicitly exonerate Paul: "We find nothing wrong in this man" (Acts 23:9). Second, they allow that Paul may have had an audition from a spirit or an angel. The reader is quite aware that these words allude to Paul's experience on the road near Damascus. But Paul relates his audition to the crowd in 22:6-10 rather than to the Sanhedrin.[14] The Pharisees affirm the possibility of Paul's revelation, although they have not been informed about it. Third, Luke breaks off the pondering of the Pharisees in mid-sentence giving stress to their contention. The Pharisees hover on the brink of confirming Paul's revelation from the risen Christ. They virtually acknowledge the resurrection of Jesus.

In the Gospel two tendencies stand out. One is the tendency to reduce conflict in comparison with parallels. Although Luke preserves controversial encounters and the theological distance between Jesus and the Pharisees,[15] he views them as capable of acting rather benevolently toward each other. The second is the tendency to juxtapose Jesus and the Pharisees. Taken together the two tendencies produce a juxtaposition that does not presuppose hostile opposition. Rather, Luke contrasts the views of Jesus and the Pharisees, as if a reader who looks at the two will easily recognize the superiority of the former without condemning the latter conclusively.

But in Acts the Pharisees assume a more positive status than in the Gospel. Some are believers, arousing controversy and needing correction perhaps, but nevertheless believers (Acts 15:5). Three times Paul appeals to Pharisaism in his own defense. Whereas in the Gospel the Pharisees are primarily a sounding board for the voice of Jesus, in Acts the voices of Pharisees speak favorably on behalf of Christianity and Paul. Why does Luke present the

[14] Overbeck, *Kurze Erklärung*, 405.
[15] Ziesler, "Luke and the Pharisees," 153.

Pharisees as even more favorable toward Christianity during the period of the church than he does for the time of Jesus?

The Pharisees' Position of Respectability and Authority in Luke-Acts

In order to account for the ambivalent role of the Pharisees, Jack Sanders identifies the Pharisees who encounter Jesus in controversy with the believers who belong to the party of the Pharisees in Acts 15:5. He hypothesizes then that they are prototypes of Jewish Christians for whom Luke harbors a profound dislike and for whom Luke holds no hope of salvation. According to Sanders, friendly Pharisees in Acts stand in a derivative relationship with friendly Pharisees in Luke and underscore the link between Christianity and the religion of Israel.[16]

Sanders's essay is quite helpful in some details. He demonstrates effectively that in the stories where Pharisees enter into conflict with Jesus, Luke disagrees with the Pharisaic *halakah*. Their interpretation of Torah (namely, their emphasis on proper behavior rather than on repentance, contrition, and belief) is therefore wrong from Luke's perspective.[17] Sanders also correctly notes that Luke can distinguish individual Pharisees or groups of Pharisees (e.g., "one of the Pharisees," "some of the Pharisees") in contrast to Mark who refers stereotypically to "the Pharisees." Thus Luke does not view all the Pharisees as opposed to Jesus.[18]

Nevertheless, Sanders's overall conclusion that Luke employs the Pharisees in order to combat Jewish Christianity runs aground. Without sufficient evidence Sanders dismisses the hope of salvation for Pharisaic Christians (for him, Jewish Christians) in Acts 15:5, even though Luke calls them believers. Sanders also speaks almost axiomatically of Luke's dislike for Jewish Christianity.[19] Although he notes that Paul claims to be a Pharisee in order to emphasize fidelity to Torah and belief in the resurrection, he fails to take those claims seriously as characterizations of Paul. He dismisses Paul's claim before the Sanhedrin in 23:6 as a tricky ploy and sees 26:5 as establishing continuity between Christianity and Israelite religion. He calls Paul then a Christianized Pharisee as

---

[16] Sanders, "Pharisees in Luke-Acts," 141–88. Sanders claims that there has been no thorough study on the Pharisees in Luke-Acts. I take it that he overlooks my dissertation, "The Pharisees in Luke-Acts: Luke's Address to Jews and His Irenic Purpose" (Ph.D. diss., Princeton Theological Seminary, 1978). In addition now Salmon ("Hypotheses") contributes to the study of the Pharisees in Luke-Acts.

[17] Sanders, "Pharisees in Luke-Acts," 153, 158–59, 170, 174–86.

[18] Ibid., 149, 156–69. Cf. Ziesler, "Luke and the Pharisees," 151–52.

[19] Sanders, "Pharisees in Luke-Acts," 159, 179–88.

distinct from a Pharisaic Christian.[20] This does injustice to the
entire theme of Paul's solidarity with the hopes of Israel of which
his relationship with Pharisaism is a part.

But beyond these incorrect turns, Sanders misses the point that
Luke writes in an environment where the Pharisees hold a rather
respectable position for both Luke and his readers. And this
accounts for the positive way the Pharisees function in Luke-Acts.

In Luke the Pharisees provide a contrast with Jesus to his
advantage. In Acts Gamaliel and some Pharisees of the Sanhedrin
give warrant to Christianity, its apostles, and Paul. In a fashion
Luke returns the favor. He holds the Pharisees in high regard.
Rudolf Bultmann attributes to Luke a general tendency to increase
hostility toward the Pharisees. There are two obvious reasons: (1)
Luke preserves conflict stories in which Pharisees encounter
Jesus; (2) Luke alters the traditions available to him to give more
prominence to the Pharisees. With this evidence there is no
quarrel. What is debatable is the assumption that the two are
causally connected. Does increased exposure imply increased
controversy? An appreciable amount of evidence points in a quite
different direction, namely, that the augumented role of the Pharisees is due to their function as rather respected and authoritative
representatives of Judaism.

Ellis Rivkin portrays the Pharisees as active protagonists of
unwritten law with enough influence to transform Judaism from its
orientation toward the written law alone to dependence upon the
two-fold law. According to Rivkin, Josephus, the NT, and Tannaitic literature concur in presenting the Pharisees as a class of
scholars enjoying power and prestige who champion the two-fold
law.[21] Over against Rivkin, Jacob Neusner theorizes that the
Pharisees evolved from a political party to a table-fellowship sect
whose prestige later Tannaim embellished.[22] Rivkin assumes
continuity of identity and character, so that the portrait of the
Pharisees remains consistent regardless of the date or nature of the

---

[20] Ibid., 149, n. 23, 165–66.

[21] E. Rivkin, A Hidden Revolution (Nashville: Abingdon, 1978) 28–123.

[22] J. Neusner, From Politics to Piety: The Emergence of Pharisaic Judaism (New
York: Ktav, 1979). On Neusner's debate with Rivkin see also J. Neusner, "Review
of A Hidden Revolution, by Ellis Rivkin," Ancient Judaism: Debates and Disputes
(Chico, CA: Scholars, 1984) 183–84; cf. idem, "The Use of the Later Rabbinic
Evidence for the Study of First-Century Pharisaism," Approaches to Ancient
Judaism: Theory and Practice (ed. W. Green, Missoula: Scholars, 1978) 215–28;
idem, The Rabbinic Traditions about the Pharisees before 70. Part III. Conclusions (Leiden: Brill, 1971) 320–66. Neusner ("Use of the Later Rabbinic Evidence," 223, 228, n. 22) does not wish to present the Pharisees as solely a
table-fellowship sect.

source material, whereas Neusner advocates historical criticism to get behind tendentious portrayals of the Pharisees.

Neusner correctly steers the debate to the question of the veracity of the sources, a question to which Rivkin pays insufficient attention. Moreover, Rivkin approaches the sources with an a priori definition of the Pharisees as opponents of the Sadducees. Nevertheless, Rivkin picks up corroborating evidence from multiple independent sources which Neusner weighs inadequately. Thus Rivkin says more than the sources allow about the consistent character of the Pharisees, while Neusner says less than the sources allow about the social position of the Pharisees.

Whether Pharisees champion a two-fold law or comprise a table-fellowship sect has little bearing on this discussion. Furthermore, the posture of the Pharisees prior to 70 C.E. (Neusner's primary concern) also lies beyond its scope, even though I will cite some evidence from Philippians and rabbinic literature that points to their prestige before 70. What is pertinent is the Pharisees' status in Luke's environment.

Josephus attests the Pharisees' position of respectability and authority in the first century. But Neusner joins Morton Smith in contesting the factuality of Josephus's accounts of the eminence of the Pharisees.[23] Their comparisons of Josephus's picture of Pharisaism in J.W. (ca. 75 C.E.) with his description of them in Ant. (93 C.E.) demonstrate that Josephus enhances the image of the Pharisees in the latter. They may be correct that the embellished portrait serves as propaganda for the Romans. And so when Josephus avows that the Pharisees have the support of the masses in their controversies with the Sadducees, while the Sadducees gain the confidence of the wealthy alone (Ant. 13.10.6 §298), he is scarcely credible.

But even though Josephus embellishes his portrait of the Pharisees in order to impress their status onto a larger Greco-Roman audience, that does not mean that he would have had to convince an audience in a narrower Jewish environment of such. In fact, he could hardly have created their status ex nihilo. In order to avoid immediate disconfirmation, he must have based his claims on some convincing reality.

At least a part of that reality is the rise to power of the Pharisees after 70 C.E. When Josephus discusses the break of Hyrcanus with

---

[23] M. Smith, "Palestinian Judaism in the First Century," *Israel: Its Role in Civilization* (ed. M. Davis; New York: Harper & Row, 1956) 71–78. Smith argues that the Pharisees had little support among the masses and actually encountered hostility from them. See also Neusner, *Rabbinic Traditions*, 3.329–30; idem, *From Politics to Piety*, 52–65.

the Pharisees in *Ant.* 13.10.5 §288, he describes their political power in an aside that apparently applies to his own era rather than to the time of Hyrcanus. He shifts abruptly from past to present verb forms and remarks, "And so great is their influence with the masses that even when they speak against a king or a high priest, they immediately gain credence." Therefore, by the end of the first century Josephus can present a convincing argument in his environment for the prominence of the Pharisees.[24]

Josephus corroborates the eminent status of the Pharisees in his environment by the way he himself claims to have been a member of the party (*Life* 2 §9-12, shortly after 100 C.E.). He professes his adherence to Pharisaism in a context where he establishes his pedigree from a noble priestly family, lauds his own intellectual abilities, and asserts his position of respect among his peers. According to him, his personal investigation of Jewish sects enabled him to select the "best," that is, Pharisaism. Hence, the claim advances Josephus's status. At this point he is not attempting to legitimate the Pharisees. Rather, he is taking advantage of Pharisaism's legitimacy to enhance his own posture. He is able to do so only because Pharisaism holds a place of respect and authority at the end of the first century.

Josephus's tendentious portrayal of the Pharisees warrants suspicion about its complete accuracy, especially when he reads their power and popularity back into their pre-70 history. But in fact, Josephus does not only present the Pharisees as eminent in *Ant.* but also in his earlier report in *J.W.* He asserts that the Pharisees hold the preeminent place in comparison with the Sadducees and Essenes (*J.W.* 2.8.14 §162). According to him, the Pharisees attempt to establish positive associations with the larger Jewish community, whereas the Sadducees care little about public relations (*J.W.* 2.8.14 §166).

Josephus also agrees with rabbinic literature and the NT in attesting the prestige of the Pharisees. Two rabbinic passages in

[24] W. Buehler (*The Pre-Herodian Civil War and Social Debate* [Basel: Reinhardt, 1974] 30, 33, 58–59, 68–69) attempts to identify the Pharisees as prominent in the period 76–40 B.C.E. by Josephus's application of οἱ πρῶτοι to them. This fails to consider that the title reflects Josephus's perspective and his own evaluation of the party. Indirectly, it does indicate Josephus's estimate of the Pharisees in his own period. With the emergence of Rabbinic Judaism at Yavneh after 70 C.E. there be little doubt of the respectability and authority of the Pharisees. G. Moore (*Judaism in the First Centuries of the Christian Era* [Cambridge: Harvard University Press, 1927] 287) hypothesizes that the influence that Josephus attributes to the Pharisees likely developed out of their control of popular education through the synagogue.

particular demonstrate popular support for the Pharisees.[25] *M. Menaḥ.* 10:3 preserves the tradition of a controversy between the Pharisees and the Boethusians (Sadducees, see below p. 108) over the proper procedure to be followed for the ritual of the cutting of the sheaf of barley for the meal offering on the second day of Passover. The reaper exaggerates the ritual by repeating questions about the proper procedure. Significantly, this exaggerated ritual receives broad public support. All the inhabitants of the nearby towns gather as spectators for the cutting of the sheaf. Moreover, they participate as respondents in the repetitive antiphony that pointedly distinguishes the Pharisaic ceremony from the Sadducean. Therefore, the general populace supports the Pharisees over against the Sadducees.

The second passage illustrates a similar loyalty to Pharisaic *halakah* on the part of the *'amme ha'areṣ. T. Sukk.* 3:1 gives a tradition that the waving of the willows takes precedence over the sabbath at the end of the Feast of Tabernacles. The Boethusians do not accept that the willows take precedence over the sabbath. On one occasion they attempt to enforce their ruling surreptitiously by hiding the willow branches under large rocks that the Pharisees would not move on the sabbath. The *'amme ha'areṣ* feel no compunction about moving the rocks on the sabbath and come to the aid of the Pharisees in their controversy with the Sadducees. So the Pharisees are able to rally popular support.[26]

[25] *M. Menaḥ.* 10.3; *b. Sukk.* 43b = *t. Sukk.* 3.1. The Pharisees are not actually mentioned in either pericope, and the authoritative *halakah* is anonymous in both cases. The Pharisees, however, are to be understood as the promulgators of the *halakah* because of the juxtaposition of the *halakah* to the position of the Boethusians (Sadducees), and because the *halakah* is identical with the Pharisaic position in other texts where the Pharisees are explicitly the promulgators of the *halakah*. So E. Rivkin, "Defining the Pharisees," *HUCA* 40–41 (1969–70) 222, 223, 226; idem, *Hidden Revolution*, 130–75. The geographical location of the tradition cannot be determined with precision. The controversy with the Boethusians implies a date before 70 C.E.

[26] *B. Soṭa* 22b contains a criticism of seven types of Pharisees that appears to indicate disdain for them on the part of the rabbis. But the parallel in *y. Ber.* 9.7 = *Soṭa* 5.5 plays one honorable type off against six dishonorable imitators. The Babylonian counterpart is elaborated by Babylonian Amoraim from the third and fourth centuries. Thus, the Palestinian Talmud actually preserves the high estimate of the Pharisees reflected in Josephus. *B. Pesaḥ.* 49b preserves a tradition of conflict between the Pharisees and the *'amme ha'areṣ.* But in the tradition only R. Eliezer's urge to kill comes from around the end of the first century, and it is an exception to the rule of positive or at least neutral relations between the Pharisees and the *'amme ha'areṣ.* The evidence appears to confirm the thesis of A. Büchler (*Der galiläisch 'Am-ha 'Areṣ des zweiten Jahrhunderts* [Vienna: Holder, 1906] passim) that the conflict between the *'amme ha'areṣ* and the *ḥaberim* escalated only after the activity of the rabbinic academy at Usha. On the problem of

The eminence of the Pharisees also carries over into the Christian community. In spite of the encounters between them and Jesus which are preserved in the synoptic tradition, the title "Pharisee" continued to confer special status upon its claimants in the life of the early church. This is quite clear even in Paul's claim to have been a Pharisee in Phil 3:5.

The polemic in Philippians 3 has a dual function. It is an attack upon opponents, and it clarifies the legitimacy of Paul's authority. As an attempt to recoup his losses, Paul's polemic gives direct and indirect information about him and his antagonists that shows that by ordinary standards the claim to be a Pharisee was a claim to special standing.

Paul's claims to status in Judaism are explicitly analogous to the assertions of his opponents. The opponents may even have claimed to be Pharisees.[27] Regardless of the nature of the boasts of the opponents, this much is clear: The purpose of their boasting was to establish their superior standing among the Philippians.

Paul himself selects the title Pharisee in order to boost indirectly his standing to a level that supersedes ordinary claims to status. In spite of the disclaimers that he puts little stock in Jewish standards of legitimation (Phil 3:3, 7-8), Paul shows that he is able to match his opponents' claims. Initially, Paul does not argue that circumcision, Hebraic racial identity, and Pharisaic adherence to the law are offensive. He uses them to establish his right to confidence in the flesh. Only at that point does he turn the tables. He introduces a sudden reversal of values that shows his legitimacy to be far superior. The old criteria are superseded to the extent that they are considered vile filth by comparison. Such an

---

identifying the Pharisees in rabbinic literature see J. Bowker (*Jesus and the Pharisees* [Cambridge: Cambridge University Press, 1973] 1–15) and Rivkin ("Defining the Pharisees," 205–49 and *Hidden Revolution,* 164–67). Bowker points to the wide scope of meaning possible for *pārûš* and attempts to coordinate Josephus and the NT with rabbinic references. Rivkin develops an ingenious though defective methodology for defining the Pharisees by their juxtaposition to the Sadducees. Rivkin assumes that the Pharisees are monolithic and that their role never varies. Defining the Pharisees by their juxtaposition to the Sadducees is tantamount to an a priori elimination of their juxtaposition to the ʿam haʾareṣ. His method provides some certainty for references where the juxtaposition to the Sadducees must imply the identity of the Pharisees, but the method is faulty in other instances where references may identify them.

[27] W. Schmithals ("Der Irrlehrer des Philipperbriefes," *ZTK* 54 [1957] 316, n. 3) argues that the opponents could not have claimed to have been Pharisees since Paul asserts the superiority of his claims. Against Schmithals, Paul similarly maintains the superiority of his claims in 2 Cor 11:21–23 although they are identical to those of his opponents.

argument can proceed only in an environment where the Pharisees continue to win respect. From Paul to Josephus to Tannaitic sources, the prestige of the Pharisees stands out, not only explicitly, but also as an unintentional indirect presupposition.

Luke writes in such an environment. When Luke introduces the Pharisee Gamaliel in Acts 5:34, he describes him as a teacher of the law highly regarded by all the people. Does Luke so characterize Gamaliel because he stands over against Luke's ordinary evaluation of the Pharisees or because he represents Luke's typical view? 5:33-40 is a conflict story. The leadership of Christianity encounters the leadership of Judaism. The Christian leadership is unified and undifferentiated. In contrast, the Jewish leadership is not monolithic. To be sure, the Sanhedrin as a body orders the apostles to cease their activity in 4:18. But even at that point the people stand over against the council (v 21). The official leaders do not adequately represent the people.

In Acts 5:34 Gamaliel comes onto the stage as a genuine representative of the people. He is an authentic Jew, nothing less than a Pharisee and a teacher of the law, who is honored by all the people. This revered Pharisee comes to the defense of the apostles. His advice stands in contrast to the earlier orders of the court. Furthermore, Gamaliel wins the day. Thereafter, the apostles are free to teach and preach daily. In this conflict story, therefore, Gamaliel and the apostles stand united against the high priest and the Sadducees.

Luke not only allies Gamaliel with Christianity, but also dissociates him from the company of inauthentic leaders of Judaism. There is a contrasting parallel between the rising up of the high priest and Sadducees in Acts 5:17 and the rising up of Gamaliel in v 34. Later, Gamaliel warns them against opposing God (v 39). But since Luke has already portrayed the high priest and Sadducees as full of jealousy ($\zeta\tilde{\eta}\lambda o\varsigma$, v 17), Gamaliel's speech, viewed from Luke's perspective, shows that the high priest and Sadducees are indeed opposing God. As part of the same Lucan design, later in Acts Paul designates himself before his conversion as $\zeta\eta\lambda\omega\tau\grave{\eta}\varsigma$ $\acute{\upsilon}\pi\acute{\alpha}\rho\chi\omega\nu$ and for that reason a persecutor of the church in league precisely with the priestly party (22:3-5). According to Luke, the leaders of Judaism who oppose Christianity, like Paul before his conversion, do a disservice to Judaism. They fight against the God for whom ostensibly they stand. The Sadducees, therefore, do not represent the genuine tradition of Israel.[28]

---

[28] A. Loisy, *Les Actes des Apôtres* (Paris: Nourry, 1920) 284.

Luke has constructed a complex apologetic device.[29] On the one hand Gamaliel is positive toward Christianity. For Luke's audience history has confirmed what Gamaliel suspects, namely, that Christianity is from God. On the other hand, Gamaliel unmasks a segment of Jewish leadership as inauthentic. Gamaliel is the genuine Jew on the verge of affirming Christianity. Thus, the conflict in Acts 5 is between the Sadducees on the one hand and Gamaliel in league with Christianity on the other.

Gamaliel functions in this way only because he is an authoritative leader highly regarded by all the people, including Luke and his audience. Acts takes advantage of Gamaliel's respectability already firmly established in Jewish tradition in order to bestow respectability on Christianity.

Luke again takes advantage of Gamaliel's high standing to legitimate Paul in Acts 22:3. It is a commonplace that Paul's contact with both Hellenism and Judaism gives him the best of both worlds. But in fact, Luke encounters difficulty establishing Paul's Jewishness in face of his contact with the Hellenistic world. For that reason Paul begins his autobiographical sketch by asserting, "I am a Jew" (v 3). Only after claiming his Jewishness does Paul acknowledge his birth in Tarsus. Immediately after mentioning his place of birth, he again emphasizes his Jewishness. Luke frames Paul's birth with his Jewishness to counter any implication that Paul's Hellenism constitutes a denial of his Judaism.

W. C. van Unnik has demonstrated from a wide range of Hellenistic literature that the series of the three verbs "born," "brought up," and "educated" in Acts 22:3 is a fixed formula describing human development from birth to maturity. Brought up and educated refer to distinct stages of the development.[30] The sense of the sentence is that Paul was brought up in his home in Jerusalem, and when he reached mental maturity, he was educated at the feet of Gamaliel.

The main verb clause and the final participial phrase form the definitive structure for Acts 22:3: "I am a Jew . . . being a zealot for God."[31] The perfect participles "brought up" and "educated"

[29] H. Conzelmann, *Die Apostelgeschichte erklärt* (Tübingen: Mohr [Siebeck], 1972) 49; cf. H. Flender, *St. Luke: Theologian of Redemptive History* (Philadelphia: Fortress, 1967) 27; E. Zeller, *The Contents and Origin of the Acts of the Apostles, Critically Investigated* (London: Williams and Norgate, 1875) 1.231.

[30] W. van Unnik, *Tarsus or Jerusalem: The City of Paul's Youth* (London: Epworth, 1962) 19–35. F. F. Bruce (*The Acts of the Apostles*, 399–400) punctuates Acts 22:3 by placing commas after κιλικίας and after Γαμαλιηλ, implying the apposition of "brought up" and "educated." Cf. the RSV. Van Unnik (*Tarsus or Jerusalem*, 44) shows conclusively that the comma must be placed after ταύτῃ.

[31] C. Burchard, *Der dreizehnte Zeuge: Traditions- und kompositionsgeschicht-*

show Paul's background in Judaism. But the principal claim is that Paul remains a Jewish zealot. In spite of his birth in Tarsus, Paul never was anything but Jewish, and that is what he remains.

The reference to Gamaliel does far more than confirm Paul's education. Luke uses the revered rabbi to place Paul in the heart of Judaism.

The parallel between Gamaliel's defense of the apostles in Acts 5 and the defense of Paul by the Pharisees in Acts 23 includes the same type of complex apology. First, Paul clashes with Ananias and exposes him as an inadequate judge who is violating the law. Second, Paul claims to be a Pharisee. His affirmation of Pharisaism is far more than a ruse to divide the Sanhedrin. It is also a rejection of the Sadducees. The Pharisees ally with Paul against the Sadducees. This places Paul in the camp of the more faithful Jews. Paul claims Pharisaism, and the Pharisees return the favor. They defend Paul. But they defend him against the Sadducees.

Luke hardly purposes to defend the Pharisees, however. The apology is for Paul. Luke uses the Pharisees to exonerate Paul because they already occupy a position of respect and authority in his environment.

In contrast to Paul's claim to be a Pharisee in the present in Acts 23:6, in 26:5 he asserts that he has been related to Pharisaism in the past. Even if the aorist implies a termination of that relationship (which is unlikely), the point of the argument is Paul's unity with the strictest party of Judaism. Had he emphasized his break with the Pharisees, he would have illustrated his apostasy rather than his unity with Judaism.

Luke utilizes Paul's Pharisaism to locate him in the center of Judaism. Paul's conflict with the Jews is an in-house affair. Paul's biographical data strengthens the picture of an intramural conflict. Significantly, Luke places Paul in the center of a revered sphere of Judaism to exonerate his mission among gentiles.

In the only other allusion to the Pharisees in Acts, certain of them are regarded as believers (Acts 15:5). These attempt to place demands on gentile believers that Luke himself cannot accept. The decree of the Jerusalem Council shows all the more, in face of the Pharisaic believers, the compatibility of Pharisaism and Christianity.

Elsewhere in Acts, highly regarded Pharisees stand on the threshold of Christianity rather than contradicting it. They can

---

liche Untersuchungen zu Lukas' Darstellung der Frühzeit des Paulus (Göttingen: Vandenhoeck & Ruprecht, 1970) 32.

vindicate Paul, the apostles, and Christianity only because they occupy a place of high status for Luke and his audience.

Luke's attitude toward the Pharisees is not as positive in his Gospel as it is in Acts. Nevertheless, even in the Gospel the Pharisees' status of respected and authoritative leaders of Judaism is perceptible.

Luke's first reference to the Pharisees associates them with teachers of the law and depicts them as hailing from all the villages of Galilee and Judea and from Jerusalem (Luke 5:17). To digress momentarily, exegetically there is no basis for inferring antagonism in this introduction, but the widespread notion that Luke places them here as enemies from the beginning necessitates a disclaimer. Rather, Luke provides a comprehensive geographical base for the Pharisees and the teachers of the law. Their connection with Jewish territory in its entirety indicates two things. First, they are present as an organized body. Their gathering is coordinated. The reference to Jerusalem breaks the form of a triad in series. The first two members of the series associate villages with territory, whereas Jersualem stands alone over and above the villages. Therefore, it may be added specifically to imply official status. Second, the broad geographical base introduces the Pharisees and teachers of the law as representing all the territory of the Jewish people.[32]

When Luke introduces Gamaliel in Acts 5, he portrays him favorably as highly regarded by all the people. The allusion to the broad geographical base of the Pharisees in Luke 5 serves a similar, if less flattering, function. In the healing of the paralytic that follows, Luke juxtaposes the authority of respected leaders of Israel to the authority of Jesus.

Pharisees extend Jesus invitations to be their guest at table on three occasions. The setting at a meal in the home of Simon in Luke 7:36-50 presupposes conviviality. The dialogue reflects the amenities of proper social relationships. Jesus politely addresses Simon; Simon reciprocates by calling Jesus teacher (v 40). The strong affinity between 7:36-50 and the genre of the Hellenistic symposium, shows that Simon provides the foil for Jesus' teaching about forgiveness. Simon fulfills the role of the host in the symposium, who is typically highly regarded especially for his

---

[32] G. Vermes (*Jesus the Jew: A Historian's Reading of the Gospels* [New York: Macmillan, 1973] 56–57) suggests that there were few Pharisees associated with Galilee in the first century. He basically argues from silence, and he fails to deal with Luke 5:17. But if his argument is accurate, Luke's identification of Pharisees with Galilee is all the more an effort to provide the region with respected and authoritative representatives.

wealth and learning.[33] But more is at stake. Simon's disdain for the woman who is a sinner demonstrates Luke's awareness that the Pharisees refuse table fellowship with sinners. And so indirectly the fellowship between Jesus and the Pharisees distinguishes Jesus from the outcasts even though he often associates with them. A subsidiary theme, then, is that Jesus is acceptable at the table of the Pharisee.

E. Springs Steele has recently accounted for the composition of Luke 11:37-54 also on the basis of the genre of the Hellenistic symposium.[34] Although the host is simply designated a Pharisee, the prominence of Pharisees (as demonstrated above) and the topoi of the genre enable us to argue cautiously that this Pharisee holds a position of honor. And again, the setting at the table implies cordiality.

Jesus' unmitigated attack on the Pharisees, however, appears to eclipse the cordiality. Luke clearly intends to present Jesus as a strong opponent to the behavior of the Pharisees *en masse*. After this encounter, the Pharisees purposefully attempt to entrap Jesus. Even at that, the break with the Pharisees is not final. Jesus still enters into dialogue with them. They never appear as opponents of Jesus in Jerusalem or in connection with the passion. Rather, the principal opponents are the priestly hierarchy.

Moreover, as I have indicated earlier, immediately after the woes, Luke cites a saying of Jesus to interpret the reprehensible behavior of the Pharisees as hypocrisy (Luke 12:1). The saying not only culminates the woes against the Pharisees but also introduces an exhortation to Christian fidelity. The Pharisees illustrate the same kind of hypocrisy as Christian apostasy.

The entrance upon the scene of tens of thousands of people in Luke 12:1 abruptly alters the setting, but it does not signal a complete break in the narrative as is clear from the allusion back to the woes in the hypocrisy of the Pharisees. Although Luke has just described the most severe opposition between Jesus and the Pharisees that he reports, he immediately counters the impression that Jews reject Jesus by relating the overwhelming support of the people. Although the masses stand over against the Pharisees here, and although the Pharisees have a serious flaw of character, Luke

---

[33] X. de Meeûs, "Composition de Lc. XIV et genre symposiaque," *ETL* 37 (1961) 862–63; J. Delobel, "L'onction par la pécheresse: La composition litteraire de Luc 7.36–50," *ETL* 42 (1966) 459. For examples see Plato *Symposium* 173–75; Xenophon *Symposium* 1.1–8; *Letter of Aristeas* 180–85; Plutarch *The Dinner of the Seven Wise Men* 146 D.

[34] E. Steele, "Luke 11:37–54—A Modified Hellenistic Symposium?" *JBL* 103 (1984) 379–394.

circumscribes the woes so that they do not repudiate Pharisaism as such.

After this most severe opposition of the Pharisees to Jesus in the entire Gospel, Luke allows the Pharisees to return to a more positive relationship with Jesus at Luke 13:31. Although the motives of the informants in warning Jesus about Herod lie concealed, they appear as benevolent protectors who act in the interest and safety of Jesus. The Pharisees identify the problem as Herod's desire to kill Jesus. They apprise Jesus of the threat and offer him a solution to the problem—leaving Herod's jurisdiction.

Table fellowship with Pharisees sets the scene for four pericopes in Luke 14:1-24. Although the question, "Is it lawful to heal on the sabbath, or not?" (v 3) is on the lips of Jesus, it voices the skepticism of the Pharisees who are "watching him" (v 1). Since the question concerns the legality of healing on the sabbath, the discussion moves to the level of *halakah*.[35] The silence of the Pharisees indicates their perplexity. A negative answer stands in conflict with benevolence; a positive one calls their sabbath *halakah* into question. Their *inability* to respond, however, highlights Jesus' perspective as authoritative (v 6). Healing not only suspends the sabbath but is lawful in a positive sense. It is the thing to do.

In this case Luke makes the prominence of the host explicit. He is a ruler of the Pharisees. Luke uses the eminence of the Pharisees on this occasion to the advantage of Jesus. Even they can offer no opposition to Jesus' rationale. Our inability to determine more precisely the meaning of "ruler" in this case indicates all the more that it is designed to convey the eminence of the host. That is, Luke prepares him for his function in the pericope rather than trying to define his status, for example, in the synagogue or Sanhedrin. Thanks to his prominence, Jesus appears in even better light.

The meal with the ruler of the Pharisees sets the stage for three additional pericopes that are linked together by the theme of eschatological reversal of status. But significantly, the presence of the Pharisees at the table with Jesus provides the occasion for

---

[35] J. Roloff (*Das Kerygma und der irdische Jesus: Historische Motive in den Jesus-Erzählungen der Evangelien* [Göttingen: Vandenhoeck & Ruprecht, 1970] 80) argues that by the time of Luke the sabbath question was no longer a live issue in Christian circles. Interest in the priority of sabbath laws appears in *b. Yoma* 85a–85b. R. Eleazar, R. Ishmael, and R. Akiba are mentioned in the discussion. This dates the pericope close to the end of the first century. The problem of Luke 14:1–6 was a live issue for rabbinic debate in the period roughly contemporaneous with Luke.

rather than the illustration of the reversal of status. Although the editorial transition in v 12 directs Jesus' advice to receive the poor, the maimed, the lame, and the blind to the host, the eschatological sense insures a general application.[36]

Even the attempt of the guests to secure a place of prominence serves as the occasion for the saying of Jesus (v 11) rather than as an illustration of it.[37] Because it is eschatological, the inversion in v 11 becomes universal, no longer applying exclusively to the Pharisees.

The parable of the banquet implies that the Pharisees are potential candidates for exclusion from the eschatological feast in the kingdom of God. But by the same token, they are potential candidates for participation, provided they are willing to enter the present manifestation of the eschatological order. Indeed, the ruler of the Pharisees could even serve as a paradigm for present participation in the eschatological order. He invites Jesus into his own home to share a meal without hope of reciprocation after the pattern of Jesus' advice to him in vv 12-14.

In naming the Pharisees φιλάργυροι (Luke 16:14), Luke adopts a Hellenistic literary device as I have already shown. From the point of view of an original conflict, Luke 16:14 appears to be an unmitigated *ad hominem* rebuke of the Pharisees. But from Luke's point of view, the juxtaposition of the φιλάργυροι with Jesus enables him to make a comparison between two orders. 14:7-24 makes a similar comparison between the present order and the eschatological order. In this case the comparison is between the present earthly order and the contemporaneous heavenly order. The Pharisees' self-justification, apparently connected with wealth as a sign of God's blessing, represents human values over against divine values. Commitment to human values over against divine values, therefore, is a part of the flawed character of the Pharisees.

From the perspective of Luke's readers, Jesus' announcement of this reversal of values takes on the character of proclamation, exhortation, and an appeal to adopt God's values. H. J. Cadbury correctly notes that this address to the Pharisees expresses Luke's concern for the "oppressor rather than . . . the oppressed" and that for Luke the words of Jesus serve "as a technique for social betterment" and an "appeal to conscience and sense of duty."[38]

---

[36] So A. Jülicher. *Die Gleichnisreden Jesu* (Tübingen: Mohr [Siebeck], 1910) 2.252.

[37] The significance of places at the table is a topos in the Hellenistic symposium. Steele, "Luke 11:37–54," 384. E.g., Plutarch *The Dinner of the Seven Wise Men* 148 E–F, 149 F.

[38] Cadbury, *The Making of Luke-Acts*, 262–63.

These words of Jesus to the Pharisees, which appear to be so caustic and biting, serve as a warning about self-justification and wealth as its evidence. But they also issue a call to adopt the divine scale of values.

Luke 17:20 employs another Hellenistic device for providing a setting for authoritative teaching. The literary form of v 20 corresponds to a typical technique for introducing apothegms—the passive participle introducing an inquiry that is then the occasion for the climactic saying.[39] For Luke, Pharisees formulate the inquiry[40] and thereby become the sounding board for the teachings of Jesus.

The key for the interpretation of Luke 17:20-21 is the meaning of ἐντὸς ὑμῶν. Lexically, the most probable meaning for ἐντός is "within." This implies that the kingdom of God is immanent within individuals. Interpreters often allege presumptively that the antipathy between the Pharisees and Jesus proscribes the location of the kingdom "within" them. True, Luke probably does not mean that the kingdom is immanent, but this conclusion rests on other grounds. Luke presupposes no hostility or sinister motives on the part of the Pharisees. He does not exclude the Pharisees a priori. Elsewhere in Luke, however, the kingdom is present more in the cosmic and external manifestations of the power of God.[41] In this pericope the Pharisees function at worst as neutral inquirers who give occasion for Jesus' teaching, at best as recipients of the kingdom.

The objection of the Pharisees to the christological acclamation from Jesus' disciples occasions Jesus' public confirmation of his messianic identity (Luke 19:39-40). The praise of God on the lips of disciples provokes their opposition.[42] Over against Mark and

---

[39] This is the classical pattern for introducing apothegms according to W. Gemoll, *Das Apophthegma: Literarhistorische Studien* (Wein/Leipzig: Freytag, 1924) 2. Gemoll gives examples from Xenophon and pottery inscriptions. I have examined over 100 examples of this form in sayings from Socrates, Diogenes, Plato, Zeno, Cleanthes, and Chrysippus. Examples of Greek apothegms are collected in G. von Wartensleben, *Begriff der griechischen Chreia und Beiträge zur Geschichte ihrer Form* (Heidelberg: Winter's Universitätsbuchhandlung, 1901).

[40] Bultmann (*History*, 53) denies the interest of Pharisees in eschatological matters. W. D. Davies ("Apocalyptic and Pharisaism," *Christian Origins and Judaism* [Philadelphia: Westminster, 1962] 19–30) has accounted for apocalyptic concerns among some Pharisees.

[41] A. Rustow, "'Εντὸς ὑμῶν ἐστίν: Zur Deutung von Lukas 17:20–21," ZNW 51 (1960) 197–224.

[42] K. Rengstorf (*Das Evangelium nach Lucas: Übersetzt und erklärt* [Göttingen: Vandenhoeck & Ruprecht, 1952] 218) and G. Caird (*The Gospel of St. Luke* [Baltimore: Penguin, 1963] 216) contend that the proclamation of Jesus as king would have been interpreted by the Romans as an act of sedition, and that the

Matthew, Luke mentions explicitly that *disciples* of Jesus cele-
brate at the descent from the Mount of Olives (v 37). In keeping
with the identification of the celebrants, the Pharisees direct their
opposition against the behavior of the disciples rather than against
Jesus, just as they do in 5:30 and 6:2.

Moreover, Luke indicates clearly what the Pharisees find
objectionable. In comparison with Mark and Matthew, Luke elaborates the description of the celebrants' behavior and specifies that
they are praising God (19:37). The Pharisees object to the occasion
and the content of that praise. The disciples' retrospective consideration of the mighty works of Jesus gives rise to the occasion; the
content is that Jesus is the messianic king. Among the synoptists
only Luke places the title "king" on the lips of the celebrants (v
37). The Pharisees imply, therefore, that the mighty works of Jesus
constitute an inadequate basis for messianic claims. But even
though the Pharisees question Jesus' messianic identity, their
interruption of the celebration enables Jesus to confirm it.

In all probability, Luke understands Peter's confession of Jesus
as "the Christ of God" (Luke 9:20) as an unequivocal identification
of Jesus as the messiah. There, however, Jesus commands his
disciples to tell no one. In contrast, his reply to the Pharisees in
19:40 validates the christological confession as a divine necessity:
If the disciples are silent, the stones will cry out. The Pharisees
oppose the confession of the disciples. Jesus, however, contradicts
their objection in order to affirm his messianic kingship. The
Pharisees in v 39 are the audience for the christological identity of
Jesus.

Conclusion

Luke takes over the Pharisees in a historical, cultural, and
religious context in which they demand admiration and assigns
them a commensurate role. In Acts they legitimate the apostles,
Paul, and Christianity. In Luke, they legitimate even Jesus. They
can fulfill their function in Acts only because they occupy a
position of respect and authority. In Luke, their status is not
absolutely necessary for their juxtaposition to Jesus. But the higher
the status, the better the contrast. Luke's Jesus will make slight
impression on his readers if his antagonists are opponents of straw.
Because Luke can count on their prestige, Jesus' *halakah* is all the
more convincing. Still the Pharisees are flawed in character. Even
Gamaliel, the Pharisaic defenders of Paul, and the believers in

---

Pharisees act benevolently to preclude trouble with Rome. According to Pilate,
however, the claim to messianic kingship is not a criminal offense (Luke 23:2–4).

Acts 15:5 are incomplete. Not until like Paul they believe in the resurrection of Jesus and accept the accession of the gentiles to God's salvation will they be faithful to the hopes of Israel as Luke understands them. But flawed character and all, they nevertheless command the respect of Luke and his readers. On the basis of their status in Luke's environment, he can use them to set Jesus and Christianity off to advantage.

CHAPTER SEVEN
SADDUCEES, PRIESTS, AND TEMPLE

With the possible exception of Josephus, all of the information from antiquity about the Sadducees comes from their opponents. Sadducees appear rather incidentally as foes of the Pharisees in rabbinic literature. They make brief dramatic appearances as stereotyped opponents of Jesus in Mark and Matthew. In Luke-Acts, though relatively more prominent as adversaries of Jesus and the early Christian community, they still remain rather peripheral. Josephus claims to be able to describe the Sadducees as an insider—he once went through the disciplines of the Jewish sects (*Life* 2 §10-12). But since in the last analysis he decides against the Sadducees in favor of the Pharisees, he too is no exception.

Since in the literature of antiquity the Sadducees never speak for themselves, investigation of who they really were always stands under a methodological caveat. Tendentious prejudices in the primary sources have to come under consideration. In contrast, an attempt to determine Luke's view of them, bias and all, escapes the strictures of such caution. But inasmuch as comparison of Luke's portrait with a more objective picture highlights his perspectives, this inquiry pursues both to some degree.

Sadducees and Chief Priests

Acts 4:1 associates the Sadducees with the priests and the captain of the temple. At the same time, it distinguishes between them. What Luke has in mind with his reference to priests is quite ambiguous. Since they are responding to a turbulent hubbub in the temple, they are temple priests. Along with the Sadducees, they are annoyed at the proclamation of the resurrection, and, in league with the captain of the temple, they have some authority to arrest the apostles (v 2). Thus, Luke creates a complex pattern of relationships between priests and Sadducees. How can we sort out these relationships?

When the Sadducees appear on the scene of history, they have political concerns and are not a priestly group (Josephus *Ant.*

13.10.6 §293-98). Although during the first century of our era the high priesthood was in their hands, it is a premature judgment which too quickly equates them with the temple functionaries. And so the Sadducees as such cannot be said to administer the temple.[1] It is possible for high priests to call themselves Sadducees (Josephus *Ant.* 20.9.1 §197-203; *b. Yoma* 19b),[2] but the perspective cannot be reversed. The movement is far broader than the priesthood and encompasses concerns far beyond the temple.

Rabbinic tradition frequently uses the terms "Sadducee" and "Boethusian" interchangeably. But an elaboration of a mishnaic tradition, in which R. Gamaliel remembers living in the same alley with a Sadducee, makes a distinction between them: "If a man lives [in the same alley] with a gentile, a Sadducee or a Boethusian, these impose restrictions upon him" (*b.'Erub.* 68b). Such a text prohibits a direct identification of the two and actually leaves room to argue that they are separate groups. The most felicitous solution to the apparent ambiguity of the evidence, however, is that the Boethusians were one of the constituent groups of the Sadducees.[3]

As such, the Boethusians were a priestly group, as they were from inception. A tradition in *The Fathers According to Rabbi Nathan* 5 (= Version B 10) claims that the Boethusians owe their origin to a certain Boethus, a disciple of Antigonus of Soko. In all likelihood, that is an anachronistic speculation. Rather, the group derives from Simon b. Boethus whom Herod the Great appointed high priest in 22 B.C.E. Josephus relates that Herod made the appointment in order to facilitate his marriage to Simon's daughter (*Ant.* 15.9.3 §320-22; according to 19.6.2 §297-98, she may be his sister). But since Simon's father was an Alexandrian, Herod may have been attempting to divorce the high priesthood from Jerusalem families. At any rate, from the time of Herod the Great until the destruction of the temple, eight high priests are related to the

---

[1] As does C. Burchard, "Sadduzäer," *Paulys Realencyclopädie der classischen Altertumswissenschaft*, Supplementband 15 (1978) 473. Cf. J. LeMoyne, *Les Sadducéens* (Paris: Gabalda, 1972) 346–48; E. Schürer, *The History of the Jewish People in the Time of Jesus Christ* (Edinburgh: T. & T. Clark, 1885–90) 2.2.29–30. V. Eppstein ("When and How the Sadducees Were Excommunicated," *JBL* 85 [1966] 213–14) argues that the fundamental relationship between the Sadducees and the temple must be rejected. In contrast M. Mansoor ("Sadducees," *EncJud* 14 [1971] 622) still contends that the *raison d'être* of the Sadducees was bound up with the temple.

[2] G. Hölscher's thesis (*Der Sadduzäismus: Eine kritische Untersuchung zur späteren jüdischen Religionsgeschichte* [Leipzig: Hinrich, 1906] 54–70), that in authentic historical traditions, the Sadducees are not associated with the high priesthood but only secondarily in later traditions, cannot be sustained.

[3] LeMoyne, *Sadducéens*, 337, cf. n. 3.

family of Boethus.[4] The family of Boethus is so associated with the high priesthood that even though Boethus himself was not a high priest, Josephus can refer to a certain Matthias son of Boethus as claiming high priestly ancestry (*J.W.* 5.13.1 §527). Thus, the Boethusians can be identified as a priestly circle within the Sadducees. Other high priestly families of the NT era were also associated with the Sadducees. From this perspective, it is easy to understand how Luke associates the Sadducees with the high priests, even though they encompass a much broader group.

The nascent Christian community encounters no opposition until Acts 4. When Luke introduces opponents, they are first of all priests, the captain of the temple, and the Sadducees. This is the only occasion in all of Luke-Acts where the author uses the unqualified term "priests" to refer to adversaries of Christianity. Not until the interrogation before the Sanhedrin on the following day does Luke mention the high priest (v 6). Although Luke makes no direct identification between the priests of v 1 and the gathering of the Sanhedrin on the following day, the context certainly implies a connection. Luke, therefore, associates the priests of v 1 with the high-priestly family of v 6. In the context he further describes one of the constituent groups of this Sanhedrin as chief priests (v 23). Although these may not be identical with the priests involved in the arrest, they are closely related. Thus, Luke associates the priests of v 1 with the high priestly party.

Elsewhere Luke consistently specifies that the priestly opponents of Jesus and the church are *chief* priests. He thereby makes a distinction between a high priestly circle and the ordinary priests.

In doing so, Luke shares a perspective that surfaces elsewhere in antiquity. *B. Pesaḥ.* 57a relates a tradition about the chief priests forcefully seizing more than their share of the skins of sacrificial animals from the priests who served one week at a time, thereby depriving the later of a source of their livelihood. Josephus reports with respect to the Sadducees that they are quite harsh in their behavior toward others and appeal only to the aristocrats (*J.W.* 2.8.14 §166; *Ant.* 13.10.6 §298; 18.1.5 §17). Necessary changes being made, we can apply Josephus's judgment to the chief priests and deduce that they constitute a priestly aristocracy separate from the ordinary priests.[5] Thus, the Sadducees are in league with the

---

[4] E. Smallwood, "High Priests and Politics in Roman Palestine," *JTS* 13 (1962) 31–34. She speculates that Simon and Boethus may be one and the same.

[5] J. Wellhausen, *Die Pharisäer und die Sadducäer: Eine Untersuchung zur inneren jüdischen Geschichte* (Greifswalk: Bamberg, 1874) 51–52; J. Jeremias, *Jerusalem in the Time of Jesus: An Investigation into Economic and Social*

chief priests, but both may be distinct from priests of lesser prominence.

Luke's portrait of ordinary priests is at worst neutral and at best rather positive. To be sure the good Samaritan stands over against a priest and a Levite, but inasmuch as for Luke the parable answers the captious lawyer, it is he who appears in bad light (Luke 10:25-37). Allegedly, Luke 5:14 might also reflect negatively on priests. In this case Jesus instructs a leper to show himself to a priest and to make an offering εἰς μαρτύριον αὐτοῖς. When εἰς μαρτύριον is used with the dative of the person for whom the witness is significant, it is usually a witness against that person.[6] But since αὐτοῖς has no antecedent, the matter is quite uncertain.

Fortunately, the comparable situation in Luke 17:14 sheds light on this case. Jesus commands ten lepers who are cleansed to show themselves to the priests. Here the narrative assumes as self-evident that the function of the priests is to confirm the successful cure.[7] The close parallel to Luke 5:14 implies the same role for the priest there. Both stories acknowledge a system in which the priest legitimates the cure of leprosy (Lev 14:2-3). Furthermore, the priest in Luke 5:14 fulfills the function of attesting the miracle, a consistent part of healing miracles as form criticism has shown. And so αὐτοῖς refers to the people at large rather than indicating a negative testimony against the priests. The priests in both stories of the healing of lepers are at worst neutral authorities who authenticate the miracle.

In two passages Luke exhibits a rather complimentary view of priests. In Acts, Luke portrays them positively enough that there is nothing incompatible about their becoming Christians. In fact, Luke states emphatically that a great crowd of the priests were obedient to the faith (Acts 6:7). His description of Zechariah and Elizabeth is all the more affirmative. Not only does Luke specify twice that Zechariah is a priest (Luke 1:5, 8), but he also implies the priestly pedigree of Elizabeth. She is from the daughters of Aaron (v 5). Luke then gives them the highest commendation—

Conditions During the New Testament Period (Philadelphia: Fortress, 1969) 180, 198; LeMoyne, *Sadducéens*, 106.

[6] H. Strathmann, "μάρτυς," *TDNT* 4.503, cf. n. 75.

[7] H. D. Betz, "The Cleansing of the Ten Lepers (Luke 17:11–19)," *JBL* 90(1971) 317; W. Bruners, *Die Reinigung der zehn Aussätzigen und die Heilung des Samariters Lk 17,11–19: Ein Beitrag zur lukanischen Interpretation der Reinigung von Aussätzigen* (Stuttgart: Katholisches Bibelwerk, 1977) 210. Bruners develops the thesis that Luke has composed the incident on the basis of Mark 1:40–45 and the healing of Naaman in 2 Kgs 5. If so, the redaction in Luke 17:14 clarifies all the more Luke's intention in 5:14.

they walk in all the commandments of the Lord and are righteous and blameless (v 6).

In contrast, the chief priests are always opponents. Jesus initially refers to them in the first passion prediction as among those who will reject him (Luke 9:22). True to that prediction, they appear on the scene at Jesus' arrival at the temple seeking to destroy him (19:47). Thereafter, they are prominent antagonists in both Luke and Acts.

Unexpectedly, among the opponents of Christianity in Ephesus are seven sons of a Jewish high priest named Sceva (Acts 19:14). Since no primary sources from antiquity attest such a Sceva among the high priests of Jerusalem, it has become customary to soften the surprise by making him a member of a high priestly family.[8] Since Josephus calls Matthias a high priest when in fact he is only from the high priestly family of Boethus (*J.W.* 4.9.11 §574; cf. 5.13.1 §527), it may be accurate to attribute to Sceva nothing more than high priestly ancestry. But Luke uses this reference to intensify the attempt to pervert Christianity. No less than sons of a high priest outrageously transform Christianity into sorcery. But their incantations backfire. They are repudiated and Paul is exonerated.

To summarize up to this point, Luke associates the Sadducees with the high priestly party. Together they earn a negative assessment from Luke. On the other hand, Luke distinguishes ordinary priests from Sadducees and high priests, and he views them rather positively.

The alliance between the Sadducees and the chief priests was not merely a social phenomenon. It was also closely related to political realities. In the first century of our era until the fall of Jerusalem, the high priest was the primary leader of the Jewish theocracy. Within the confines of Roman domination, he presided over the Sanhedrin, the principal agency of the limited self-government of the Jews. According to Josephus, at the time of the revolution against Rome, the Sanhedrin contained elements of the leading citizens, chief priests, and prominent Pharisees (*J.W.* 2.17.3 §411; cf. 2.14.8 §301). Acts stands in basic agreement. Acts 4:5-6 implies that the council is composed of rulers and elders and scribes under the leadership of the high priest. When Peter has opportunity to respond to their inquiry, he addresses them as "rulers of the people and elders" (v 8). Upon release Peter and John summarize what the chief priests and elders had said to them (v 23). In 5:17 the high priest, supported by Sadducees, arrests the

8 Among many, Schürer, *History*, 2.1.203–205.

apostles and convenes the Sanhedrin (v 21). The high priest leads
the proceedings (v 28). Furthermore, at least one prominent
Pharisee is present, namely, Gamaliel (vv 34-40).

Acts 23 supposedly reflects a situation more than two decades
later. The high priest still presides over the council, which counts
among its members chief priests (22:30), Sadducees, and Pharisees
(at least some of the Pharisees are also called scribes) (23:2-3, 6-9).
Later in the same chapter some Jews plot against Paul and confide
in chief priests and elders who apparently are members of the
council (vv 14-15). If the elders of Acts correspond to the prominent citizens to whom Josephus refers (and they probably do), then
Luke and Josephus stand in close proximity in their concepts of the
council.

Since the Pharisaic element of the Sanhedrin sides with Paul
in Acts 23:6-10, Joachim Jeremias identifies the elders in Acts
23:14 wth the Sadducees in vv 6-10.[9] That is correct insofar as it
applies to this particular incident. But it is impossible to generalize
that "elders" represent Sadducean adversaries in Luke-Acts. In
Luke 7:3 elders enter into a positive relationship with Jesus on
behalf of the centurion of Capernaum. In Acts, Luke presupposes
the existence of Christian elders. When the congregation at
Antioch sends relief to Judea, Barnabas and Paul deliver it to "the
elders" who up until that point have not been introduced (11:30).
Thereafter, Luke refers rather frequently to elders who are obviously Christian. On the other hand, when elders are allied with the
chief priests, they are antagonists.

One might deduce from the fact that Gamaliel carries the day
in Acts 5:35-40 and from the apparent standoff between Pharisees
and Sadducees in Acts 23:7-10 that the Pharisees are at least the
equals of the Sadducees. According to t. Para 3:6, opponents,
presumably Pharisees, force Ishmael b. Phiabi, a Sadducean high
priest sometime in the first quarter of the first century of our era, to
pour out ashes of a red heifer prepared under his own standards of
purification and to burn another red heifer under the standards of
purification of his opponents. Another tradition in t. Yoma 1:8 tells
of a Boethusian who burns incense outside the holy of holies in
contrast to the teachings of the sages. He boasts that he has done it
correctly over against his predecessors who accommodated to the
sages. But his predecessors anticipate that he will soon die
because of his actions. Not thirty days later, he was buried.
Josephus claims that even though the Sadducees are in power,

---

[9] Jeremias, *Jerusalem*, 230. Cf. LeMoyne, *Sadducéens*, 131; E. Lohse,
"συνέδριον," *TDNT* 7.864.

they submit to what the Pharisees say since otherwise the masses would not tolerate them (*Ant.* 18.1.4 §16-17).

But in spite of this array of evidence about the influence of the Pharisees, there are indications that the high priestly element dominated the council. It is not completely without significance that the Sanhedrin met in the chamber of hewn stone in the temple precincts, an indication of the influence of the temple authorities on the council as well as vice versa. In addition, rabbinic traditions about the dominance of the Pharisees betray legendary accretions reflecting the subtle (and somewhat humorous) one-upmanship of a group that is out of power. Ishmael b. Phiabi must pour out the ashes prepared his own way. The naive Boethusian does things "right" only to invite his untimely death. For his part, Josephus obviously exaggerates in his reports that the Sadducees acquiesce so much that they accomplish "nothing so to say" (*Ant.* 18.1.4 §17).

Moreover, Josephus relates the execution of James the brother of Jesus at the hands of the Sadducee Ananus in 62 C.E. (*Ant.* 20.9.1 §199-203). Although fair-minded citizens (probably Pharisees) react, and King Agrippa deposes Ananus, the incident still shows the jurisdiction of the judicial system in the hands of the high priest. A mishnaic tradition proves the same point in an indirect way. When Rabbi Eleazar was young enough to be carried on his father's shoulders (about the middle of the first century), he observed the capital punishment of a priest's daughter condemned for "prostitution." The execution was carried out according to Sadducean procedure (*m. Sanh.* 7:2). In the middle of the first century, therefore, the Sadducees controlled the Sanhedrin.

On the basis of this evidence, it is likely that in the last decades before the destruction of the temple, the Sadducees did accommodate toward the Pharisees. But to make them virtual pawns of the Pharisees is an exaggeration. In spite of some adjustments, the high priestly party remained in control.[10]

In referring to a contingent of the Sadducees as a αἵρεσις (Acts 5:17), Luke uses the same terminology as Josephus. Although αἵρεσις may be translated "sect," both Luke and Josephus view the Sadducees as a segment integral to Judaism. Acts uses the same word in reference to both Pharisees and Christians who, according

---

[10] Schürer (*History*, 2.1.179) and Jeremias (*Jerusalem*, 159) exaggerate the influence of the Pharisees in the Sanhedrin. Cf. S. Safrai, "Jewish Self-Government," in *The Jewish People in the First Century: Historical Geography, Political History, Social, Cultural and Religious Life and Institutions* (ed. S. Safrai and M. Stern; Philadelphia: Fortress, 1974) 386. For a more critical appraisal see J. Blinzler, *Der prozess Jesu* (Regensburg: Pustet, 1969) 216–29; LeMoyne, *Sadducéens*, 249–62, 269–74, 279.

to Luke's view, come under the canopy of Judaism. The radical view of Gustav Hölscher that the Sadducees are sectarians who reject Jewish piety and Jewish law[11] is slightly regarded today. Both Acts and Josephus describe the Pharisees as the strictest party, but the proliferation of their rulings accounts for that. They are likely neither more nor less committed to their law than are the Sadducees. The high priestly Sadducees have their villains, but in general they adhere to a basic pentateuchal tradition. They take seriously the practice of the temple cultus, and they follow their own understanding of Torah with religious scrupulosity.[12] Viewed from their own perspective, they dwell squarely within Judaism. In fact, as the head of the temple cultus, the high priestly party constitutes the religious leadership of Judaism.

Socially, politically, and religiously the chief priests and the Sadducees stand at the forefront of Judaism. Luke's irony is all the more stinging, therefore, in that for him they cannot be taken seriously as representatives of the people. Luke-Acts preserves the memory of the high priestly opposition to Jesus and to the early church. But by the time of Luke, the chief priests and Sadducees had experienced their demise. They were no longer the principal adversaries of Christianity. Nevertheless, Luke portrays them as inauthentic Jews who menace Jesus and the church.

In Mark 12:13 Pharisees and Herodians put Jesus to the test with the question of paying tribute to Caesar. Luke mentions nothing of the Pharisees and Herodians (Luke 20:19). It is significant for Luke that Jesus has arrived at the temple and is teaching in the temple precincts when this incident occurs. Accordingly, Luke speaks instead of scribes and chief priests. From this point on they are the chief antagonists. Other Jews can raise opposition to Stephen and Paul, and the death of James the brother of John pleases anonymous Jews (Acts 12:2-3). But until the end of Acts organized official opposition comes from the chief priests and Sadducees.

Although the chief priests and the Sadducees oppose Jesus and the church physically, Luke's quarrel with them is primarily theological. He has two major arguments with them: (1) They deny the resurrection,[13] and (2) they reject the involvement of God in

---

[11] Hölscher, Sadduzäismus, 10–27.

[12] R. Leszynsky, Die Sadduzäer (Berlin: Mayer & Müller, 1912) 24–25; Jeremias, Jerusalem, 230, n. 36; LeMoyne, Sadducéens, 16, 33, 103–104, 117.

[13] The Sadducees advocate a particularist temple state as the fulfillment of God's promise and therefore reject its eschatological fulfillment. R. Meyer, "Σαδδουκαῖος," TDNT 7.44; J. Leipoldt, W. Grundmann et al, Umwelt des Urchristentums:

human affairs. Luke clashes with the first of these head on; the second he encounters more indirectly.

Like Mark 12:18, Luke 20:27 introduces the Sadducees as if their characteristic mark is denying the resurrection. Because of the scarcity of information from antiquity, we may not know what their central concerns were, but undoubtedly they were primarily occupied with the theocratic temple state.[14] Therefore, the debate about the resurrection is all the more clearly the interest of the Evangelists. The Sadducees deny the resurrection, and yet they test Jesus by asking a question about the resurrection. The Sadducean opponents thinly veil their motives in a *reductio ad absurdum*. Jesus sees through their ploy, rejects their premise that there is marriage in the resurrection, and supports his case by arguing rather obliquely from Moses.[15] Significantly, in material peculiar to Luke, some scribes agree with Jesus and acknowledge that he has vanquished his opponents, who no longer dare to question him. Thus, Luke not only stresses the perspicuity of Jesus, as does Mark, but also his theological kinship to these scribes along with the radical dissimilarity between Jesus and the Sadducees.

In spite of the fact that this is Luke's only conflict between Jesus and the Sadducees, it does not stand alone. In Acts, Peter and John encounter opposition because they proclaim the resurrection. Acts 4:1 specifies that at least some of the opponents are Sadducees. It is unlikely that mere proclamation of the resurrection would have incurred such opposition since the opponents would have had to arrest a large number of Pharisaic proponents of the resurrection as well.[16] This demonstrates again that the resurrection represents Luke's quarrel with the Sadducees.

Later, Paul declares before the Sanhedrin that he is a Pharisee on trial because of his hope in the resurrection. That incurs the hostility of the Sadducees but draws support from the Pharisees. The incidents in Acts are of a piece with Jesus' dispute with the Sadducees. In all three there is some agreement with scribes or Pharisees and conflict with Sadducees and/or chief priests. Thus,

---

Darstellung des neutestamentlichen Zeitalters (Berlin: Evangelische, 1982) 1.268–69.

[14] Leszynsky, *Sadduzäer*, 89.

[15] Are the patriarchs already resurrected, or is their future resurrection assured? E. Ellis ("Jesus, the Sadducees and Qumran," *NTS* 10 [1963–64] 274–79) makes the case for the assured future resurrection.

[16] G. Baumbach, "Das Sadduzäerverständnis bei Josephus Flavius und im Neuen Testament," *Kairos* 13 (1971) 28–29.

from Luke's perspective, Christians approach the views of some, Jews while they are estranged from the Sadducees.

This is especially clear in Paul's further explanation of his relationship with Judaism in Acts 24:14-15. His hope of the resurrection accords completely with worship of the God of *our* fathers and with the law and the prophets. If this pericope is internally consistent, Paul even alleges his agreement with the high priest Ananias, elders accompanying him, and Tertullus (v 1). That is, he claims that his accusers share his hope in the resurrection (v 15). But it is unlikely that Paul is entirely consistent. He alludes to his accusers once again in v 20 and by implication associates them with those who opposed his confession of the resurrection before the Sanhedrin. The parallel passage in 26:6-8 confirms this interpretation. There Paul again defends his belief in the resurrection as the promise made by God to *our* fathers and envisions it as a view shared by the twelve tribes, that is, by Jews in general. The sense of 24:15 is that Jews for the most part concur with Paul's belief. His immediate opponents deny it.

This means that Jewish leadership embodied in the Sadducees and the high priestly party reject the essential hope of Judaism. For Luke, ironically those sitting at the head of Judaism are its traitors. In this he agrees essentially with *m. Sanh.* 10:1: "All Israelites have a share in the world to come. . . . And these are they that have no share in the world to come: he that says that there is no resurrection of the dead. . . ." Since R. Akiba adds a saying to this tradition, it likely existed at the end of the first century and probably includes the Sadducees. Therefore, Luke perhaps found the Sadducees as ready-made apostates for his portrait of inauthentic Jews.

Luke betrays his second point of dispute with the Sadducees only indirectly. In Acts 5:34-39 he uses the Pharisee Gamaliel to confront the Sadducean element of the Sanhedrin with God's direction of human history. Without information in Josephus, this conflict would be far less evident. Josephus claims that the Sadducees deny the existence of fate. Human beings determine their own destiny by free choice (*J.W.* 2.8.14 §164-65; *Ant.* 13.5.9 §173). It is clear in his discussions that fate represents his equivalent to God's involvement in history. He uses the term fate because he accommodates his description to popular Hellenistic philosophy.[17] Nevertheless, he indicates clearly that the Sadducees distance God from the course of history.

---

[17] D. Flusser, "Josephus on the Sadducees and Menander," *Immanuel* 7 (1977) 61–67.

As Luke's spokesperson, Gamaliel takes on the Sadducees precisely with an argument based on God's control of history. The previous chapter has already argued that Gamaliel's speech presents Luke's view of God's control of history. Since from Luke's perspective Christianity has not collapsed like the movements of Theudas and Judas, history has confirmed Gamaliel's intuition that Christianity likely is from God. Accordingly, Luke has Gamaliel term dissenters from the opinion that God is working out human history θεομάχοι. For anyone who knows that Sadducees deny the involvement of God in history, Gamaliel's advice virtually identifies them with the enemies of God.

Luke's picture of the high priest Ananias further illustrates the extent to which he views the alleged leaders of Israel as inadequate representatives of the people. Ananias appears briefly in Acts 23:2-4. His only action is to command that Paul be struck. After issuing his command, he plays no role in the remainder of the story other than appearing in passing as one of Paul's stereotyped accusers (24:1). His presence in 23:2-4 is solely for the purpose of juxtaposing him to Paul. Ananias breaks the law in commanding that Paul be struck. Paul confesses allegiance to the law. The accused is a law keeper; the judge is a law breaker.

Paul applies Exod 22:28 to the high priest. Viewed from the author's perspective, this means that Luke thinks of the high priest as the ruler. Moreover, it reflects Luke's positive evaluation of the high priesthood but his negative opinion of its occupant. A high priest like Ananias cannot be taken seriously as the representative of the people.

In summary, Luke distinguishes the Sadducees from the high priestly party but also views them as closely allied. Together they constitute the primary opponents of Christianity. In contrast, Luke differentiates ordinary priests from the high priestly aristocracy. The former take at worst a neutral stance toward Christianity and at best a complimentary one. Luke ironically reverses the noble status of the chief priests and Sadducees. They are not only opponents of Jesus and early Christian preachers, but also detractors from Judaism. By denying the resurrection and God's control of history, they commit apostasy. They are inauthentic Jews and inadequate leaders of Israel. The high priest Ananias sets an appalling example. In spite of outrage at Ananias's lawlessness, Luke maintains a high evaluation of the high priesthood. The office has fallen into the wrong hands, and consequently also the oversight of the temple. But this final point will become clear only after the next section.

Luke and the Temple

The prominence of the temple in Luke-Acts goes far beyond the actual number of references. Since the Galilean ministry of Jesus and the diaspora mission of Paul exclude contact with it, the role of the temple is necessarily subdued in major segments of Luke-Acts. Nevertheless, Luke structures his material so that the Gospel begins and ends in the temple, and the early chapters of Acts center on it.[18]

At the beginning of his Gospel, Luke raises the curtain on a scene in the temple. Zechariah receives an angelic vision beside the altar of incense (Luke 1:1-23). After the birth of Jesus, Bethlehem recedes into the background and the infancy narratives focus on the temple in Jerusalem (Luke 2). From the time of Jesus' descent from the Mount of Olives, it becomes the center for his teaching (19:47). Furthermore, as long as Acts deals with the Jerusalem community, the temple is the center of Christian prayer and proclamation (Acts 2:46; 3:1, 11; 4:1; 5:12, 20, 42). At the end of his career Paul attempts to consummate his purification there (21:23-26). In a defense speech he also relates a vision that he received in the temple shortly after his conversion (22:17-21).

On the other hand, the temple comes under sharp attack in Luke-Acts. Jesus drives out the merchants (Luke 19:45) and announces the destruction of the temple (21:6), and Stephen plays Solomon's temple off against the tabernacle as a sign of Israel's rebellion (Acts 7:45-50). To what do we owe this ambiguous fascination with the holy place of Israel?

The answer is bound up with the centrality of Jerusalem for Luke. Whereas after the tragic events of the passion, Mark anticipates and Matthew describes a shift to Galilee, Luke fixes his gaze upon Jerusalem. The lingering of the apostles in Jerusalem spans the interval between the Gospel and Acts. After persecution scatters the Jerusalem congregation, there is a constant reciprocation between the exterior and Jerusalem.[19] Jerusalem is the place of revelation where the prophet must die (Luke 13:33) and from which the gospel must go out (Luke 24:47; Acts 1:8).[20]

Lloyd Gaston has shown that Jewish eschatological hope could

[18] H. Flender, *St. Luke: Theologian of Redemptive History* (Philadelphia: Fortress, 1967) 107; L. Johnson, *The Literary Function of Possessions* (Missoula: Scholars Press, 1977) 188. Against Johnson, I see no special significance in the climax of the temptations at the temple in Jerusalem.
[19] See above, p. 35–36.
[20] H. Conzelmann, *The Theology of St. Luke* (New York: Harper & Row, 1961) 133.

focus on Jerusalem without the temple.[21] But he incorrectly infers from this a dichotomy between the city and the sanctuary. Actually, the two go together hand in glove as a sacred place. Granted, there is a line of Jewish tradition that links God's promises with the city and with the throne of David. For example, according to Psalm 132, the transfer of the ark of the covenant to Jerusalem and the establishment of the Davidic dynasty guarantee God's presence in Jerusalem; conversely, God's presence guarantees the dynasty and the city. But to read such traditions as the transfer of God's presence from the temple to the city, as Gaston does, is to fail to understand temple imagery.

Judaism shared views with many people of antiquity that compare the architecture of the temple to the structure of the universe. The outer sanctuary corresponds to the earth and the inner sanctuary to the heavens. Josephus describes the construction of the tabernacle and explains that its three parts correspond to the system of the world. The holy of holies represents heaven, and consequently, it is reserved for God alone. The other two parts, opened to the priests, symbolize the sea and the land (*Ant.* 3.6.4. §123; 3.7.7 §180-87). God's habitation extends to the dimensions of the cosmos. And so at the consecration of the temple, Josephus's Solomon acknowledges the inadequacy of the sanctuary and beseeches that some *portion* of God's spirit dwell in it (*Ant.* 8.4.3 §114-17). In the face of the threat of Titus to destroy the Herodian temple, Josephus even allows the Zealots to dispense with the temple by declaring that the entire world is a better temple for God (*J.W.* 5.11.2 §458-59). Similarly, Philo claims that the genuine temple is the whole cosmos, and the most holy part of reality is heaven. Corresponding to the genuine temple is the other one made by the hand of human beings (*On the Special Laws* 1.66-67; cf. *On Noah's Work as a Planter* 126; *Moses* 2.88). Hebrews employs similar imagery in describing Jesus' entrance into heaven as an entrance into the genuine sanctuary (Heb 9:12, 24).[22]

Since the temple is a model of the cosmos, in the eschatological Jerusalem God can be present without a temple. The eschaton

---

[21] See L. Gaston, *No Stone on Another: Studies in the Significance of the Fall of Jerusalem in the Synoptic Gospels* (Leiden: Brill, 1970) 105–112. Gaston (365–369) later acknowledges the close relationship between Jerusalem and the temple in Luke-Acts. Cf. G. Fohrer, "Σιών," *TDNT* 7.304–306.

[22] G. MacRae, "Heavenly Temple and Eschatology in the Letter to the Hebrews," *Semeia* 12 (1978) 187-88. Some Jewish eschatological hopes envision the restoration of the temple, e.g., *Jub.* 1:28–29, *1 Enoch* 90:28–29. Cf. J. Levenson, *Sinai and Zion: An entry into the Jewish Bible* (Minneapolis: Winston, 1985) 141.

means stripping away the partition between heaven and earth. And so Rev 21:22 specifies that there is no temple in the new Jerusalem because God dwells with humanity. But that does not constitute a transfer of God's presence from the temple to the city. Rather, God's immediacy renders the temple's imperfect representation of the divine presence superfluous.

Luke is in touch with a kindred tradition. Stephen debates the relationship between the temple and the presence of God and concludes that God does not dwell in houses made with hands. Stephen applies this axiom particularly to Solomon's temple, and by extension, certainly also to the Herodian temple. He follows that up with a quote from Isa 66:1-2 that ascribes cosmic proportions to God's habitation: " 'Heaven is my throne, and earth my footstool. What house will you build for me, says the Lord, or what is the place of my rest?' " (Acts 7:49).

Nevertheless, Luke also shares the prominent belief of Jews of his age that the temple is the place of prayer *par excellence*.[23] Luke adds an incidental note to the story of Zechariah's vision describing a great crowd of people praying (Luke 1:10). The prophetess Anna prays day and night in the temple (2:37). The parable of the Pharisee and the publican presupposes that the temple is the supreme place of prayer (18:9-14). On his entrance into the temple, Jesus claims that it shall be a house of prayer rather than a den of robbers (19:46). Acts 3:1 assumes as normal that Peter and John observe the hour of prayer in the temple.

But Luke also makes it the place of teaching and proclaiming *par excellence*. The Spirit inspires Simeon's canticle when he comes into the temple (Luke 2:27-35). Jesus' typical activity when he arrives in Jerusalem is to teach in the temple (19:47, 21:37). The early Christian preachers not only take opportunity to preach in the temple, but an angel of the Lord commands them to do so (Acts 3:11, 5:19-20). That then becomes their regular behavior (v 42). The temple is a particularly appropriate setting for public teaching from Jesus and the early Christians.[24]

In brief, Luke makes the temple as a place of prayer and proclamation completely compatible with his refusal to imprison God's presence within it.

How, then, do the temple critiques of Jesus and Stephen fit into the picture? The conventional wisdom is that Luke rejects Judaism's central institution and announces God's judgment upon

[23] Jeremias, *Jerusalem*, 75; G. Schrenk, "ἱερός," *TDNT* 3.243.
[24] M. Bachmann, *Jerusalem und der Temple: Die geographisch-theologischen Elemente in der lukanischen Sicht des jüdischen Kultzentrums* (Stuttgart: Kohlhammer, 1980) 265–72.

the Jews, that is, that Luke buries the Jews under the rubble of the decimation of the primary symbol of their relationship with God.

It is doubtful, however, that Stephen attacks the temple at all. Of course, the light of Jesus' announcement of the destruction of the temple (Luke 21:6) and of the events of 70 C.E. fall on Stephen's speech. The occasion of the speech is the accusation that Stephen speaks against the temple and the law (Acts 6:13). At the climax of the speech Stephen charges his audience with rebellion on the heels of alluding to the temple. Thus, an impressive array of scholars interprets Stephen's speech as a rigorous attack on the temple.[25] Marcel Simon thinks that Stephen juxtaposes the tabernacle and the temple in such a way that the very construction of the temple is a falling away from the best of Israel's tradition.[26] In this sense Stephen expresses a nostalgia for the tabernacle in the wilderness.

But there are three reasons that this argument fails to fit the evidence. (1) Stephen prefixes his recollection of the tabernacle with a tirade about disobedience and idolatry during the wilderness wandering (Acts 7:38-43). That is, Stephen uses the wilderness wandering as an example of rebellion rather than of Israel's golden age.[27]

(2) The structure of the entire speech establishes a cycle between God's acts of mercy and Israel's rebellion. In that structure, David's desire for a temple is a sign of God's favor, just as was the prior presence of the tabernacle. The problem of Stephen's view of the temple is complicated by a textual variant in Acts 7:46. The best MSS have οἴκῳ Ἰακώβ, whereas the competing reading has θεῷ in place of οἴκῳ. Οἴκῳ is preferred as the most difficult reading.[28] A. F. J. Klijn has also defended this reading on the basis of some parallels in 1QS, arguing that Stephen understands the tabernacle as a place for the people of Israel to serve God, whereas Solomon's temple became misunderstood as God's dwelling place.[29] But in spite of Klijn's suggestion, οἴκῳ makes little sense

---

[25] Among others, L. Goppelt, *Christentum und Judentum im ersten und zweiten Jahrhundert: Ein Aufriss der Urgeschichte der Kirche* (Gütersloh: Bertelsmann, 1954) 78; Gaston (*No Stone*, 154) thinks that Stephen represents opposition to the temple among certain Jewish groups for whom the destruction of the temple by the messiah is a clear case. See also Johnson, *Literary Function*, 188.

[26] M. Simon, "Saint Stephen and the Jerusalem Temple," *JEH* 2 (1951) 127.

[27] On the theme of rebellion see A. F. J. Klijn ("Stephen's Speech—Acts VII.2–53," *NTS* 4 [1957–58] 25–27).

[28] B. Metzger, *A Textual Commentary on the Greek New Testament* (Stuttgart: United Bible Societies, 1971) 351–53.

[29] Klijn, "Stephen's Speech," 29–31.

in the text.[30] Furthermore, some details in the context favor the reading θεῷ. For one thing, it is the antecedent for αὐτῷ in v 47. Solomon obviously builds a house for God and it is difficult to construe the syntax in such a way as to make θεοῦ in v 46 the antecedent for αὐτῷ in v 47. For another, the last half of v 46 stands in parallel to the first half,[31] so that finding favor before God corresponds to finding a habitation for God. In addition, the line of argument in v 49 moves to the issue of the dwelling place of God, rather than to whether a house of worship is a place for the people or for the divinity. Θεῷ is the proper reading, and the sense is: Although David desired to build a dwelling for God, Solomon actually completed the project.[32]

Since David finds favor in asking permission to build a temple, so also its building is a sign of God's mercy. The problem is not the temple, but the behavior of the people to whom God has given the temple.[33] Stephen's abrupt shift to the attack in v 51 makes sense only if a parallel is seen between the rebellion of the people to whom God had given the tabernacle (past) and the rebellion of the people to whom God has given the temple (present). The last great act of God's mercy in this cycle is the coming of the Righteous One, whom the rebellious audience has killed (v 52).[34] The audience then falls into the same cycle by killing Stephen who is full of grace (6:8, 7:58).

(3) Luke takes pains to show that the charge that Stephen attacks the temple comes from *false* witnesses (Acts 6:13).[35] They accuse him of claiming that Jesus would destroy the temple and change the customs of Moses. Over against those allegations, Stephen actually appeals to Moses and the temple for support, turns the tables on his adversaries, and indicts them for opposing the temple and Moses. Stephen, thus, remains positive toward the temple.

Three points characterize Jesus' connection with the temple:

[30] Haenchen (*Acts*, 285, n. 2) comments, "Luke . . . would not have been understood by any reader in the sense proposed by Klijn."

[31] E. Richard, *Acts 6:1–8:4: The Author's Method of Composition* (Missoula: Scholars, 1978) 132.

[32] Haenchen, *Acts*, 285, n. 2.

[33] F. Weinert ("The Meaning of the Temple in the Gospel of Luke" [Ph.D. diss., Fordham University, 1979] 27, 84, 127) argues correctly that Jesus' attitude in Luke similarly opposes the wrong behavior of people associated with the temple, rather than the temple or cult themselves.

[34] On the structure of Stephen's speech see Richard, *Acts 6:1–8:4*, 182–206, 264–66.

[35] J. Jervell, "The Acts of the Apostles and the History of Early Christianity," *ST* 37 (1983) 24.

He makes a claim on it as a place of prayer, he uses it as the forum for his teaching in Jerusalem, and he announces its destruction. Jesus' entry into the temple is commonly called "the cleansing of the temple." But that nomenclature is misleading. Jesus corrects behavior in the temple, but performs no act of cleansing. Hans Conzelmann envisions the act as taking possession of the temple.[36] That too is misleading. Jesus acts with reckless abandon and with a mysterious authority. His opponents cannot withstand him in the temple and they dare not arrest him there. But he does not behave as proprietor. More correctly, he makes a claim on it as a place of prayer. Significantly, in Acts (as indicated above) his followers actually make it a place of prayer, but, surprisingly, Jesus himself does not. Rather, he exercises his prerogative of teaching in it.

To regard the entry as assuming possession leads Conzelmann into a second error, namely, that the temple is profaned because it is in the wrong hands.[37] This then becomes the alleged basis for Jesus' pronouncement of judgment and the wrath of God upon the temple. But the support of the temple reflected in the stories of Zechariah, the early life of Jesus (Luke 1-2), the purification of Paul (Acts 21:24-26), and the worship of early Christians shows that Luke does not think of the temple as profaned.[38]

In order to understand Luke's view of the destruction of the temple, it must be considered along with the destruction of Jerusalem, because the two are of one piece for Luke. Luke, by way of a false etymology, apparently associates ἱερός or ἱερόν with Ἱεροσόλυμα.[39] And so Luke is capable of using the temple and Jerusalem virtually interchangeably. At the end of the Gospel, Jesus commands his disciples to remain in the *city*. Luke then describes their wait as continually blessing God in the *temple* (Luke 24:52-53). According to Acts 5:25, the apostles are teaching in the *temple*. The same activity is later summarized as filling *Jerusalem* with their teaching (v 28). In 24:11 Paul claims that he went up to *Jerusalem* to worship. In the context he obviously alludes to going up to the *temple* for his purification. In each of these cases Jerusalem and temple stand in close parallel.

---

[36] Conzelmann, *Theology*, 76. Johnson (*Literary Function*, 188) follows Conzelmann and makes the idea of possession even more emphatic.

[37] Conzelmann, *Theology*, 165.

[38] Bachmann, *Jerusalem und der Temple*, 149, 181–87. Luke sanctions the temple and views priestly service there positively.

[39] Ibid., 63–64. Such an understanding of the name of Jerusalem surfaces among others of Luke's contemporaries. Josephus explains that the name of the city originally was Σόλυμα until Melchizedek built a temple there, whereupon it became Ἱεροσόλυμα (*J. W.* 6.10.1 §438; cf. *Ant.* 1.10.1 §180).

But the connection between the temple and Jerusalem is even more direct in the context of Luke 21:6. Here Jesus announces the destruction of the *temple*. His audience asks him when this will take place (v 7). Jesus answers with the fall of *Jerusalem* (vv 20-24). That in turn is connected thematically with Jesus' laments in Luke 13:34-35 and 19:41-44, with his parable of the pounds in 19:11-27, and with his warning to the daughters of Jerusalem in 23:26-31.[40] In each of these cases, punishment comes as a result of unbelief. 13:34-35 links the destruction of Jerusalem in the first instance with repeated rejection of the prophets, but secondarily with the implied rejection of Jesus. Jesus identifies himself with the prophets and anticipates his own destiny in Jerusalem.[41] Jesus wishes to gather the children of Jerusalem, but Jerusalem refuses. For this the dwelling of Jerusalemites is forsaken (Luke 13:34-35).[42] This lament shares close ties with 19:42-44. Jerusalem's eyes do not perceive the time of her visitation by the one just declared the king who comes in the name of the Lord (v 38). Jesus' prophetic judgment here stops short of announcing Jerusalem's death knell, and Jesus actually expresses a compassionate attitude toward Jerusalem. Still he predicts out-and-out calamity for the city.[43] In 19:11-27 the journeying nobleman who has received his kingdom returns for blood revenge on his enemies who did not want him to reign over them. The parable is so closely associated with Jesus' entry into Jerusalem, which results in his crucifixion, that the citizens in the parable must be an allegory of the Jerusalemites who reject Jesus.[44] 23:31 interprets Jesus' warn-

[40] The splitting of the temple curtain in Luke 23:45 is not included as a reference to the destruction of the temple because, in spite of efforts to so interpret the incident, the temple obviously continues to function with Luke's approval at least through Paul's experience in the temple in Acts 21:26–36. D. Sylva ("The Temple Curtain and Jesus' Death in the Gospel of Luke," *JBL* 105 [1986] 239–50) has shown, on the grounds of Jesus' communion with God, that the tearing of the temple curtain does not represent the destruction of the temple.

[41] D. Tiede, *Prophecy and History in Luke-Acts* (Philadelphia: Fortress, 1980) 71–76.

[42] K. Baltzer ("The Meaning of the Temple in the Lucan Writings," *HTR* 58 [1965] 272–273) has an interesting thesis, that since οἶκος in the LXX is the common term for the temple, then in Luke 13:35 it also refers to the temple. But he misreads the evidence, since the LXX could call the temple οἶκος θεοῦ, or οἶκος τοῦ κυρίου but hardly οἶκος ὑμῶν.

[43] C. Giblin, *The Destruction of Jerusalem According to Luke's Gospel: A Historical-Typological Moral* (Rome: Biblical Institute, 1985) 55. This otherwise excellent study suffers under the methodology of trying to distill a typological moral from Luke's presentation of history. In the final analysis this type of moralism is Giblin's hermeneutic of history rather than Luke's.

[44] Tiede, *Prophecy and History*, 79–80.

ing to the daughters of Jerusalem. Jesus' crucifixion is what "they" do when the wood is green, that is, in the face of Jesus himself. In the future, "their" behavior will net judgment with severe consequences for the weeping women.

But to whom does "they" in v 31 refer? Whereas "they" in v 30 is associated with the daughters of Jerusalem, in v 31 it is distinguished from them. The most obvious reference is to those who crucify Jesus, as in v 33. Jerusalem, then, experiences God's wrath and vengeance (including the destruction of the temple) because of unbelief and because of the crucifixion of Jesus. From his vantage point, Luke has interpreted the fall of Jerusalem as the stern and dreadful judgment of God.

Is this judgment upon Jerusalem and the temple final? Helmut Flender argues that with the passion of Jesus, Jerusalem becomes completely secular, no longer the bearer and guardian of divine promises.[45] But although the fall of Jerusalem is an unmitigated disaster, the judgment upon Jerusalem is not definitive. In the first place there is a temporal limit implied by Luke 21:24: "Jerusalem will be trodden down by the gentiles until the times of the gentiles are fulfilled." This is Luke's own interpretation of the destruction of Jerusalem in which he sets forth a brief outline of future salvation history. The gentiles are the agents of the destruction of Jerusalem, and their ascendency has a purpose for their own fulfillment. But the end of the time of the gentiles also anticipates the restoration of God's mercy to Jerusalem. 21:24 bears uncanny verbal resemblances to Ezek 39:23 and Zech 12:3.[46] There the apocalyptic perspective clearly includes both the judgment upon Jerusalem by the gentiles and the restoration of God's mercy upon the city. Luke has taken over that apocalyptic perspective and, therefore, views the limit to the era of the gentiles as the time of the renewal of God's mercy for Jerusalem.

In the second place, Luke not only blames those who crucify Jesus, he also exonerates them. The perpetrators of Jesus' execution, designated "they" in Luke 23:31, are the cause of a severe warning against Jerusalem. But (if the textually disputed v 34 is

[45] Flender, *St. Luke*, 17–18, 108, 113–14.
[46] F. Flückiger, "Luk. 21,20–24 und die Zerstörung Jerusalems," *TZ* 28 (1972) 388–89. Flückiger is correct on this point, although his dating of Luke does not follow from the allusions to Ezekiel and Zechariah. Giblin (*Destruction of Jerusalem*, 89–90) argues that Luke 21:24 cannot be interpreted in optimistic light of Israel's conversion or ultimate vindication. But he reads ἄχρι οὗ as implying the completion of the destruction of Jerusalem rather than as a temporal restriction of it, and that is tied up with his historical-typological moral schema in which the fate of the gentiles is cast typologically by Jerusalem's fate. See n. 43 above.

accepted) even the instigators of the crucifixion also come under Jesus' prayer for forgiveness, for "they" in 23:31 is identical with "they" in v 34. Even if Jesus' prayer is not original, Acts manifests a similar attitude. Peter attributes the crucifixion to the ignorance of people he calls "brethren." He even explains the behavior of their rulers by ascribing it to ignorance (Acts 3:17). Although 13:27 is a little less generous, it also excuses the crucifixion on the grounds of misunderstanding.[47]

In the third place, Luke's severe interpretation of the fall of Jerusalem is quite compatible with Jewish traditions of both the vengeance and vindication of Israel. David Tiede has adduced particularly impressive evidence of Jewish traditions that explain the fall of Jerusalem both to the Babylonians and to the Romans in terms remarkably consonant with Luke's interpretation of divine judgment. What is more, passages such as Deuteronomy 32, Zech 12:3, Amos 9:13-14, Joel 3-4 (LXX), 1 Macc 4:11, and 2 *Apoc. Bar.* 67-68 balance God's harsh vengeance with the divine vindication of Israel. Therefore, far from signaling a final repudiation of Jerusalem, Luke's portrayal of Jerusalem's destiny fits more accurately within an environment of typical Jewish debates about how the fall of Jerusalem was to be understood, including the restoration of the city.[48] In fact, against Flender, Jerusalem does continue to function as a special holy place after the crucifixion. The disciples must tarry in Jerusalem until they receive divine power (Luke 24:49, Acts 1:4-8). And Jerusalem is the necessary starting point for Christian preaching (Luke 24:47, Acts 1:8). Moreover, the temple remains the hub of the early Christian community (Luke 24:53, Acts 2:46, 3:1, 5:20). What does Luke have in mind by centering Christianity upon the temple and Jerusalem?

Doubtless there is truth in the frequent response that Jerusalem is a salvation-historical center for Luke.[49] It is the place where significant acts for salvation take place. But that only invites the further question: Why, for Luke, do significant acts for salvation occur in Jerusalem? There is equal truth in another common answer to the effect that Luke wishes to demonstrate continuity with Israel. He does. In fact, Hans Conzelmann is entirely correct when he says that the authentic Jew is compelled to become a Christian in order to remain a Jew.[50] But continuity can be

---

[47] J. Houlden, "The Purpose of Luke," *JSNT* 21 (1984) 56–57.

[48] Tiede, *Prophecy and History*, 66, 80–96.

[49] Many scholars follow Conzelmann, *Theology*, 73–94, 132–34. See, e.g., Gaston, *No Stone*, 96.

[50] H. Conzelmann, *Die Apostelgeschichte erklärt* (Tübingen: Mohr [Siebeck], 1972) 147. For another proponent of salvation-historical continuity, see K. Löning,

maintained apart from remaining focused on Jerusalem as the Gospel of Matthew shows. There is also truth in the claim that Jerusalem is central because the twelve reside there.[51] But Jerusalem eminates an aura before the twelve reside there. Jesus must orient his "going up" toward Jerusalem (Luke 9:51). Furthermore, it is also central for the twelve themselves. They must remain there to be empowered. Michael Bachmann's suggestion, that for Luke Jerusalem and the temple represent the universal holy place for the Jews, fills in even more of the puzzle.[52]

But in order to perceive how Jerusalem and the temple function for Luke, we need to empathize with the perspective of a Hellenistic reader contemporaneous with Luke. Projecting ourselves into the mind-set of antiquity, we trip upon the point where the divine intersects with the human. Mircea Eliade considers the belief in the sacred city or the temple as the meeting point between heaven and earth typical of the mythological worldview.[53] A broad distribution of the belief in antiquity confirms Eliade's contention and establishes a milieu for interpreting Luke's view of the temple. Against that background, virtually any reader from antiquity would have recognized in the centrality of Jerusalem Luke's tacit assumption that it is the *axis mundi*.

Aeschylus, who dates from the sixth to the fifth century B.C.E., speaks of the defilement of Apollo's sanctuary and laments the pollution of blood on the navel of the earth (*Eumenides* 166). In the fifth century B.C.E. Pindar, referring to the oracle at Delphi, identifies it as words spoken beside the central navel of the three-clad mother, namely, earth (*Pythian Odes* 4.74). Euripides alludes to Delphi as the navel of the earth that sings in prophetic strains (*Medea* 666). Plato calls Apollo the god who sits in the center of earth on the navel (*Republic* 427 C). Around the turn of the centuries into the Common Era, Strabo attributes the eminence of the temple at Delphi to its central location in Greece and to the belief that it is the center of the world. He too calls it the navel of the earth (9.3.6). At about the same period, Livy identifies Delphi as the common oracle of the human race, the navel of the world (38.48.2). Perhaps a century later Pausanias explains that what the people of Delphi call the navel is a white stone that they

---

Die Saulustradition in der Apostelgeschichte (Münster: Aschendorf, 1973) 188–93.
[51] J. Tyson, *The Death of Jesus in Luke-Acts* (Columbia, SC: University of South Carolina Press, 1986) 96.
[52] Bachmann, *Jerusalem und der Temple*, 215–16, 297–302.
[53] M. Eliade, *Cosmos and History: The Myth of the Eternal Return* (New York: Harper & Row, 1959) 12–16.

say is the center of all the earth (10.16.3). Thus, the prominence of the Delphic oracle derives from its location at the *axis mundi*, the very point of contact between the divine and human.

In Babylonia, the same type of belief can be deduced from the names of temples. Temples were given names such as "the house which is the link between heaven and earth," "the mooring post of heaven and earth," and "the foundation platform of heaven and earth."[54] This is also reflected in the architecture of Babylonian temples. They followed a typical pattern of two buildings, one of which was level, the other of which was a tower that constituted a stylized sacred mountain, a ziggurat. The top of the ziggurat was the point of descent for the deity.[55]

Egyptian temples too carried with them the claim that they represented the *axis mundi*. The holy of holies where the image of the god resided was regarded as the initial point of creation where earth first arose from the primeval waters.[56]

The widely diffused belief in a specific location as the *axis mundi* invaded Jewish thought as well. Ezek 38:12 describes the plotting of Gog to battle against Jerusalem and attributes to him the design to carry away spoils from the people who live at the navel of the earth. In *1 Enoch* 26:1, Enoch visits Jerusalem and calls it the center of the earth. *Jub.* 8:12 alludes to Palestine as the middle of the earth and then in v 19 calls Mt. Zion the center of the navel of the earth. This view also probably lies behind the elevation of Jerusalem as the center to which all nations must aspire, as in Isaiah 60.[57]

According to rabbinic tradition, Jerusalem had its own stone that marked the *axis mundi*. M. *Yoma* 5:2 relates that in the temple there was a stone, where the ark was, that had been there since the time of David and Solomon. It was called *shetiyah*, that is, "foundation stone." Elaborating on this, *b. Yoma* 54b says that it is called *shetiyah* because it is the original point from which the rest of the world was created. This tradition is associated with R.

[54] G. Wright, "The Significance of the Temple in the Ancient Near East. III. The Temple in Palestine-Syria," *BA* 7 (1944) 67.

[55] A. Oppenheim, "The Significance of the Temple in the Ancient Near East. II. The Mesopotamian Temple," *BA* 7 (1944) 54. A. Wensinck (*The Ideas of the Western Semites Concerning the Navel of the Earth* [Amsterdam: Müller, 1916]) documents the location of the sanctuary at the center of the earth in the OT and rabbinic thought; he also traces it in later Islamic traditions.

[56] H. Nelson, "The Significance of the Temple in the Ancient Near East. I. The Egyptian Temple," *BA* 7 (1944) 48.

[57] H. Wenschkewitz, *Die Spiritualisierung der Kultusbegriffe: Temple, Priester und Opfer im Neuen Testament* (Leipzig: Pfeiffer, 1932) 11. Cf. Levenson, *Sinai and Zion*, 111–114.

Eliezer, a rough contemporary of Luke. A later tradition from R. Aḥa b. Ḥaninah, a third generation Amoraim, identifies the meeting place of the Sanhedrin in the temple as the navel of the world (*b. Sanh.* 37a). The foundation stone of the temple is probably identical to the monolith that today lies at the center of the Dome of the Rock Mosque. When *m. Yoma* 5:2 is taken at face value, the stone is considered to have formed the floor of the holy of holies. But the size of the rock exceeds the probable dimensions of the holy of holies so that it likely lay elsewhere within the temple.[58]

Although the *axis mundi* could be specifically identified with a stone, the point of contact was not confined to it. As a sacred city Jerusalem claimed the same distinction. Moreover, the status of a sacred precinct was especially extended to the Mount of Olives. During Passover in order to accommodate pilgrims, the city district was enlarged to include Bethphage, taking in the Mount of Olives.[59] A causeway was constructed across the Kidron Valley from the temple to the Mount of Olives. Across it the high priest led the red heifer to the Mount of Olives to be burned for the ashes of purification (*m. Para* 3:6; *Šeqal.* 4:2; *Yoma* 6:4). After the preparation of the ashes, some of them were deposited on the Mount of Olives so that people intending to enter the temple could purify themselves there (*m. Para* 3:11). When the Sanhedrin was banished from the Chamber of Hewn Stone in the temple, it moved to the Mount of Olives (*b. Roš. Haš.* 31a).[60] Thus, both Jerusalem and the Mount of Olives shared in the sanctity of the *axis mundi*.

It is this strategic location of the temple at the very center of the world that renders opponents of the temple-functionaries powerless to raise a competing sanctuary. Although in the sixth century B.C.E. some Jews in Egypt consecrated another temple in Elephantine, and Onias IV erected a rival temple at Leontopolis when Alcimus had superseded him, Jews from all over the

---

[58] For discussions on the stone, see F. Filson, "The Significance of the Temple in the Ancient Near East. IV. Temple, Synagogue, and Church," *BA* 7 (1944) 81; R. Patai, *Man and Temple in Ancient Jewish Myth and Ritual* (London: Nelson and Sons, 1947) 85; S. Terrien, "The Omphalos Myth and Hebrew Religion," *VT* 20 (1970) 317; P. Schäfer, "Tempel und Schöpfung: Zur Interpretation einiger Heiligtumstraditionen in der rabbinischen Literatur," *Kairos* 16 (1974) 123–25.

[59] J. Jeremias, *The Eucharistic Words of Jesus* (New York: Scribner's, 1966) 43, 55.

[60] For secondary references see J. Derenbourg, *Essai sur l'histoire et la géographie de la Palestine* (Paris: Imperiale, 1867) 466–67; V. Eppstein, "The Historicity of the Gospel Account of the Cleansing of the Temple," *ZNW* 55 (1964) 47–49.

diaspora continued to be loyal to the temple in Jerusalem. Because the temple is the point of contact between heaven and earth, the Qumran community could not simply build a competing temple of their own. And so they spiritualized temple symbolism and applied it to the community itself.[61] Synagogues could be proliferated anywhere Jews settled. They could even be built adjacent to each other in apparent rivalry. But temples could not be multiplied because the Jerusalem sanctuary stood at the navel of the earth.

Even though explicit references in Luke fail to name the temple or Jerusalem the *axis mundi*, Dennis Sylva has recently uncovered a bit of evidence that supports such an understanding of Luke's symbolism of temple and holy city. Sylva appeals to the correspondence between the death of Jesus and the stoning of Stephen and notes that Acts 7:56 refers to an opening in the heavens into the presence of God in parallel with the splitting of the temple curtain in Luke 23:45.[62] In the tearing of the temple curtain Jesus gains direct access to God, comparable to the opening above Jerusalem through which Stephen sees the glory of God and Jesus standing at the right hand of God.

But explicit references aside, the belief in a specific location for contact between heaven and earth so pervades antiquity, that it provides the vantage point for understanding the place of the temple and Jerusalem in Luke-Acts. Jerusalem stands at the center of salvation-history because it also stands at the central point of contact between heaven and earth. Almost any of Luke's contemporaries would have seen beneath the symbolism of Jerusalem the presupposition that it marked the *axis mundi*.

It is with this kind of assumption that Luke ushers his readers into the temple in the story of Zechariah. The temple is not the only place of visions as the subsequent angelophany of Mary illustrates (Luke 1:26-38; cf. Luke 2:9, Acts 5:19, 8:26, 10:3, 12:7-11, 27:23). But the sacred location adds to its weight. Gabriel, the very angel who stands in the presence of God, appears to Zechariah precisely at the right side of the altar of incense (Luke 1:11, 19). The message comes straight from God because Gabriel has just stepped down from the heavenly realm. With that Luke authorizes the beginning of his Gospel as divine truth, and both warrants and limits the place of John the Baptist (vv 14-17).

Also when Mary and Joseph dedicate the infant Jesus in the

---

[61] B. Gärtner, *The Temple and the Community in Qumran and the New Testament* (Cambridge: Cambridge University Press, 1965) 15–16.
[62] Sylva, "Temple Curtain," 244–45.

temple, they bring him to the *axis mundi*. Simeon's canticle, therefore, takes on the character of a temple oracle.

Paul's temple vision is closely related. On this occasion the Lord himself appears to Paul (Acts 22:18-21). Again, appearances of the Lord are not confined to the temple (cf. 9:5, 10; 10:13-15; 18:9; 23:11). Nevertheless, the location bears significant import for legitimizing Paul's mission among gentiles. That is, Paul claims to have received his commission at the very window of heaven.

The same light illuminates Luke's view that as a prophet Jesus must die in Jerusalem (Luke 13:33). Jesus leaves the Galilean hinterlands and travels to Jerusalem to be received up (9:51) because that is the point of entry into heaven. A moment before Jesus' death, the temple curtain is torn giving Jesus direct access to God to whom he commits his spirit (23:45-46).[63] After the resurrection Jesus appears in the environs of Jerusalem, including the walk to Emmaus. Since the disciples are enjoined to remain in Jerusalem, and since they are the ones who receive appearances, by implication the appearances are confined to Jerusalem (24:49, Acts 1:1-4). Finally, Jesus ascends into heaven from the Mount of Olives, the highest point in the sacred complex from which to enter the doorway of heaven (1:9-12).

This is also part of the reason the apostles must tarry in Jerusalem in order to receive power from on high (Luke 24:49, Acts 1:4-8). To be sure, the Spirit can descend upon Jesus in the region of the Jordan (Luke 3:22). But Luke wishes to warrant the Christian enterprise by establishing its divine empowerment at the point of contact between heaven and earth. And so at Pentecost Luke specifies that visible and audible manifestations from heaven attend the coming of the Spirit (Acts 2:2-3). The sound comes from the portals of heaven, and the tongues of fire mark the place where the Spirit alights. In this way the Gospel goes forth from the center of the earth at the gates of heaven.

Further, the martyrdom of Stephen testifies to the direct access at the threshold of heaven. When the heavens open, Stephen can actually see inside. He observes the glory of God and Jesus at the right hand. On the one hand, he sees the glory of the God who cannot be confined to the temple. On the other, he suggests that Jerusalem is the point where the earth is God's footstool (Acts 7:48-50). Significantly, he claims to see into heaven before he is thrown out of the city. That implies two things. First, it places Jesus at the entrance of heaven directly above Jerusalem. But second, that constitutes an astounding claim over against

---

[63] Ibid., 245.

Stephen's opponents. It is the momentous assertion that Jesus has occupied the place of God's power, rather than an alleged critique of the temple, that immediately precipitates Stephen's death (vv 56-58).

But can Luke think of Jerusalem and the temple as lying at the navel of the earth if from his historical vantage point the city and the sanctuary have been destroyed? Precisely. In Israel's tradition judgment upon the sacred center should not be unforeseen but expected. When Ezekiel envisions the wrath of God upon Jerusalem, it begins at the sanctuary (Ezek 9:6). But later Ezekiel anticipates the restoration of Israel (36:8-38). The glory of the Lord that has forsaken the temple in 9:3 returns to it in 43:2-5.

Similarly, Luke 21:24 limits the time of the gentiles. Although this evidence is sparse, Luke may anticipate the restoration of God's favor on the sacred city. In fact, Luke's presupposition that Jerusalem is the *axis mundi* may mean that he is in touch with a tradition that Jerusalem is the eschatological center of the Kingdom of God. Of course that speculates about a future that is unavailable in Luke-Acts. But at least Jerusalem's renewal is not excluded by a supposed assumption on the part of Luke that God has definitively rejected the Jews and transferred the center of Christianity to Rome.

Conclusion

Luke portrays the chief priests and Sadducees as archenemies of Jesus and Christianity. With other Jews Luke claims a common heritage. The authentic hope of Judaism, as Luke envisions it, is fulfilled in the resurrection of Jesus. But the chief priests and Sadducees have forsaken that genuine hope of Judaism. Since they are unworthy leaders who have betrayed Judaism, there is little surprise that they also oppose Christianity. Luke carefully distinguishes the high priestly circle from ordinary priests who are at least neutral if not favorable toward Christianity.

The hostility of the aristocractic temple-coterie toward Jesus and Christianity does not nullify the sacredness of the temple and city. Luke warrants the Christian enterprise by establishing its divine empowerment at the *axis mundi*, that is, at the very point of contact between heaven and earth. The destruction of the city and the temple is more a sign of rather than an obstacle to their holy function. Unbelief among the Jews invites the wrath of God upon the navel of the earth. But the only groups of Jews predisposed toward unbelief that Luke identifies concretely are the chief priests and the Sadducees.

CHAPTER EIGHT
THE JEWISH POPULACE

Although high priestly circles constitute the chief adversaries of Jesus and the church, anonymous masses can fall under their sway or appear as godless choruses even without official influence. They are equally capable of marveling at Jesus and his successors with exceptional approval. Is this merely an unstructured way of heightening the drama? Or does Luke employ the crowds in a definable pattern?

According to Martin Dibelius, in the early strata of developing traditions, reactions to events are placed in the mouths of anonymous crowds in order to simplify the story. Their role in the narrative, therefore, is not to be attributed to the evangelists.[1] But however much undifferentiated multitudes may belong to earlier strata of the tradition, Luke has adopted them into his cast of characters. That is, they play roles in the plots of Luke-Acts. They do not merely shed light on the development of the action but perform a function in motivating it.[2]

The Lucan view of the crowds, however, is hidden behind his portrayal of them as representatives of the furthest extremes of both credence and disbelief. The first multitude that the reader encounters is a crowd of pious Jews praying at the temple (Luke 1:10). Other multitudes who hear John the Baptist all repent and accept baptism (3:7–21). At the beginning of his ministry, Jesus is glorified by all (4:15). Not until anonymous citizens of Nazareth reject Jesus does the reader glimpse the other side. But this behavior is hardly just another facet of their character. Since they attempt to kill Jesus, they are but a step away from the crowds who demand the crucifixion (23:18–23).

In Acts the crowds also fall into these contrasting variations of

[1] M. Dibelius, *From Tradition to Gospel* (New York: Scribner's, 1965) 53, 57.
[2] J. Tyson ("The Jewish Public in Luke-Acts," *NTS* 30 [1984] 577) distinguishes between the crowds in Luke-Acts and the Greek chorus, in that the former participate in the plot. Aristotle (*Poetics* 18.19–20) says that the chorus should be regarded as one of the actors and should share in the action.

behavior. On the one hand, they give support to Christianity over against the high priestly opponents (e.g., Acts 4:21), and an astonishing number become believers (e.g., 2:41, 47; 4:4). On the other hand, a mob, now allied with diaspora Jews and the high priestly circle, lynches Stephen (6:12, 7:57–58). Another tries to do the same to Paul (21:30–31). This kind of ambiguity makes it difficult to formulate a Lucan view of the masses. What can one make of the contrasting, if not contradictory, images?

Jacob Jervell has developed the thesis that the gospel divides Israel into the repentant and the unrepentant.[3] According to him, Luke juxtaposes references to mass conversions of the Jews with reports about their rejection of the Christian message and its messengers in order to portray true Israel as that portion of Jews who believe. The successful aspect of the mission among Jews means the restoration of Israel. Where it fails, it means the repudiation of unbelievers, a kind of purging of the people of God.

Jervell confines his study to Acts. But Augustin George supplies what is lacking for the Gospel of Luke by painting a similar picture of the way in which Luke presents Israel's response to Jesus.[4] Since Luke confines the mission of Jesus to Israel alone and reserves the mission to the gentiles for Acts, the Gospel particularly depicts the response of Jews to Jesus. In Luke 2:34 Simeon anticipates what the remainder of the Gospel clearly shows: Jesus provokes the division of Israel.[5]

Luke Johnson advances beyond recognizing and describing the division of Israel by considering it a developed dramatic pattern.[6] The reaction of the hearers plays a crucial role in the movement of the plot and forms a significant part of the structure of Luke-Acts. For example, Stephen provokes a negative response in Jerusalem (Acts 6–7), Philip a positive one in Samaria (8:5–24). The significance of this for Johnson is that it is part of a larger pattern of prophet and people. Spirit-filled representatives of Christianity in Acts experience acceptance and rejection after the pattern of Jesus the prophet.[7]

Recently, Joseph Tyson has attempted to refine this ac-

---

[3] J. Jervell, *Luke and the People of God* (Minneapolis: Augsburg, 1972) 41–74.

[4] A. George, "Israël dans l'oeuvre de Luc," *RB* 75 (1968) 481–525. George's study also analyzes the material in Acts with more emphasis on Jewish rejection of the gospel than Jervell.

[5] Ibid., 492–506.

[6] L. Johnson, *The Literary Function of Possessions in Luke-Acts* (Missoula: Scholars, 1977).

[7] Ibid., 48–69, 95–126.

ceptance/rejection pattern.[8] He suggests that Luke consistently employs the crowds as a device to show initial acceptance and final rejection. Tyson finds a comparable analogy in Aristotle's description of the sudden reversal from favor to disfavor in Greek tragedy. Luke shapes the pattern *in nuce* in the rejection of Jesus at Nazareth (Luke 4:16–30), then develops it on a large scale by portraying crowds initially supporting Jesus until finally rejecting him at his trial. Similarly, in Acts the pattern is repeated in smaller units when Paul preaches. In the broader dimension Tyson sees the Jewish public as favorably disposed toward Christianity early in Acts but changing precipitously at the end in turning against Paul. Thus, whereas Johnson envisions the pattern as possibly simultaneous reactions in the face of the prophet, Tyson sees the pattern as sequential with the second possibility carrying the day.

Tyson's thesis raises a series of questions, the answers to which should cast light on Luke's view of the Jewish populace. In the first place, in what sense does Luke-Acts partake of the genre of tragedy so that Aristotle's pattern of reversal should find reverberations there? Tyson refers to Aristotle not to classify Luke-Acts generically as tragedy but to establish that Luke's work contains elements of tragedy.[9]

But the resurrection of Jesus and Paul's providential survival of potential calamities align Luke-Acts with the comic genre.[10] Nevertheless, it is also true that the emphasis on conflict and death in Luke-Acts betrays elements of tragedy. As David Tiede says with respect to the death of Jesus:

> The bitter tears of Peter ([Luke] 22:62), the laments of the women (23:27) and the beating of the breasts by the multitudes (23:48) all represent Luke's tragic vision of a people swept along in a current of intrigue and betrayal as they recognize the inevitable consequences of their participation too late to alter them (23:49).[11]

---

[8] Tyson, "Jewish Public," 574–83. A revised form of Tyson's article appears in J. Tyson, *The Death of Jesus in Luke-Acts* (Columbia, SC: University of South Carolina Press, 1986) 29–47.

[9] Tyson, *Death*, 16, 29, 169.

[10] D. Via (*Kerygma and Comedy in the New Testament: A Structuralist Approach to Hermeneutic* [Philadelphia: Fortress, 1975] 45–46, 93–99) sees resurrection as a characteristic of comedy and calls Mark tragicomedy. Luke is even more emphatic about the resurrection than Mark. D. Tiede (*Prophecy and History in Luke-Acts* [Philadelphia: Fortress, 1980] 117, 125) shows how God's dominion transcends the tragedy.

[11] Tiede, *Prophecy and History*, 104–105.

Acts traces a comparable flow of the predicament of misdirected people. Peter accuses the people of Judea and diaspora Jews dwelling in Jerusalem of crucifying Jesus, the very one attested by God (Acts 2:22–23; cf. 3:14). Lamentable resistance to God's plan snares even Paul. He consents to the death of Stephen, a man full of faith, grace, power, and of the Holy Spirit (6:5, 8; 8:1). Then as the table turns, rejection of the gospel pivots repeatedly on Paul.

If, then, it is granted that tragedy provides some precedent and ambience for Luke-Acts, there are other elements in Aristotle's *Poetics* that come into play. Tyson's use of Aristotle's reversal as an indication of a final rejection of Jesus by the Jewish public might find additional support in Aristotle's description of the ideal character. According to Aristotle, the exemplary hero is not pre-eminently virtuous and comes to reversal by some great flaw (13.5). Luke's protagonists are pre-eminently virtuous and come to reversal not by a flaw,[12] but by sinister opposition. The opponents in Luke-Acts, therefore, come under severe judgment.

On the other hand, Aristotle thinks that tragedy at its best links reversal with recognition. For its part, recognition signifies a change from ignorance that produces either friendship or hatred from those who are destined for success or ill fortune (*Poetics*, 11.4). Admittedly, Aristotle is somewhat ambiguous here. But he probably means that recognition produces a *division* into friends and enemies among those who experience the recognition depending on whether they are destined for good fortune or ill. In other words, in spite of implications of severe judgment upon those who do become enemies, Aristotle's *Poetics* would more strongly support an interpretation of Luke-Acts that describes a division among the Jewish populace with respect to Jesus, rather than a final rejection of him.[13]

In the second place, is the crowd always identical in Luke-Acts or does it wear different masks? Certainly Tyson has correctly called attention to the dramatic shift in the behavior of the people at large. After the messianic acclamations of the crowds on the Mount of Olives (Luke 19:38), the attention that the people give to Jesus' teaching in the temple (v 48, 21:38), and the fear of the authorities to test Jesus' popular support (19:48; 20:19, 26; 22:2), the reader is unprepared to find the masses calling for the crucifixion (23:13, 18–23).

But as abrupt as the change in attitude is, Luke does not allow

[12] Tyson, *Death*, 14, 29.
[13] Tyson (*Death*, 29–45) notes a type of division but insists on final rejection.

a direct identification of all the crowds.[14] He specifies that those who confess Jesus on the Mount of Olives are disciples (Luke 19:37). When Jesus teaches in the temple, Luke very clearly makes a distinction between the people and the high priestly circle (20:19, 26; 22:2). In contrast, when Luke introduces the multitudes at the trial, he allies them with the chief priests (23:4). Can these all be the same? Apparently not. Otherwise, it is impossible to account for the multitude that immediately follows Jesus to the crucifixion and bewails and laments him (v 27).

It is true that Luke does make some indiscriminate identification of the crowds. In Acts 2:23, 36 Peter lays responsibility for the crucifixion of Jesus upon his audience. He does the same thing at 3:14–15. But simultaneously, Luke also differentiates among the crowds. When Peter refers to the actual perpetrators of the crucifixion, he distinguishes them from his audience as lawless ones (2:23). In 3:17 Peter again makes a distinction between the people and the rulers. In so doing, he has intimated that the crowd at the trial of Jesus is under the influence of the high priestly party. By 4:2 the people once again stand over against the high priestly party, and the Sanhedrin must capitulate to them (4:21).

Tyson's methodology does not differentiate among the crowds but allows them to stand symbolically for Israel at large. There is linguistic support for this position. Luke can use ὄχλος and λαός interchangeably, and, as Nils Dahl has shown, Luke limits λαός to Israel with the exception of Acts 15:14 and 18:10.[15] On this basis one could easily consider Jewish crowds symbolic for Luke's view of the Jews as a whole. But Dahl also shows that in Luke λαός is fluid. It can refer to Israel as a totality or to a given group of Israelites without any high degree of precision. In addition, Jerome Kodell has demonstrated that in Luke 19:28–24:53, λαός distinguishes people friendly toward Jesus from the leaders who

---

[14] P. Minear ("Jesus' Audiences According to Luke," NovT 16 [1974] 81–89) shows that Luke carefully distinguishes his audiences. Chapter 6 above should provide a corrective for Minear's failure to distinguish the Pharisees as a particular audience with distinctive characteristics. Tiede (*Prophecy and History*, 105–118) indicates that the role of the people is carefully differentiated in the passion narrative. Tyson (*Death*, 171) notes the transformation of roles but insists that Luke controls the Jewish public by a literary pattern of initial acceptance and final rejection.

[15] N. Dahl, "'A People for His Name'," NTS 4 (1957–58) 324–26. Minear ("Jesus' Audiences," 85–86) argues that ὄχλος is not really interchangeable with λαός (the permanently elect people of God who are always redeemable), but that Luke takes ὄχλος as an equivalent from his sources. This attributes too little responsibility to Luke as an intentional author.

take the lion's share of the blame for the crucifixion.[16] In fact, the Gospel of Luke never presents the people as a concerted group acting on its own initiative except when they appear in favorable light.[17] Luke's view of a group of Israelites does not necessarily reflect his view of all Israel.

The way in which some Jews are related to "the Jews" is particularly crucial for the programmatic sermon of Jesus in Nazareth. Since the Nazarenes are Jews, Tyson understands their rejection of Jesus as anticipating the Jewish response to Jesus at the end of Luke.[18] But this fails to take into consideration how the rejection of Jesus by the people of Nazareth functions. I have shown in chapter 2 that Jesus is rejected by his hometown because he is a prophet, in accordance with the proverb that no prophet is acceptable in his πατρίς. The function of the rejection is to confirm Jesus' prophetic identity rather than to anticipate the rejection of all Israel. Elsewhere, the prophet encounters the pattern of acceptance and rejection (Johnson), so that the reaction in Nazareth is atypical of the Jews as a whole. Thus, the people of Nazareth cannot be identified indiscriminately with the crowds in Jerusalem who call for Jesus' crucifixion.

Although Tyson recognizes the complexity of Luke's views, he fails to distinguish the character of various crowds. This failure leads him to posit a logical inconsistency in the behavior of the people—the same crowds that repudiate Jesus enthusiastically embrace early Christians. According to Tyson, this is due to Luke's commitment to the literary pattern of initial acceptance and final rejection in both Luke and Acts.[19] Granted, Luke identifies two of Peter's audiences with those who demand the crucifixion. But a process of transformation also distinguishes them. Power from on high has come upon the apostles, the crowd has gathered at the sound of speaking in tongues, and Peter calls for them to repent (Acts 2). Those who do are no longer indeterminate and undefined Jewish people.

The repentant crowd now becomes a growing company of believers. Accordingly, they can be distinguished from the crowd that is involved in Stephen's death. Luke carefully stipulates that

---

[16] J. Kodell, "Luke's Use of *LAOS*, 'People,' Especially in the Jerusalem narrative (Lk 19, 28–24, 53)," *CBQ* 31 (1969) 328–31, 341, 343.

[17] C. Giblin, *The Destruction of Jerusalem According to Luke's Gospel: A Historical-Typological Moral* (Rome: Biblical Institute, 1985) 96.

[18] Tyson, "Jewish Public," 577–78; idem, *Death*, 32–33.

[19] Tyson, "Jewish Public," 581; idem, *Death*, 42.

opposition to Stephen originates with diaspora Jews.[20] These antagonists conspire to bring false accusations against Stephen precisely to stir up the people along with the elders and scribes (Acts 6:9–14). That is, this crowd is differentiated by coming under the sway of Stephen's opponents.

In brief, on occasion Luke has some sense of continuity in the identity of the crowds, but he can also create them without any interrelationship. Moreover, the crowds frequently are distinguished by coming under the sway of other more clearly defined characters. Even when the crowds are identical, Luke can differentiate them by having them undergo a transformation. Therefore, the role of the crowds is fluid and they wear different masks.[21]

In the third place, is the rejection of Paul by *some* Jews a sign of the rejection of Christianity by Judaism at large? Tyson cites Acts 25:24 as part of his support for taking Paul as the representative of the gospel. Here Festus explains to Agrippa II that all the multitude of the Jews have accused Paul.[22] As I have shown, Luke frequently uses πᾶς not in a strictly literal sense, but to refer to a large number. When in 25:2, 7 Luke confines Paul's accusers to the high priestly circle, he shows that as the author of Festus's words he cannot have in mind the whole Jewish people. I have also already demonstrated that Paul appears in Acts as Paul and is no cipher for Christianity. Paul's problems in Jerusalem (21:28) belong to him rather than to Christianity at large. Even if the Jewish rejection of him should prove to be final, it would not be equivalent to the rejection of Christianity.

Here Tyson once again fails to differentiate the crowds. Paul's problems come from Jews in Asia who trump up false charges. The mob is made up of Jerusalemites who have come under the sway of these Asian conspirators (Acts 21:27). But it does not maintain its definition by submission to the Asians, because Paul addresses the throng and triggers his own opposition. He identifies the God of the patriarchs as the one who sent him to the Gentiles (22:21). With that, the horde harbors its own complaint against Paul. Still, it is far from representing a total Jewish reaction. In subsequent chapters, opposition once again contracts to high priestly circles, including

---

[20] On the identity of Stephen's opponents, see G. Schneider, *Die Apostelgeschichte* (Freiburg: Herder, 1980) 1.435, cf. n. 19.

[21] The failure to differentiate among Jews is also the problem of N. Petersen's depiction of a literary pattern of confrontation between God's messengers and God's people in Jewish sanctuaries. (*Literary Criticism for New Testament Critics* [Philadelphia: Fortress, 1978] 85–91).

[22] Tyson, "Jewish Public," 581; idem, *Death*, 40–41.

the more than forty who plot to kill Paul (23:6–10, 12–14; 24:1; 25:2).

An integral part of this question is the way Jewish rejection of Paul functions. I appeal to my argument in chapter 5 that the rejection of Paul by *some* Jews explains, from an empirical perspective, the motivation for Paul's turning to Gentiles. Additionally, the opposition to Paul in Jerusalem explains how he comes to Rome. This precludes Paul all the more from being a sign of the rejection of the gospel.

In the fourth place, do Luke and Acts actually end on a final note of opposition by the people? The crux of Tyson's argument is that Luke follows a pattern of final rejection. For him, the animosity toward Jesus at his trial and the antagonism toward Paul in Jerusalem represent the final response of Jewish crowds.[23] Is that actually the case?

Tyson can maintain that the behavior of Jews at the trial of Jesus represents their definitive attitude only by failing to consider adequately two texts.[24] In one case, a great multitude of the people and of women follow Jesus and bewail and lament him (Luke 23:27). The women are not distinguished from the people here but are particular representatives of them (one article controls two genitives: τοῦ λαοῦ καὶ γυναικῶν).[25] The entire crowd of the people mourns the fate of Jesus. Jesus responds with an announcement of severe judgment that nevertheless does not indict the people and women.[26] Rather, Jesus envisions that the mourners and their children will suffer catastrophe as part of the punishment upon Jerusalem for which others are held accountable.[27] Therefore, Luke differentiates the mourners from the crowd that calls for the crucifixion.

The final response of the multitudes to Jesus comes from witnesses at the crucifixion who return home beating their breasts (Luke 23:48). On the one hand, the people stand in contrast to the rulers from whom they have already been distinguished in v 35. The rulers scoff at Jesus; the multitudes return home beating upon their breasts. Beating upon themselves is a sign of repentance as

---

[23] Tyson, "Jewish Public," 582; idem, *Death*, 37, 41–42.

[24] Tyson, ("Jewish Public," 577, 583, n. 13) refers to both in a note but makes substantive use of neither. Tyson (*Death*, 35–36) does give some attention to these texts.

[25] Giblin, *Destruction of Jerusalem*, 97. BDF §276(1).

[26] Against J. Neyrey, "Jesus' Address to the Women of Jerusalem (Lk. 23.27–31)—A Prophetic Judgment Oracle," *NTS* 29 (1983) 75–84.

[27] Giblin, *Destruction of Jerusalem*, 100–104.

the repentant publican in 18:13 shows.[28]

But the people also stand in solidarity with the repentant criminal (Luke 23:40–41) and the centurion (v 47) who declare Jesus innocent. Before the crucifixion Pilate pronounces Jesus innocent three times (vv 4, 14, 22). Luke takes pains to point out to the reader that Pilate makes the declaration for the third time. After the crucifixion, the criminal, the centurion, and the people who beat their breasts form the counterpart, a corresponding triple judgment against the perversion of justice.[29] The final function of the Jewish crowd in the Gospel of Luke is to beat upon their breasts in order to signify their own repentance in recognition of the innocence of Jesus. The final response of the people in Luke is not the rejection of Jesus.

Tyson actually recognizes that neither does Acts end on a final note of rejection by the Jews. Paul's preaching in Rome produces a division among them. And so Tyson substitutes Paul's final words to the Jews of Rome for their alleged rejection of the gospel. He judges those words to be the author's controlling concept—the negation and suppression of the earlier acceptance of Jesus and the early church.[30]

Jack Sanders renders an even harsher judgment about the ending of Acts. According to him, Paul's preaching produces no converts among Roman Jews. He bases his conclusion on Luke's use of πείθω to describe the more positive response of the Jews in Rome. He argues that some Jews may be persuaded, but persuasion is not conversion.[31] Here he succumbs to the fallacy of

[28] K. Rengstorf, *Das Evangelium nach Lukas* [Göttingen: Vandenhoeck & Ruprecht, 1937] 257. Tyson (*Death*, 36, 46, n. 13) rejects the notion that beating the breast is a sign of repentance as unsuitable to the Lucan context and literary structure. But the parallel in 18:13 and the correspondence to Pilate's third declaration of Jesus' innocence shows that it is suitable to the context and literary structure. See the subsequent discussion in the text and n. 29.

[29] Recently R. Karris ("Luke 23:47 and the Lucan View of Jesus' Death," *JBL* 105 [1986] 65–74) presents the argument that the centurion pronounces Jesus "righteous" rather than "innocent." But there are two points in particular that Karris overlooks. One is the symmetrical architectonic structure where the responses of the criminal, the centurion, and the people balance Pilate's thrice repeated declaration of Jesus' innocence. The other is the inherent ambiguity of δίκαιος. Although we may need to translate with preference to "righteous" over "innocent" or vice versa, the Greek can and does sustain both meanings at the same time. Jesus, therefore, fits into the Lucan schema of both an innocent martyr and the suffering righteous one.

[30] Tyson, "Jewish Public," 582; idem, *Death*, 42–43.

[31] J. Sanders, "The Salvation of the Jews in Luke-Acts," *Luke-Acts: New Perspectives from the Society of Biblical Literature Seminar* (ed. C. Talbert; New York: Crossroad, 1984) 107–109. Cf. H. Hauser, *Structuren der Abschlus-*

defining Luke's terminology by a word study that restricts the function of the term within its context. Sanders is correct that πείθω often does not imply belief, but incorrect that it never does. On the basis of this fallacy he concludes that none of the Jews in Rome believe. But here he overlooks the antithesis between ἐπείθοντο and ἠπίστουν (Acts 28:24). If πείθω in this case does not imply belief, how can it stand in contrast to unbelief? The failure to interpret πείθω more accurately within its context is part of the misleading evidence Sanders marshalls in support of an alleged universal and pervasive hostility of the Jews toward the gospel.

Whereas Tyson pictures Luke-Acts repeating acceptance/rejection patterns in crowd responses, Robert Tannehill proposes that the entire plot development of Luke-Acts moves toward tragic disappointment of the hope of Israel.[32] The early chapters of Luke heighten expectation for the redemption of Israel. But, Tannehill argues, Luke leaves these expectations largely unfulfilled. Individual pericopes in Luke-Acts mirror the same pathetic lack of fulfillment of the hope of Israel. For example, in his defense speeches, Paul implies that the Jews have rejected their own hope. To take another case in point, Stephen's speech describes the course of Israel's history according to a pattern of tragic reversal that prefigures Israel's rejection of Jesus. And so, according to Tannehill, Acts ends on a tragic note with the hope of Israel unfulfilled.[33]

It is symptomatic of the methodology of Sanders, Tannehill, and Tyson (among many) that they do not distinguish among various groups of Jewish people. Tannehill differentiates among the Jews to a degree before Stephen's speech,[34] but he deals with the Jews in Rome at the end of Acts as monolithic in rejecting the hope of Israel, and he identifies them with Israel at large. But do the Jews in Rome represent their people as a whole? On the one hand, Paul's allusion to Isaiah's audience as "your fathers" (Acts 28:25) could be adduced as a sign of their solidarity with the entire people. In addition, his conclusion that the salvation of God has been sent to the gentiles appears to play gentiles off against Jews as a whole. On the other hand, additional details of the passage show that Luke does differentiate the Jews in Rome. He initially designates Paul's audience as the leaders of the Jews in Rome

---

serzählung der Apostelgeschichte (Apg 28, 16–31) (Rome: Biblical Institute, 1979) 64–66.
[32] R. Tannehill, "Israel in Luke-Acts: A Tragic Story," *JBL* 104 (1985) 69–85.
[33] Ibid., 78–82.
[34] Ibid., 74.

(whom Paul addresses as brethren, v 17). Although they return in even greater numbers (v 23), Paul as a prisoner does not have access to the Jews at large.[35] Since Paul's preaching produces a division among them, only a part of the representative leaders refuse to believe.

Tannehill is correct that Paul's defense speeches imply the ironic rejection of the hopes of Israel by Jews themselves. But he fails to see that Paul distinguishes his accusers from other Jews. In Acts 23 Pharisees rally around Paul against the Sadducees in support of the hope of the resurrection of the dead. In 24:18–21 Paul identifies his opponents as Asian Jews and the high priestly, Sadducean coalition, the latter represented in this context by Ananias and Tertullus. Moreover, Paul's repeated claim that the real issue of his arrest is the hope of Israel establishes him as a model of a Jew in whom the hope of Israel has been fulfilled.

To understand the place of the Jews in Acts 28, the declaration that God's salvation goes to the gentiles must also be interpreted in its context. That context is Paul's defense before the Jewish leaders in Rome. The theme of Paul's speech, as Ernst Haenchen points out, is "I."[36] Acts 28:17–20 has a chiastic structure that emphasizes Paul's innocence. Paul's innocence stands at the center of the chiasm and is framed by denials of any opposition on his part against his people.[37] Paul explicitly tells the Jewish leaders that he wishes to explain that his arrest stands for the hope of Israel. The unspoken question that stands behind all of this is how to explain Paul's mission among gentiles (22:21–22, 26:20–21). That is answered, again on the empirical level, by the unbelieving portion of Paul's audience. In this context, Paul quotes Isa 6:9–10 and announces salvation for the gentiles in order to warrant his mission among the gentiles. This forms one-half of Luke's double explanation for why the thoroughly Jewish Paul nevertheless goes to gentiles (see above pp. 70–78).

Furthermore, Acts actually ends, not with Paul's citation of Isa 6:9–10, but with the narrator's summary of Paul's next two years. Paul welcomes all, and he preaches quite openly and unhindered (Acts 28:30–31). If "all" is consistent within its context, it would include Jews, both the curious and the believers. At any rate, *Paul's preaching no longer rouses Jewish opposition in Rome.* Is Paul at peace because Luke has written off the Jews, or because Luke wishes to leave the impression that Paul's mission among

---

[35] Schneider, *Apostelgeschichte*, 2.414, n.2.

[36] E. Haenchen, *The Acts of the Apostles: A Commentary* [Philadelphia: Westminster, 1971] 722.

[37] Hauser, *Structuren der Abschlusserzählung*, 23.

gentiles has been adequately explained? Since the second half of Acts concentrates on Paul and his mission in the diaspora, including a mission among gentiles, and since the last quarter of Acts focuses on a defense of Paul, is not the second possibility the only viable one? Against Tyson, neither Luke's Gospel nor Acts ends on the final note of Jewish rejection.

Luke emphatically differentiates the Jewish public in the parable of the vineyard in Luke 20:9–19. Since in the context of Jesus' daily teaching the cursing of the fig tree does not interrupt 19:47–20:19, the Evangelist has created an integrated series of episodes with a more unified thematic development than the parallel in Mark; a common thread running all the way to 20:45–47 is the indictment of opponents among the leaders, especially the scribes and chief priests.[38] According to 19:47 the chief priests, the scribes, and the principal men *of the people* seek to kill Jesus. But they cannot because *all the people* hang upon his words.

In Mark, Jesus addresses the parable to the chief priests, the scribes, and the elders (Mark 11:27, 12:1). By way of contrast, Luke stipulates that Jesus tells the parable to the people (Luke 20:9). The reaction of the horrified people in v 16 has no parallel and, therefore, is a significant clue to Luke's view of the Jewish public in this instance. When the parable predicts the destruction of the tenants and the transfer of the vineyard to others, the audience responds fearfully with μὴ γένοιτο. They understand that the parable brings them under scrutiny. They share in the larger destiny of their people,[39] and the parable foreshadows dire consequences for them.[40] Against this backdrop, Jesus' further explana-

---

[38] C. Talbert, *Reading Luke: A Literary and Theological Commentary on the Third Gospel* (New York: Crossroad, 1982) 188–89; Giblin, *Destruction of Jerusalem*, 59.

[39] Tyson (*Death*, 103) thinks that the vineyard stands allegorically for the temple rather than the nation. But the background of the vineyard as a stock metaphor in the OT, particularly in Isaiah 5, and the fearful response of the people in Luke 20:16, showing that the judgment in the parable impinges significantly upon them, indicate that the vineyard symbolizes Israel as the people of God. K. Snodgrass, *The Parable of the Wicked Tenants: An Inquiry into Parable Interpretation* (Tübingen: Mohr [Siebeck], 1983) 60, 74–76; Giblin, *Destruction of Jerusalem* 66–67.

[40] E. Schweizer (*The Good News According to Luke* [Atlanta: Knox, 1984] 304) says that Luke distinguishes the people from the officials in v 16. That is not precisely accurate. Rather, the parable refers to "those tenants" whereas the evangelist describes the response of the hearers. But this leaves room for the same type of distinction between the people and the scribes and chief priests that is made in v 19. E. Klostermann (*Das Lukasevangelium* [Tübingen: Mohr (Siebeck), 1929] 193) perceives the differentiation of people and authorities, although he

tion interprets Ps 118:22 as a warning to those who reject him but leaves the fate of repentant people ambiguous. Luke 20:19–20, however, once again distinguishes the people from the scribes and chief priests. The authorities explicitly interpret the parable as judgment upon themselves over against the people who in v 19 play a role in support of Jesus.[41] Thus, Luke brackets the parable with the strong opposition of chief priests and scribes who are in conflict with the people who support Jesus (19:47–48, 20:19). This framework "merits detailed attention, the better to situate the central episode (the parable) as forcefully warning the people, but not as prophetically charging them with a crime or attacking their own current attitude or conduct."[42]

Luke 24:20 and Acts 4:11 provide Lucan commentaries on the culpability of the Jewish leaders. In a kind of literary flashback, Cleopas and the other disciple explain to the risen Jesus, who is traveling to Emmaus incognito, that the chief priests and rulers delivered Jesus up to be condemned to death and crucified him (Luke 24:20). In Acts 4:11 Peter quotes Ps 118:22 against the Sanhedrin. They are the builders who have rejected the stone which has become the head of the corner. The citation comes as a proof text to explain the resurrection of Jesus who was crucified (Acts 4:10). Luke, however, is not merely interested in proving God's affirmation of Jesus by way of the resurrection, because he also pointedly identifies the perpetrators of the crucifixion. In v 10 he uses ὑμεῖς to make the agents of the crucifixion emphatic. Then in v 11 he specifies that the stone is rejected ὑφ' ὑμῶν, a variation from both the MT and the LXX. Luke's version has been attributed to early Christian testimonia,[43] even though Mark 12:10, Luke 20:17, and 1 Peter 2:7 all have the LXX form. Whatever the source, the parallel between ὑμεῖς in Acts 4:10 and ὑφ' ὑμῶν in v 11 shows

identifies the authorities as members of the Sanhedrin. Similarly, W. Grundmann, *Das Evangelium nach Lukas* (Berlin: Evangelische, 1961) 372.

[41] I. Marshall (*The Gospel of Luke: A Commentary on the Greek Text* [Grand Rapids: Eerdmans, 1978] 726) interprets Luke 20:19 as clarifying the impact of the parable on the religious leaders. Therefore, it warns the people against their leaders. F. Danker (*Jesus and the New Age According to St. Luke: A Commentary on the Third Gospel* [St. Louis: Clayton, 1972] 199) thinks that the distinction between the leaders and the people in Luke 19:47–48 means that Israel as a whole has not renounced Jesus. Cf. G. Schneider, *Das Evangelium nach Lukas Kapitel 11–24* (Gütersloh: Mohn, 1977) 398–400; Snodgrass, *Parable of the Wicked Tenants*, 46, 91.

[42] Giblin, *Destruction of Jerusalem*, 60.

[43] So e.g., Schneider, *Apostelgeschichte*, 1.347–348. Cf. B. Lindars, *New Testament Apologetic: The Doctrinal Significance of the Old Testament Quotations* (London: SCM, 1961) 81–82, 170.

intentional emphasis on the members of the Sanhedrin as the agents of the crucifixion.

But Luke provides further commentary on the agents of the crucifixion by recording the response of the Christian community to the experience of Peter and John before the Sanhedrin (Acts 4:23–28). The congregation quotes Ps 2:1–2 as a chorus and interprets it in chiastic order. According to the interpretation, Jesus is the Lord's anointed, Herod and Pilate correspond to the kings of the earth and the rulers. Curiously, the interpretation ignores the parallelism of Psalm 2 and therefore takes the "peoples" of v 1 to be Israelites, whereas in the parallelism they are gentiles. Furthermore, the kings and the rulers in v 2 are parallel to the raging gentiles and the plotting peoples in v 1. *Midr. Tehillim* on Psalm 2 shows that this most obvious view of the parallelism dominated rabbinic tradition. The midrash gives as examples of the raging peoples of v 1 Pharaoh, Sisera, and Nebuchadnezzar, and even anticipates the apocalyptic uprising of Gog and Magog. In addition, the "peoples" explicitly stand over against the Israelites. But Luke disregards the parallelism in order to demonstrate a point by point fulfillment of the Psalm as prophecy according to his own account of the passion.

Equally as curious, Luke also takes the reference to gathering together to include the gentiles and people as well as the kings and rulers. And so the application of the Psalm to the crucifixion of Jesus envisions a confederacy of Herod, Pilate, gentiles, and the peoples of Israel.[44] In this case there is no distinction between Jewish leaders and people. Is Luke then indicting the people as a whole?

This passage and the Gospel account of the crucifixion mutually explain how Luke understands the confederacy. Luke alone relates the trial of Jesus before Herod and notes at the end that Herod and Pilate became friends (Luke 23:12). They are the kings and rulers who set themselves against the Lord and against the Lord's anointed. But who in the passion story corresponds to the gentile collaborators? The only possible answer appears to be the soldiers who mock Jesus (23:36).[45] Luke does not specify that they are gentiles, but elsewhere he refers to the temple police as στρατηγοί, whereas here he uses the term στρατιῶται. To complete the picture, the peoples of Israel allude to the Jewish multitudes who call for the crucifixion.

[44] Luke specifically uses the plural of λαός here to correspond to the peoples of Psalm 2:1.
[45] See Haenchen, *Acts*, 227.

There are three main pieces of evidence that restrict this reference to the people from indicting all Israelites. One is the corresponding case of the gentiles. Their participation in the conspiracy against Jesus does not mean a repudiation of all gentiles. In fact, only a few soldiers who make a cameo appearance are adequate to fulfill the prophecy. Second, Acts 4:28 shows that Luke's interest is to vindicate the passion of Jesus as a realization of the plan of God confirmed by fulfillment of the prophecy. Third, Acts 4:29 reverts to the opposition from the Sanhedrin[46] and anticipates an uninterrupted mission to the Jews in Jerusalem, a mission that continues to bear fruit.

Thus, in spite of Luke's use of undefined crowds of Jews, he is also able to distinguish them. They wear different masks particularly when they stand over against high priestly circles as opposed to coming under their sway.

To recapitulate, this discussion has established (1) a larger literary context for understanding the parable of the wicked tenants within the framework of distinguishing the Jewish public from their leaders and (2) a broader Lucan commentary on the differentiation of Jewish leaders from the people at large in the rejection of Jesus. This background also sheds light on Luke's parable of the pounds (Luke 19:11–27). As is well known, Luke fuses the parable of the throne claimant with the parable of the pounds. Whereas the parable of the pounds alone emphasizes rewards for productive and punishment for unproductive servants, the parable of the throne claimant adds severe judgment against the nobleman's enemies. If these enemies symbolize the Jews,[47] we would have to stop developing a picture of Luke's differentiation of the Jewish public. But several considerations raise objections to interpreting the king's command to kill his enemies as Luke's repudiation of the Jews.

For one thing, the fused parables distinguish the hostile citizens from the nobleman's servants. Future judgment is far more severe for the hostile citizens than for the unproductive servant.[48] This distinction between servants and enemies could easily symbolize the distinction between Christians and Jews were it not for another detail in the context. Luke 19:11 ties the fused parables to the story of Jesus and Zacchaeus. Zacchaeus has just been cited,

---

[46] Αὐτῶν refers to the Sanhedrin in Acts 4:29. Haenchen, *Acts*, 228.

[47] J. Sanders ("The Parable of the Pounds and Lucan Anti-Semitism," *TS* 42 [1981] 666–67) argues that Luke dissociates the kingdom from Jerusalem and adds the throne claimant, the point of which is the destruction of the Jews.

[48] Grundmann, *Evangelium nach Lukas*, 363; Giblin, *Destruction of Jerusalem*, 45.

rather ironically, as an example of a lost son of Abraham who has been saved. This vindicates Jesus against the murmuring crowd for associating with Zacchaeus. Calling Zacchaeus a saved son of Abraham implies including him within the people of God on the basis of repentance, rather than excluding him on the basis of social standing. Zacchaeus becomes an exemplary saved Jew who could hardly be lumped together with the alleged Jewish enemies of the parable of the throne claimant. Because Luke links the fused parable to the Zacchaeus incident, the distinction between servants and enemies fits Luke's pattern of differentiation within Judaism.

Luke Johnson's refreshing interpretation of this pericope corroborates my contention that in it Luke differentiates the Jewish public.[49] Over against the typical exegesis of the parable as an allegory of the ascension and the delayed parousia, Johnson reads it as referring to the kingship of Jesus already accomplished. The rewards for the productive servants of ruling over cities alludes, therefore, to the participation of Christian leaders within the king's realm in Luke's own present.[50] Further, Johnson suggests that the ambiguity of the audience in Luke 19:11 indicates that Luke intends for the parable to address the general crowds, the disciples, and the opponents each in distinct ways.[51] Against that background, the parable confirms the expectation of the audience in v 11 that the kingdom of God will be declared upon the arrival of Jesus in Jerusalem. Therefore, at the climactic arrival, anticipated since 9:51, Jesus is declared king by the disciples in 19:38, a close parallel to 19:15.[52] The parable has the capacity of proclaiming the kingdom to the disciples, of calling the crowds in general to repentance, and of announcing judgment upon the leaders who reject Jesus. In this regard, the parable fits the Lucan motif of a division within Israel caused by Jesus' proclamation with the attending new leadership for the believing portion.[53] And so the parable of the pounds, rather than suspending our developing picture of Luke's differentiation of the Jewish public actually is a part of it.

Luke also leaves clues of his perspectives toward the Jewish

---

[49] L. Johnson, "The Lukan Kingship Parable (Lk. 19:11–27)," *NovT* 24 (1982) 139–59.

[50] Ibid., 143–44. Johnson argues that nothing indicates a temporal delay. For the opposing view see J. Dupont, "La parabole des talents (Mat. 25:14–30) ou des mines (Luc 19:12–27)," *RTP* 19 (1969) 382.

[51] Johnson, "Lukan Kingship Parable," 145.

[52] Ibid., 145–58.

[53] Ibid., 153.

public in the way he deals with the synagogue. Ambiguity in this case also makes it difficult to define his views. Luke portrays Jesus as customarily attending the synagogue on the sabbath (Luke 4:16). Even when Jesus' incursion into the synagogue at Nazareth culminates in his expulsion, Luke still presupposes that Jesus has access to the synagogue. When Luke introduces Jesus' ministry in Capernaum, he describes him teaching on the sabbath, and then coincidentally mentions that he is in the synagogue (v 33). When elders in Capernaum intercede for the centurion, they commend him for building their synagogue in such a way as to imply both the approval of Jesus and the author (7:5).

Acts similarly presupposes that Christians have access to synagogues, although Christians are never actually placed in the synagogue in Jerusalem. True, Stephen debates with opponents identified by their synagogue affiliation, but no direct information places him in the synagogue. It is well known that Paul consistently follows a pattern of going into the synagogue upon arrival at a new location. Like Jesus, he customarily attends the synagogue (Acts 17:2). Surprisingly, although Paul's difficulties arise virtually always from Jews, opposition seldom arises directly with the synagogue.

There is another side to the coin. In addition to the incident in Nazareth, Jesus encounters opposition within the synagogue on another occasion. He rouses the indignation of a ruler of a synagogue by healing an infirm woman on the sabbath (Luke 13:14). In Acts there is only one specific case of opposition within the synagogue. When Paul debates in the synagogue at Ephesus for three months, some opponents speak evil of Christianity before the congregation and Paul withdraws (Acts 19:8–9). Yet the case in Corinth is so similar, involving also withdrawal from the synagogue, that it too must be seen as opposition within the synagogue (18:4–7).

Acts narrates a lot of mob violence toward Christianity on the part of Jews, but official opposition from the synagogue is conspicuous by its absence. This is all the more surprising since two sayings of Jesus in Luke anticipate persecution from the synagogue. In the context of counsel against apostasy, Jesus recommends reliance on the Holy Spirit in order for his disciples to know what to say before the synagogues, the rulers, and the authorities (Luke 12:11). Jesus gives the same advice in an apocalyptic context when he foretells that persecution will precede eschatological signs. Jesus predicts that believers will be delivered up to synagogues and prisons and will be brought before kings and governors

(21:12).[54] Acts 4–5, 6–7, and 23–26 relate instances that correspond closely to arraignment before rulers, authorities, kings, and goverors. But little fulfills the prediction of being hauled up before synagogues. Peter and John, the apostles, Stephen, and Paul all face trials before the Sanhedrin, but not before the synagogue. The closest fulfillment of these predictions is the persecution from Paul before his conversion.

Paul, identified here as Saul, secures official permission from the high priest to arrest Christians in the synagogue (Acts 9:1–2). He later recalls his persecution of believers, claiming that he imprisoned and beat them in synagogues (22:19). In 26:11 he recalls imprisoning believers and even executing them, but also punishing them in the synagogues. But the former persecutor, who punished Christians in the synagogue, actually enjoys markedly positive relationships in the synagogue. Even when the sailing is not smooth, Paul is the one who abandons the synagogue.

Paul does not merely exploit the synagogue as a strategy to find sympathizers. He views it as the necessary starting point theologically. And so he explains to the congregation in Antioch of Pisidia that the resurrection of Jesus fulfills the promise of God to the children of Abraham and the patriarchs.[55] That is why it is necessary for the gospel to be spoken first to Jews (Acts 13:26, 32–33, 46). Whereas for the Jews the synagogue is primarily the place of the torah,[56] for Luke it is primarily the place of the gospel.

To repeat, Luke 12:11 and 21:12 anticipate opposition and persecution in the first instance from the synagogue. Something like that materializes in the persecution from Paul. But in Acts the synagogue is primarily the place where Paul proclaims the gospel to Jews,[57] and it has lost its menacing disposition. As far as Paul is

---

[54] W. Schrage ("συναγωγή," TDNT 7.834) sees a polemical thrust against the synagogue in Luke 12:11 and 21:12. Josephus (Life 56–59 §293–304) and m. Mak. 3:12 (an undated tradition) attest to the synagogue as a place of judicial inquiry and punishment.

[55] K. Hruby, Die Synagoge: Geschichtliche Entwicklung einer Institution (Zürich: Theologische, 1971) 62–63.

[56] Schrage, TDNT 7.821. Schrage argues (829) that "synagogue" is not used to designate Christian congregations because of such close associations with the law. That may be true historically, and it is even reflected in Acts 15:21. But Luke associates the synagogue most closely with the gospel.

[57] A great deal is made of a Lucan theme that the state is at worst harmless to Christianity and at best its protector. So recently P. Walasky, "And So We Came to Rome": the Political Perspective of St. Luke (Cambridge: Cambridge University Press, 1983); C. Talbert, Acts (Atlanta: Knox, 1984). But as far as a Pauline role model is concerned, the synagogue is not the place of persecution envisioned in Jesus' prophecy, but the place of proclamation of the Christian gospel.

concerned, the threat has been transferred to Jewish mobs and the high priestly circle.

The law, as a rather diaphanous symbol, also evidences Luke's attitude toward the Jews. In a recent monograph on *Luke and the Law*, Stephen Wilson documents yet another mixed bag. On the one hand, Luke's Jesus keeps the law and denounces disobedience. On the other hand, he critiques it and moves beyond it. There is a similar duality in Acts. The law is inadequate as a means of salvation and holds no validity for gentiles. Nevertheless, it is the proper way of life for Jews and Jewish Christians.[58]

Does all the ambiguity relegate Luke's view of the Jews to muddleheaded confusion? Unlikely. Luke's general artistry and precision call for integrating the diversity into a sensible pattern. A rather standard solution is to consign Luke's positive appraisal of Judaism to the past while his disparaging sentiments represent the present.[59]

But three difficulties hamper this explanation. (1) Luke's actual presentation of stages of development in the past, (2) the accommodation of Paul and the gentile mission toward Judaism as Luke understands it, and (3) the focus on Paul as Paul.

(1) To summarize a previous argument, contrary to the standard line, Luke does not describe a progressive development of the church from a Jewish to a gentile entity. He portrays the development of an essentially Jewish sect, that in fulfillment of God's promises to Israel includes gentiles. The only church Acts knows still has the umbilical cord attached.

(2) There is a recurring pattern of conciliatory action on the part of those engaged in gentile mission for the sake of unity with Jewish Christians.[60] As a response to the conversion of Cornelius (Acts 10:1–11:18) and of gentiles in Antioch (11:20–21), Cyprus, and Asia Minor (13:4–14:27), the Jerusalem Council requests gentile believers to obey the minimal laws required to maintain table fellowship with Jewish Christians. In a thorough discussion of the apostolic decree, Stephen Wilson argues that it advocates

---

[58] S. Wilson, *Luke and the Law* (Cambridge: Cambridge University Press, 1983) 27–102, 114–15.

[59] See, e.g., P. Richardson, *Israel in the Apostolic Church* (Cambridge: Cambridge University Press, 1969) 160–65; F. Bovon, "Luc: Portrait et projet," *Lumière et vie* 30 (N. 153/54, 1981) 12; Wilson, *Luke and the Law*, 115–16. Hauser (*Structuren der Abschlusserzählung*, 78, 107–110, 228) holds that the ending of Acts moves to a new phase where the gospel is proclaimed unhindered to all. The confrontation between Jews and gentiles has been overcome. He explicitly makes the Jews of Rome representatives of all Jews and hence does not differentiate among the Jews. Similarly, he makes Paul a cipher for Christianity.

[60] Talbert, *Acts*, 93.

apostolic mores rather than imposing minimal demands of the law upon gentile believers.[61] Although he places the decree in the context of the debate over the imposition of the Jewish law upon gentile converts, he fails to appreciate its importance as a reaction to the issue of *relations* between Jews and gentiles. The debate in Jerusalem hinges on circumcision according to the custom of Moses (15:1). In response, the Council stipulates that Jewish Christians are not to demand circumcision, but gentiles are to mold their behavior according to the prohibitions that are concessions to Jews. Further, 21:20–25 provides a Lucan commentary on the meaning of the decree. In that context James implies that Paul should demonstrate his allegiance to the law, even as the gentiles do what the law demands of them. Thus, the apostolic decree is an accommodation toward Jewish Christians in the interest of church unity.

A second case of conciliatory behavior is the circumcision of Timothy. Luke presents the case as if it is well known among the Jews around Lystra that Timothy is not circumcised. Luke stipulates that Timothy is already a disciple so that the circumcision has nothing to do with Timothy's status as a believer. Rather, it is for the sake of the Jews (Acts 16:1–4). In the same context, Luke relates that Timothy and Paul promulgate the apostolic decree, another indication that the decree and Timothy's circumcision are conciliatory.

The final repetition of this pattern is Paul's support of four men under a vow and his purification along with them (Acts 21:23–26). This comes in response to suspicions among Jewish Christians in Jerusalem that Paul is encouraging diaspora Jews to give up the Mosaic law. Paul complies specifically to accommodate Jewish Christians who are zealous for the law (v 20).

(3) The scholarly opinion that Luke let his final rejection of Judaism show through his narrative rests largely on Paul's patterned reaction to unbelieving Jews. His thrice repeated decision to go to the gentiles (Acts 13:46, 18:6, 28:28) is read not as Paul's decision but as the movement of the entire enterprise of God's salvation. But the final half of Acts is a story about Paul as Paul. The story of the extension of God's salvation as a whole is another one that Luke does not tell.

Since the only type of Christianity that Luke describes maintains its relationships with Judaism, it is a blind leap off the end of

---

[61] Wilson, *Luke and the Law*, 71–101. Wilson has raised sufficient doubt about the decree's reference to Lev 17–18, that there is reason to avoid reference to it as what the law demands of gentiles. Nevertheless, it is a concession to Jews.

Acts to a Lucan church free from Judaism. If Luke writes from the perspective of the triumph of gentile Christianity over Judaism, how can he be so concerned to accommodate Paul and the mission among gentiles toward Judaism as he defines it? The methodological basis for this blind leap is another perilous step, namely, to read Paul's story symbolically as the story of Christianity. The attempt to integrate Luke's ambiguity toward Jews by a division of past and present falls with the blind leap and the perilous methodology.

An intriguing attempt to comprehend the ambiguity in Luke's view of the Jews comes from François Bovon.[62] He describes Lucan Christianity sociologically as a sect searching for identity. The emerging sect defines itself over against Judaism and legitimates itself as the genuine fulfillment of the hope of Israel. According to this view, positive evaluations of Judaism are actually signs of the historical break with Judaism, that is, Christianity appropriates the claims of Israel and thus repudiates it.

But the picture is more complex than Bovon indicates. Christianity in Acts does lay claim to the promises of God to Israel (Peter, Acts 2:14–36, 3:12–26; Stephen, 7:2–53; Paul, 13:16–41; 24:14–15; 26:6–7, 22). In that sense Christianity has identified itself by asserting its relative superiority over Judaism apart from Christ. But Luke does not simply set Christianity over against Judaism. Rather, he divides Israel into two camps—believers and unbelievers. Then, he associates certain groups more closely with one or the other of the two camps. Luke differentiates Sadducees and the high priestly circle and connects them with recalcitrant Israel. On the other hand, he presents Pharisees as on the brink of Christianity. He takes advantage of the elevated status of the Pharisees in general in order to allow them to advocate Paul. In similar fashion he exploits Gamaliel's outstanding reputation for the benefit of Paul, and uses him to lobby on behalf of the Christian enterprise. Although the Pharisees can yet be distinguished as unbelievers, they are more closely related to believing Israel than to recalcitrant Israel.

Against Bovon, Luke does not merely usurp the prerogatives of Israel; he also *includes* a significant portion of Israel and has other reputable and influential Jews waiting in the wings. Bovon's hypothetical search for Christian identity fails to do justice to this collage.

The problem of ambiguity takes on a different character when

---

[62] F. Bovon, "Israel, die Kirche und die Völker im lukanischen Doppelwerk," *TLZ* 108 (1983) 403–414.

the last half of Acts is viewed as Luke's story, and ultimately defense, of Paul. Initially in Jerusalem high priestly circles oppose the gospel. To them may be added some diaspora Jews who conspire against Stephen. A mob comes under the sway of Stephen's opponents and evidently participates in his execution. But many more believe. In the final half of Acts it is Paul, rather than Christianity as such, who attracts consistent opposition from the Jewish populace. Even in those cases, many Jews also believe. But the unbelieving segment is sufficient to motivate Paul to turn to the gentiles.

Paul is Luke's problem,[63] hardhearted Jews a part of the solution. But so are believing Jews, some Pharisees who defend Paul, and a highly regarded rabbi named Gamaliel who, so to speak, gives Paul his diploma. Believing Jews recognize Paul's gospel as the hope of Israel, and reputable representatives of the strictest party of Judaism, who have preserved that hope, stand on the brink of faith.

---

[63] Wilson (*Luke and the Law*, 108) confirms Jervell's view (*Luke*, 146) that Paul is Luke's real problem.

CHAPTER NINE
CONCLUSION

The Jews in Luke-Acts play out their roles enmeshed in an intricate pattern of theme and plot development. Little wonder that ambiguity smudges the colors scholars paint onto their portrait. Little wonder also that oversimplification engraves one outline of the image in stronger relief than another. To delineate the role of the Jews in Luke-Acts at all reduces a complex picture to a simpler one and already twists it out of shape. Yet recognizing the complexity and differentiating the distinct parts played by Jews minimize the distortion. To differentiate the roles of the Jews is to determine their literary function in theme and plot development, a task overlooked when interpreters jump straight from hostility between the Nazarenes and Jesus, for example, to antipathy between Luke and the Jews.

Therefore, the first task of the foregoing has been to repair, to pull down an old facade and to raise up another. What I have tried to pull down is the conventional theory that Luke gives up on the Jews as hopelessly hardened against the gospel and that he views them as providing antecedents for Christianity only as a part of a remote past.

But to move beyond iconoclastic antithesis, I have then offered a counter proposal, namely, that Luke responds to Jewish antagonism apologetically and proffers conciliation. I have proceeded by asking how Luke views conflict arising from Jewish sources and what his response to it is. Especially significant in this regard is the literary function of the rejection of Jesus by the people of Nazareth. Their refusal to accept Jesus establishes his identity as a prophet who is Spirit-filled and who makes messianic claims. The literary purposes of the rejection of Paul by some Jews in Asia Minor, Greece, and Rome is of equal significance. Against opponents of Pauline universalism, it explains empirically why Paul goes to the gentiles. Jewish obduracy motivates Paul to turn to the gentiles.

If there were a monolithic repudiation of Jesus and the gospel by Jews, then Jesus and Paul would be exonerated at their expense. But large islands of acceptance jut out in the midst of the opposition. Jesus wins popular support with the exception of crowds under the sway of the high priestly party. Even though such crowds call for his crucifixion, the people are finally distinguished from the high priestly party, and they beat upon their breasts in repentance. That repentance is confirmed in Acts by the crowds in Jerusalem who accept the gospel.

The Pharisees match the ambiguity of the people. They dispute with Jesus and stand over against the multitudes that accept him. They earn rebukes from Jesus, and he pronounces woes upon them. In contrast, they also host Jesus and they warn him against Herod. But again what is significant is how they function. In some cases they intensify the question of who Jesus is and they are the audience for announcements of his christological identity. In repeated instances they are juxtaposed to Jesus. In comparison, Jesus appears in all the more positive light because the Pharisees are highly regarded in the Lucan environment.

Acts takes advantage of the elevated status of the Pharisees to vindicate Christianity and some of its heroes. Gamaliel holds the door open for Christianity and actually betrays a preference for it. In addition, Pharisees within the Sanhedrin see nothing incredible about Paul's claims.

Not only do the Pharisees hold open the door to Christianity, but they oppose the Sadducees and the high priestly party. From the time of the passion of Jesus through the trials of Paul, Sadducees and the circle around the chief priests invariably play the role of opponents. They have given up the hopes of Israel, and Ananias, a prominent example from their number, breaks the law while judging Paul. They are inauthentic Jews who constitute the archenemies of Jesus and the early church.

The move from differentiating the roles of Jews in Luke-Acts to an address of Luke to Jews (Jewish Christians) is hazard-fraught. The risk is that, no longer dealing with literary function within the text, but with hypothetical historical reconstruction beyond the text, we reify phantoms of our mind. But the evidence is also substantial. It is clearest in Luke's portrayal of Paul.

For Luke, the image of Paul has suffered damage from detractors who claim that Paul's gospel is incomplete, and who raise suspicions among Jewish Christians that Paul teaches apostasy from Judaism. To repair the damage, Luke sketches the character of Paul in Jewish contours with Pharisaic overtones. He accommodates the Paul of the Epistles toward Judaism as he envisions it. Comparison with Paul's own testimony in Gal 1:9 and Rom 1:5, 15:18 shows that Luke also accommodates Paul's mission toward

Judaism; that is, in Acts Paul is first of all a missionary to Jews. Moreover, he himself willingly demonstrates his orthodoxy.

Luke also partially explains Paul's mission among gentiles as the result not of Paul's plans but Jewish machinations. (Parenthetically, I reiterate emphatically that the second half of Acts relates only the Pauline incursions into gentile territory rather than detailing the gentile mission in its larger scope.) To be sure, from the beginning God has destined Paul to go to gentiles as well as Jews. But recalcitrant Jews drive Paul away from themselves and provide the occasion for Paul to turn to the gentiles. Jews (Jewish Christians) suspicious of Paul and his mission among gentiles have God and recalcitrant Jews to blame. Paul himself exerts less energy in the gentile mission than in proclaiming the gospel to Jews. Do not this accommodation toward Judaism and this explanation of why Paul turns to gentiles function only for an audience suspicious of Paul's tenuous relations with Judaism?

Paul's Jewishness is also the burden of his defense speeches. He claims to be committed to the hopes of the fathers, Moses, and the twelve tribes, and he avows that he espouses the hopes of genuine Jews who are his contemporaries. He presents himself as a Pharisee who has become a believer who still claims to be a Pharisee.

Paul's Jewishness functions in context to settle apprehension and to quiet opposition raised by his relations with gentiles. In fact, Luke uses Paul's relation to Judaism to vindicate his relation to gentiles. Who is Luke's target?

Although Luke keeps his opponents well concealed, clues to their identity emerge in the Miletus address. Here Paul ostensibly warns about opponents of the future. That future, however, is Luke's present, and the opponents are no longer anticipated but real. Threats arise from without but also from within. Since external threats to Paul virtually always originate in Jewish circles, and since Luke goes on to describe Paul's arrest in Jerusalem,—a threat that the Miletus address anticipates—we can identify the external opponents as Jews. I would hazard a guess that the internal opponents are Jewish Christians, but they may be sympathetic gentiles, such as former God-fearers. At any rate, Luke attempts to counter anti-Paulinism from both Jewish and Christian (Jewish Christian?) sources.

To their complaints, the Lucan Paul offers an apology. But the portrait of Paul is also conciliatory. This is most apparent in Paul's support of four Jewish Christians under a vow and his attempt to purify himself in the temple along with them. The same type of conciliatory pattern surfaces in the circumcision of Timothy, and in this case the conciliation appears to have Jews as its object.

Beyond Paul, Luke dramatizes the conciliation in the Jerusalem Council and the apostolic decree. Over against the contentions of Pharisaic Christians, the Council sanctions the accession of gentiles to the gospel apart from the law of Moses. But then the decree enjoins gentiles to make reciprocal concessions in the patterns of their behavior.

To the evidence for conciliation may be added the implicit high regard for the Pharisees in general and the explicit esteem of Gamaliel in particular. In Luke the Pharisees set Jesus off to advantage. But Luke does not compare them as hero and villain, good against the bad. He contrasts them as superior over reputable. For Luke, Jesus rises above the Pharisees rather than repudiating them utterly. The force of Gamaliel's character gives his advice to the Sanhedrin its impact, not for his fellow jurists, but for Luke's audience. Luke appeals to Gamaliel and other Pharisees of lesser prominence for the sake of his readers. He demonstrates to them how close the strictest party of Judaism is to Christianity. In short, Luke ushers the Pharisees right up to the portals of the Christian faith,

Luke's portrait of the Pharisees intersects with his portrait of Paul. Paul is a Pharisee by training (at the feet of Gamaliel), by doctrine (belief in the resurrection), and by zeal (formerly persecuting Christians). Paul himself then becomes the example of a Pharisee most faithful to the hopes of Israel—he remains a Jew by becoming a Christian. It is difficult to resist the conclusion that in Paul as a role model of a Pharisee become Christian, Luke seeks to arouse a sympathetic response among Jews and/or God-fearers who stand on the threshold of the faith, as well as among Jewish Christians already within the church. Paul's conciliatory circumcision of Timothy for the sake of the Jews points in the same direction.

For the sake of sanity, human beings superimpose our own mental construct onto reality. Luke-Acts is what is left behind of Luke's efforts to integrate his experiences with a pattern of tradition. No interpreter can do any more than approximate Luke's integration with more or less accuracy. Therefore, a disclaimer of having spoken the last word is unnecessary. But I sound one final appeal for including Luke's conciliation within the category of accurate approximation. A part of his experience is conflict between highly regarded Jews (Jewish Christians?) and a Christian community that embraces gentiles without requiring them to become proselytes to Judaism, particularly Pauline Christianity.

In his construct of the traditions of Jesus and the early church, he draws what he considers to be authentic Jews toward Christianity and authentic Christians toward Judaism.

In short, these contours of Luke-Acts compel me to join the company of scholars who are now resisting the standard reading of Luke-Acts as a triumph of gentile Christianity over Judaism. The evidence warrants a new reading of Luke-Acts as a product of a struggle for the legacy of Israel as the people of God. In such a struggle, Luke attempts to show how Jesus qualifies as messiah in spite of his rejection by a large and influential segment of Judaism. Moreover, Paul's behavior and the mission of the church that includes gentiles are, for Luke, unequivocally appropriate to the fulfillment of Israel's destiny.

Therefore, the standard paradigm for understanding Luke's view of the relation between Christianity and Judaism should pivot 180 degrees. That is, rather than setting gentile Christianity free, Luke ties it to Judaism. And rather than rejecting the Jews, Luke appeals to them.

BIBLIOGRAPHY OF MODERN AUTHORS CITED

Adams, David. "The Suffering of Paul and the Dynamics of Luke-Acts." Ph.D. dissertation, Yale University, 1979.

Albertz, Rainer. "Die 'Antrittspredigt' Jesu im Lukasevangelium auf ihrem alttestamentlichen Hintergrund." *ZNW* 74 (1983) 182–206.

Baarlink, Heinrich. "Ein gnädiges Jahr des Herr—und Tage der Vergeltung." *ZNW* 73 (1982) 204–220.

Bachmann, Michael. *Jerusalem und der Temple: Die geographisch-theologischen Elemente in der lukanischen Sicht des jüdischen Kultzentrums.* Stuttgart: Kohlhammer, 1980.

Baer, Heinrich von. *Der Heilige Geist in den Lukasschriften.* Stuttgart: Kohlhammer, 1926.

Bajard, J. "La structure de la pericope de Nazareth en Lc. iv, 16–30." *ETL* 45 (1969) 165–171.

Baltzer, Klaus. "The Meaning of the Temple in the Lucan Writings." *HTR* 58 (1965) 263–277.

Barr, David and Wentling, Judith. "The Conventions of Classical Biography and the Genre of Luke-Acts: A Preliminary Study." *Luke-Acts: New Perspectives from the Society of Biblical Literature Seminar.* Edited by Charles Talbert. New York: Crossroad, 1984.

Baumbach, Günther. "Das Sadduzäerverständnis bei Josephus Flavius und im Neuen Testament." *Kairos* 13 (1971) 17–37.

Baur, F. C. *Kritische Untersuchungen über die kanonischen Evangelien.* Tübingen: Fues, 1847.

———. *Paulus der Apostel Jesu Christi: Sein Leben und Wirken, seine Briefe und seine Lehre.* Stuttgart: Becher & Müller, 1845.

———. *Über den ursprung des Episcopats in der christlichen Kirche.* Tübingen: Fues, 1838.

———. "Über Zweck und Veranlassung des Römerbriefs und die damit zusammenhangenden Verhältnis der römischen Gemeinde." *Tübinger Zeitschrift für Theologie* (1836) 59–178.

Betz, Hans Dieter. "The Cleansing of the Ten Lepers (Luke 17:11–19)." *JBL* 90 (1971) 314–328.

———. *Lukian von Samosata und das Neue Testament: Religionsgeschichtliche und paränetische Parallelen.* Berlin: Akademie, 1961.

Blass, F. and Debrunner, A. *A Greek Grammar of the New Testament and Other Early Christian Literature.* Translation and revision by Robert W. Funk incorporating supplementary notes of A. Debrunner. Chicago: University of Chicago Press, 1961.

Blinzler, Joseph. *Der Prozess Jesu.* Regensburg: Pustet, 1969.

Bovon, François. "Israel, die Kirche und die Völker im lukanischen Doppelwerk." *TLZ* 108 (1983) 403–414.

———. "Luc: Portrait et projet." *Lumière et vie* 30 (No. 153/54, 1981) 9–18.

Bowker, John. *Jesus and the Pharisees.* Cambridge: Cambridge University Press, 1973.

Brandon, S. G. F. *The Fall of Jerusalem and the Christian Church* London: SPCK, 1975.

Brawley, Robert L. "Paul in Acts: Lucan Apology and Conciliation." *Luke-Acts: New Perspectives from the Society of Biblical Literature Seminar.* Edited by Charles Talbert: New York: Crossroad, 1984.

———. "The Pharisees in Luke-Acts: Luke's Address to Jews and His Irenic Purpose." Ph.D. dissertation, Princeton Theological Seminary, 1978.

Bremond, Claude. "Morphology of the French Folktale." *Semiotica* 2 (1970) 248–276.

Brown, Raymond. *The Birth of the Messiah: A Commentary of the Infancy Narratives in Matthew and Luke.* Garden City, NY: Doubleday, 1977.

Bruce, F. F. *The Acts of the Apostles.* London: Tyndale, 1951.

Brunners, Wilhelm. *Die Reinigung der zehn Aussätzigen und die Heilung des Samariters Lk 17, 11–19: Ein Beitrag zur lukanischen Interpretation der Reinigung von Aussätzigen.* Stuttgart: Katholisches Bibelwerk, 1977.

Budesheim, Thomas. "Paul's Abschiedsrede in the Acts of the Apostles." *HTR* 69 (1976) 9–30.

Büchler, A. *Der galiläische 'Am–ha 'Ares des zweiten Jahrhunderts. Beiträge zur innern Geschichte des palästinischen Judentums in den ersten zwei Jahrhunderten.* Vienna: Holder, 1906.

Buehler, William W. *The Pre-Herodian Civil War and Social Debate.* Basel: Reinhardt, 1974.

Bultmann, Rudolf. *The History of the Synoptic Tradition.* New York: Harper & Row, 1963.

Burchard, Christoph. *Der dreizehnte Zeuge: Traditions- und kompositionsgeschichtliche Untersuchungen zu Lukas' Darstellung der Frühzeit des Paulus.* Göttingen: Vandenhoeck & Ruprecht, 1970.

————. "Sadduzäer." *Paulys Realencyclopädie der classischen Altertumswissenschaft,* Supplementband 15 (1978) 466–478.

Busse, Ulrich. *Dan Nazareth-Manifest Jesu: Eine einführung in das lukanische Jesusbild nach Lk 4, 16–30.* Stuttgart: Katholisches Bibelwerk, 1978.

Cadbury, Henry J. "Dust and Garments." *Additional Notes to the Commentary. The Beginnings of Christianity. Part I. The Acts of the Apostles.* Vol. 5. Edited by F. J. Foakes Jackson and Kirsopp Lake. London: Macmillan, 1933.

————. *The Making of Luke-Acts.* New York: Macmillan, 1927.

Caird, G. B. *The Gospel of St. Luke.* Baltimore: Penguin, 1963.

Combrink, H. J. B. "The Structure and Significance of Luke 4:16–30." *Neot* 7 (1963) 27–47.

Conzelmann, Hans. *Die Apostelgeschichte erklärt.* Tübingen: Mohr (Siebeck), 1972.

————. *The Theology of St. Luke.* New York: Harper & Row, 1961.

Crockett, Larrimore. "Luke 4:25–27 and Jewish-Gentile Relations in Luke-Acts." *JBL* 88 (1969) 177–183.

Cullmann, Oscar. *Christ and Time: The Primitive Christian Conception of Time and History.* Philadelphia: Westminster, 1950.

————. *Salvation in History.* New York: Harper & Row, 1967.

Dahl, Nils. *Jesus in the Memory of the Early Church.* Minneapolis: Augsburg, 1976.

————. "'A People for His Name'." *NTS* 4 (1957–58) 319–327.

Danker, Frederick. "The Endangered Benefactor in Luke-Acts." *SBLSP.* Edited by Kent Richards. Chico, CA: Scholars, 1981.

————. *Jesus and the New Age According to St. Luke: A Commentary on the Third Gospel.* St. Louis: Clayton, 1972.

Davies, W. D. "Apocalyptic and Pharisaism." *Christian Origins and Judaism.* Philadelphia: Westminster, 1962.

de la Potterie, J. "L'onction du Christ." *NRT* 80 (1959) 225–252.

de Jonge, Henk J. "Sonship, Wisdom, Infancy: Luke II.41–51a." *NTS* 24 (1977–78) 317–354.

Delobel, J. "L'onction par la pécheresse: La composition litteraire de Luc 7.36–50." *ETL* 42 (1966) 415–475.

Derenbourg, J. *Essai sur l'histoire et la géographie de la Palestine*. Paris: Imperiale, 1867.

Dibelius, Martin. *From Tradition to Gospel* New York: Scribner's, 1965.

———. *Studies in the Acts of the Apostles*. London: SCM, 1956.

Dupont, Jacques. *Les béatitudes: la bonne nouvelle*. Paris: Gabalda, 1969.

———. *Gnosis: la connaissance religieuse dans les épîtres de saint Paul*. Louvain: Nauwelaerts, 1949.

———. "La parabole des talents (Mat. 25:14–30) ou des mines (Luc 19:12–27)." *RTP* 19 (1969) 376–391.

———. "La question du plan des Actes des Apôtres à la lumière d'un texte de Lucien Samosate." *Novum Testamentum* 21 (1979) 220–231.

———. "Le salut des gentils et la signification theologique du Livre des Actes." *NTS* 6 (1959–60) 132–155.

Eliade, Mircea. *Cosmos and History: The Myth of the Eternal Return*. New York: Harper & Row, 1959.

Ellis, E. Earle. "Jesus, the Sadducees and Qumran." *NTS* 10 (1963–64) 274–279.

Eltester, Walter. "Israel im lukanischen Werk und die Nazarethperikope." *Jesus in Nazareth*. Berlin: de Gruyter, 1972.

Eppstein, Victor. "The Historicity of the Gospel Account of the Cleansing of the Temple." *ZNW* 55 (1964) 42–58.

———. "When and How the Sadducees Were Excommunicated." *JBL* 85 (1966) 213–224.

Exum, Cheryl and Talbert, Charles. "The Structure of Paul's Speech to the Ephesian Elders (Acts 20:18–35)." *CBQ* 29 (1967) 233-236.

Feldman, Louis. "Hengel's *Judaism and Hellenism* in Retrospect." *JBL* 96 (1977) 371–382.

Filson, Floyd. "The Significance of the Temple in the Ancient Near East. IV. Temple, Synagogue, and Church." *BA* 7 (1944) 77–88.

Finkel, Asher. "Jesus' Sermon at Nazareth (Luk. 4, 16–30)." *Abraham unser Vater: Juden und Christen in Gespräch über die Bibel; Festschrift für O. Michel*. Edited by Otto Betz, Martin Hengel, and Peter Schmidt. Leiden: Brill, 1963.

Fitzmyer, Joseph. *The Gospel According to Luke (I–IX): Introduction, Translation, and Notes*. Garden City, NY: Doubleday, 1981.

Flender, Helmut. *St. Luke: Theologian of Redemptive History*. Philadelphia: Fortress, 1967.

Flückiger, Felix. "Luk. 21, 20–24 und die Zerstörung Jerusalems." *TZ* 28 (1972) 385–390.

Flusser, David. "Josephus on the Sadducees and Menander." *Immanuel* 7 (1977) 61–67.

Foakes Jackson, F. J. and Lake, Kirsopp. *Prolegomena II: Criticism. The Beginnings of Christianity. Part I. The Acts of the Apostles.* Vol. 2. London: Macmillan, 1922.

Fohrer, G. "Σιών." *TDNT* 7.292–319.

Friedrich, Gerhard. "προφήτης." *TDNT* 6.828–861.

Gärtner, Bertil. *The Temple and the Community in Qumran and the New Testament.* Cambridge: Cambridge University Press, 1965.

Gaston, Lloyd. *No Stone on Another: Studies in the Significance of the Fall of Jerusalem in the Synoptic Gospels.* Leiden: Brill, 1970.

Gemoll, Wilhelm. *Das Apophthegma: Literarhistorische Studien.* Wein/Leipzig: Freytag, 1924.

George, Augustin. "Israël dans l'oeuvre de Luc." *RB* 75 (1968) 481–525.

Georgi, Dieter. "Forms of Religious Propaganda." *Jesus in His Time.* Edited by H. Schultz. Philadelphia: Fortress, 1971.

————. *Die Gegner des Paulus im 2 Korintherbrief: Studien zur religiösen Propaganda in der Spätantike.* Neukirchen: Neukirchencr, 1964. ET, *The Opponents of Paul in 2 Corinthians: A Study of Religious Propaganda in Late Antiquity.* Philadelphia: Fortress, 1985.

Giblin, Charles. *The Destruction of Jerusalem According to Luke's Gospel: A Historical-Typological Moral.* Rome: Biblical Institute, 1985.

Gnilka, Joachim. *Die Verstockung Israels: Isaias 6, 9–10 in der Theologie der Synoptiker.* Munich: Kösel, 1961.

Goldstein, J. "Jewish Acceptance and Rejection of Hellenism." *Jewish and Christian Self-Definition.* Vol. 2. *Aspects of Judaism in the Greco-Roman Period.* Edited by E. P. Sanders. Philadelphia: Fortress, 1981.

Goppelt, Leonhard. *Christentum und Judentum im ersten und zweiten Jahrhundert: Ein Aufriss der Urgeschichte der Kirche.* Gütersloh: Bertelsmann, 1954.

Goulder, M. D. *Type and History in Acts.* London: SPCK, 1964.

Grenfell, B. and Hunt, A., eds. *New Classical Fragments and Other Greek and Latin Papyri.* Oxford: Clarendon, 1897.

Grundmann, Walter. *Das Evangelium nach Lukas.* Berlin: Evangelische, 1961.

Haenchen, Ernst. *The Acts of the Apostles: A Commentary.* Philadelphia: Westminster, 1971.

Hahn, Ferdinand. *Christologische Hoheitstitel: Ihre Geschichte im frühen Christentum.* Göttingen: Vandenhoeck & Ruprecht, 1963.

Harnack, Adolf von. *The Acts of the Apostles.* New York: Putnam's Sons, 1909.

Hauser, Hermann. *Strukturen der Abschlusserzählung der Apostelgeschichte (Apg 28, 16–31).* Rome: Biblical Institute, 1979.

Hengel, Martin. *Jews, Greeks, and Barbarians: Aspects of the Hellenization of Judaism in the pre-Christian Period.* Philadelphia: Fortress, 1980.

————. *Judaism and Hellenism: Studies in Their Encounter in Palestine during the Early Hellenistic Period.* Philadelphia: Fortress, 1974.

Hill, David. "The Rejection of Jesus at Nazareth (Luke 4:16–30)." *NovT* 13 (1971) 161–180.

Hölscher, Gustav. *Der Sadduzäismus: Eine kritische Untersuchung zur späteren jüdischen Religionsgeschichte.* Leipzig: Hinrich, 1906.

Holladay, Carl. *Theios Aner in Hellenistic Judaism: A Critique of the Use of the Category in New Testament Christology.* Missoula: Scholars, 1977.

Houlden, J. L. "The Purpose of Luke." *JSNT* 21 (1984) 53–65.

Hruby, Kurt. *Die Synagoge: Geschichtliche Entwicklung einer Institution.* Zürich: Theologische, 1971.

Jeremias, Joachim. *The Eucharistic Words of Jesus.* New York: Scribner's, 1966.

————. *Jerusalem in the Time of Jesus: An Investigation into Economic and Social Conditions During the New Testament Period.* Philadelphia: Fortress, 1969.

————. *Jesus' Promise to the Nations.* Naperville, IL: Allenson, 1958.

Jervell, Jacob. "The Acts of the Apostles and the History of Early Christianity." *ST* 37 (1983) 17–32.

————. *Luke and the People of God: A New Look at Luke-Acts.* Minneapolis: Augsburg, 1972.

————. "Paulus in der Apostelgeschichte und die Geschichte des Urchristentums." *NTS* 32 (1986) 378–392.

Johnson, Luke T. *The Literary Function of Possessions in Luke-Acts.* Missoula: Scholars, 1977.

————. "The Lukan Kingship Parable (Lk. 19:11–27)." *NovT* 24 (1982) 139–159.

166   Bibliography

Juel, Donald. *Luke–Acts: The Promise of History.* Atlanta: Knox, 1983.
Jülicher, Adolf. *Die Gleichnisreden Jesu.* Vol. 2. Tübingen: Mohr (Siebeck), 1910.
Karris, Robert. "Luke 23:47 and the Lucan View of Jesus' Death." *JBL* 105 (1986) 65–74.
Keck, Leander. "Jesus' Entrance upon His Mission." *RevExp* 64 (1967) 465–483.
Kennedy, George. *New Testament Interpretation through Rhetorical Criticism.* Chapel Hill: University of North Carolina Press, 1984.
Klein, Günter. *Die zwölf Apostel: Ursprung und Gehalt einer Idee.* Göttingen: Vandenhoeck & Ruprecht, 1961.
Klijn, A. F. J. "Stephen's Speech—Acts VII.2–53." *NTS* 4 (1957–58) 25–31.
Klostermann, Erich. *Das Lukasevangelium.* Tübingen: Mohr (Siebeck), 1929.
Kodell, Jerome. "Luke's Use of *LAOS*, 'People,' Especially in the Jerusalem Narrative (Lk 19, 28–24, 53)." *CBQ* 31 (1969) 323–343.
Kümmel, W. G. *Introduction to the New Testament.* Nashville: Abingdon, 1965.
Ladouceur, David. "Hellenistic Preconceptions of Shipwreck and Pollution as a Context for Acts 27–28." *HTR* 73 (1980) 435–449.
Lake, Kirsopp and Cadbury, Henry J. *English Translation and Commentary. The Beginnings of Christianity. Part I. The Acts of the Apostles.* Vol. 4. Edited by F. J. Foakes Jackson and Kirsopp Lake. London: Macmillan, 1933.
Leaney, A. R. C. *A Commentary on the Gospel according to Luke.* New York: Harper & Row, 1963.
Leipold, Johannes and Grundmann, Walter eds. *Umwelt des Urchristentums: Darstellung des neutestamentlichen Zeitalters.* Vol. 1. Berlin: Evangelische, 1982.
LeMoyne, Jean. *Les Sadducéens.* Paris: Gabalda, 1972.
Leszynsky, Rudolf. *Die Sadduzäer.* Berlin: Mayer & Müller, 1912.
Levenson, Jon D. *Sinai and Zion: An Entry into the Jewish Bible.* Minneapolis: Winston, 1985.
Lightfoot, Robert H. *History and Interpretation in the Gospels.* London: Hodder and Stoughton, 1934.
Lindars, Barnabas. *New Testament Apologetic: The Doctrinal Significance of the Old Testament Quotations.* London: SCM, 1961.

Löning, Karl. *Die Saulustradition in der Apostelgeschichte.* Münster: Aschendorf, 1973.

Lohfink, Gerhard. *The Conversion of St. Paul: Narrative and History in Acts.* Chicago: Franciscan Herald, 1976.

————. *Die Sammlung Israels.* Munich: Kösel, 1975.

Lohse, Eduard. "συνέδριον." *TDNT* 7.860–871.

Loisy, Alfred. *Les Actes des Apôtres.* Paris: Nourry, 1920.

MacRae, George. "Heavenly Temple and Eschatology in the Letter to the Hebrews." *Semeia* 12 (1978) 179–199.

Maddox, Robert. *The Purpose of Luke-Acts.* Edinburgh: T. & T. Clark, 1982.

Mansoor, M. "Sadducees." *EncJud* 14 (1971) 620–622.

Marshall, I. H. *The Gospel of Luke: A Commentary on the Greek Text.* Grand Rapids: Eerdmans, 1978.

Meeûs, X. de. "Composition de Lc. XIV et genre symposiaque." *ETL* 37 (1961) 847–870.

Menoud, Philippe. "Le plan des Actes des Apôtres." *NTS* 1 (1954–55) 44–51.

Metzger, Bruce M. *A Textual Commentary on the Greek New Testament.* Stuttgart: United Bible Societies, 1971.

Meyer, Rudolf. "Σαδδουκαῖος." *TDNT* 7.35–54.

Michel, Hans-Joachim. *Die Abschiedsrede des Paulus an die Kirche Apg 20,17–38: Motivgeschichte und theologische Bedeutung.* Munich: Kösel, 1973.

Miles, Gary and Trompf, Garry. "Luke and Antiphon: The Theology of Acts 27–28 in the Light of Pagan Beliefs about Divine Retribution, Pollution, and Shipwreck." *HTR* 69 (1976) 259–267.

Minear, Paul. "Jesus' Audiences According to Luke." *NovT* 16 (1974) 81–89.

Moessner, David. "Luke 9:1–50: Luke's Preview of the Journey of the Prophet like Moses of Deuteronomy." *JBL* 102 (1983) 575–605.

Moore, George F. *Judaism in the First Centuries of the Christian Era.* Cambridge: Harvard University Press, 1927.

Morgan, Robert. *The Nature of New Testament Theology: The Contribution of William Wrede and Adolf Schlatter.* London: SCM, 1973.

Moulton, James Hope. *A Grammar of New Testament Greek.* Vol. 1 *Prolegomena.* Edinburgh: T. & T. Clark, 1949.

Nellessen, Ernst. *Zeugnis für Jesus und das Wort: Exegetische Untersuchungen zum lukanischen Zeugnisbegriff.* Köln: Haustein, 1976.

Nelson, Harold. "The Significance of the Temple in the Ancient Near East. I. The Egyptian Temple." *BA* 7 (1944) 44–53.

Nestle, W. "Anklänge an Euripides in der Apostelgeschichte." *Philologus, Zeitschrift für das classische Altertum* 59 (1900) 46–57.

Neusner, Jacob. *From Politics to Piety: The Emergence of Pharisaic Judaism.* New York: Ktav, 1979.

―――. *The Rabbinic Traditions about the Pharisees before 70. Part III. Conclusions.* Leiden: Brill, 1971.

―――. "Review of *A Hidden Revolution*, by Ellis Rivkin." *Ancient Judaism: Debates and Disputes.* Chico, CA: Scholars, 1984.

―――. "The Use of the Later Rabbinic Evidence for the Study of First-Century Pharisaism." *Approaches to Ancient Judaism: Theory and Practice.* Edited by William Scott Green. Missoula: Scholars, 1978.

Neyrey, Jerome. "Jesus' Address to the Women of Jerusalem (Lk. 23.27–31)—A Prophetic Judgment Oracle." *NTS* 29 (1983) 75–84.

Nock, A. D. *Conversion: The Old and New in Religion from Alexander the Great to Augustine of Hippo.* Oxford: Oxford University Press, 1961.

Nolland, John. "Words of Grace (Luke 4:22)." *Bib* 65 (1984) 44–60.

Oppenheim, A. Leo. "The Significance of the Temple in the Ancient Near East. II. The Mesopotamian Temple." *BA* 7 (1944) 54–63.

Overbeck, Franz. *Kurze Erklärung der Apostelgeschichte.* Leipzig: Hirzel, 1870.

Panier, Louis. "Comprenez vous pourquoi vous comprenez! Actes 1, 15–2:47." *Semiotique et Bible* 23 (1981) 20–43.

Parkes, James. *The Conflict of the Church and the Synagogue: A Study in the Origins of Antisemitism.* London: Soncino, 1934.

Patai, Raphael. *Man and Temple in Ancient Jewish Myth and Ritual.* London: Nelson and Sons, 1947.

Pesch, Rudolf. *Die Vision des Stephanus: Apg 7.55–56 im Rahmen der Apostelgeschichte.* Stuttgart: Katholisches Bibelwerk, 1966.

Petersen, Norman. *Literary Criticism for New Testament Critics.* Philadelphia: Fortress, 1978.

Plümacher, Eckhard. *Lukas als hellenistischer Schriftsteller: Studien zur Apostelgeschichte.* Göttingen: Vandenhoeck & Ruprecht, 1972.

Plunkett, Mark. "Ethnocentricity and Salvation History in the Cornelius Episode (Acts 10:1–11:18)." SBLSP. Edited by Kent Richards. Atlanta: Scholars, 1985.

Reicke, Bo. "Jesus in Nazareth—Lk 4, 16–30." *Das Wort und die Wörter; Festschrift Gerhard Friedrich.* Edited by H. Balz and S. Schulz. Stuttgart: Kohlhammer, 1973.

———. "πᾶς." *TDNT* 5.892–896.

Rengstorf, Karl. *Das Evangelium nach Lukas übersetzt und erklärt.* Göttingen: Vandenhoeck & Ruprecht, 1952.

Rese, Martin. *Alttestamentliche Motive in der Christologie des Lukas.* Gütersloh: Mohn, 1969.

Richard, Earl. *Acts 6:1–8:4: The Author's Method of Composition.* Missoula: Scholars, 1978.

Richardson, Peter. *Israel in the Apostolic Church.* Cambridge: Cambridge University Press, 1969.

Rivkin, Ellis. *A Hidden Revolution.* Nashville: Abingdon, 1978.

———. "Defining the Pharisees: The Tannaitic Sources." *HUCA* 40–41 (1969–70) 205–249.

Rolland, Philippe. "L'organisation du Livre des Actes et de l'ensemble de l'oeuvre de Luc." *Bib* 65 (1984) 81–86.

Roloff, Jürgen. *Das Kerygma und der irdische Jesus: Historische Motive in den Jesus-Erzählungen der Evangelien.* Göttingen: Vandenhoeck & Ruprecht, 1970.

Rustow, Alexander. "Ἐντὸς ὑμῶν ἐστίν: Zur Deutung von Lukas 17:20–21." *ZNW* 51 (1960) 197–224.

Safrai, S. "Jewish Self-Government." *The Jewish People in the First-Century: Historical Geography, Political History, Social, Cultural and Religious Life and Institutions.* Edited by S. Safrai and M. Stern. Philadelphia: Fortress, 1974.

Salmon, Marilyn. "Hypotheses about First-Century Judaism and the Study of Luke–Acts." Ph.D. dissertation, Hebrew Union College, 1985.

Sanders, James. "From Isaiah 61 to Luke 4." *Christianity, Judaism and Other Greco-Roman Cults; Studies for Morton Smith.* Edited by Jacob Neusner. Leiden: Brill, 1975.

———. "Isaiah in Luke." *Int* 36 (1982) 144–155.

Sanders, Jack T. "The Parable of the Pounds and Lucan Anti-Semitism." *TS* 42 (1981) 660–668.

———. "The Pharisees in Luke–Acts." *The Living Text; Essays in Honor of Ernest W. Saunders.* Edited by Dennis Groh and Robert Jewett. Lanham, MD: University of America, 1985.

———. "The Salvation of the Jews in Luke–Acts." *Luke–Acts: New Perspectives from the Society of Biblical Literature*

Seminar. Edited by Charles Talbert. New York: Crossroad, 1984.

Schäfer, Peter. "Tempel und Schöpfung: Zur Interpretation einiger Heiligstumstraditionen in der rabbinischen Literatur." *Kairos* 16 (1974) 122–133.

Schille, Gottfried. *Die Apostelgeschichte des Lukas.* Berlin: Evangelische, 1983.

Schlatter, Adolf. "The Theology of the New Testament and Dogmatics." *The Nature of New Testament Theology: The Contribution of William Wrede and Adolf Schlatter.* Edited by Robert Morgan. London: SCM, 1973.

Schmithals, Walter. "Der Irrlehrer des Philipperbriefes." *ZTK* 54 (1957) 297–341.

Schneckenburger, Matthias. *Apostelgeschichte: Zugleich eine Ergänzung der neueren Commentare.* Bern: Fischer, 1841.

Schneider, Gerhard. *Die Apostelgeschichte.* 2 vols. Freiburg: Herder, 1980.

———. *Das Evangelium nach Lukas Kapitel 11–24.* Gütersloh: Mohn, 1977.

Schnider, Franz. *Jesus der Prophet.* Göttingen: Vandenhoeck & Ruprecht, 1973.

Schrage, W. "συναγωγή." *TDNT* 7.798–841.

Schrenk, G. "ἱερός." *TDNT* 3.221–247.

Schubert, Paul. "The Final Cycle of Speeches in the Book of Acts." *JBL* 87 (1968) 1–16.

———. "The Place of the Areopagus Speech in the Composition of Acts." *Transitions in Biblical Scholarship.* Edited by J. Rylaarsdam. Chicago: University of Chicago Press, 1968.

———. "The Structure and Significance of Luke 24." *Neutestamentliche Studien für Rudolf Bultmann.* Edited by Walter Eltester. Berlin: Töpelmann, 1954.

Schürer, Emil. *The History of the Jewish People in the Time of Jesus Christ.* 2 vols. Edinburgh: T. & T. Clark, 1885–90.

Schürmann, Heinz. "Zur Traditionsgeschichte der Nazareth-Perikope Lk 4,16–30." *Mélanges bibliques en homage au R. P. Béda Rigaux.* Edited by A. Descamps and A. de Halleux. Gembloux: Duculot, 1970.

Schweitzer, Albert. *Das Adendmahl im Zusammenhang mit dem Leben Jesu and der Geschichte des Urchristentums.* Tübingen: Mohr (Siebeck), 1901.

———. *Paul and His Interpreters: A Critical History.* London: Black, 1912.

———. *The Quest of the Historical Jesus: A Critical Study of Its Progress from Reimarus to Wrede.* London: Black, 1954.

Schweizer, Eduard. *The Good News According to Luke*. Atlanta: Knox, 1984.

Simon, Marcel. "Saint Stephen and the Jerusalem Temple." *JEH* 2 (1951) 127–142.

Smallwood, E. Mary. "High Priests and Politics in Roman Palestine." *JTS* 13 (1962) 14–34.

Smith, Morton. "Palestinian Judaism in the First Century." *Israel: Its Role in Civilization*. Edited by M. Davis. New York: Harper & Row, 1956.

―――. "Prolegomena to a Discussion of Aretalogies, Divine Men, the Gospels, and Jesus." *JBL* 90 (1971) 174–199.

Snodgrass, Klyne. *The Parable of the Wicked Tenants: An Inquiry into Parable Interpretation*. Tübingen: Mohr (Siebeck), 1983.

Steck, Odil. "Bemerkungen zu Jesaha 6." *BZ* 16 (1972) 188–206.

―――. *Israel und das gewaltsame Geschick der Propheten: Untersuchungen zur Überlieferung des deuteronomistischen Geschichtsbildes im Alten Testament, Spätjudentum und Urchristentum*. Neukirchen-Vluyn: Neukirchener, 1967.

Steele, E. Springs. "Luke 11:37–54—A Modified Hellenistic Symposium?" *JBL* 103 (1984) 379–394.

Stolle, Volker. *Der Zeuge als Angeklagter: Untersuchungen zum Paulusbild des Lukas*. Stuttgart: Kohlhammer, 1973.

Strathmann, H. "μάρτυς." *TDNT* 4.474–514.

Strobel, August. "Die Ausrufung des Jubeljahrs in der Nazarethpredigt Jesu: Zur apokalyptischen Tradition Lc 4:16–30." *Jesus in Nazareth*. Edited by Walter Eltester. Berlin: de Gruyter, 1972.

Sylva, Dennis. "The Temple Curtain and Jesus' Death in the Gospel of Luke." *JBL* 105 (1986) 239–250.

Talbert, Charles. *Acts*. Atlanta: Knox, 1984.

―――. *Literary Patterns, Theological Themes, and the Genre of Luke-Acts*. Missoula: Scholars, 1974.

―――. *Luke and the Gnostics*. New York: Abingdon, 1966.

―――. *Reading Luke: A Literary and Theological Commentary on the Third Gospel*. New York: Crossroad, 1982.

―――. *What is a Gospel? The Genre of the Canonical Gospels*. Philadelphia: Fortress, 1977.

Tannehill, Robert. "Israel in Luke-Acts: A Tragic Story." *JBL* 104 (1985) 69–85.

―――. "The Mission of Jesus according to Luke 4:16–30." *Jesus in Nazareth*. Edited by Walter Eltester. Berlin: de Gruyter, 1972.

Terrien, Samuel. "The Omphalos Myth and Hebrew Religion." *VT* 20 (1970) 315–338.

Theissen, Gerd. *The Miracle Stories of the Early Christian Tradition.* Philadelphia: Fortress, 1983.

Tiede, David. *The Charismatic Figure as Miracle Worker.* Missoula: Scholars, 1972.

———. *Prophecy and History in Luke–Acts.* Philadelphia: Fortress, 1980.

Torrey, C. C. *The Composition and Date of Acts.* Cambridge: Harvard University Press, 1916.

Trocmé, Etienne. *Le Livre des Actes et l'histoire.* Paris: Presses Universitaires de France, 1957.

Tyson, Joseph. *The Death of Jesus in Luke–Acts.* Columbia: University of South Carolina Press, 1986.

———. "The Jewish Public in Luke–Acts." *NTS* 30 (1984) 574–583.

Unnik, W. C. van. "Der Ausdruck ἕως ἐσχάτου τῆς γῆς (Apostelgeschichte 1:8) und sein alttestamentlicher Hintergrund." *Sparsa Collecta: The Collected Essays of W. C. van Unnik.* Leiden: Brill, 1973.

———. *Tarsus or Jerusalem: The City of Paul's Youth.* London: Epworth, 1962.

Vermes, Geza. *Jesus the Jew: A Historian's Reading of the Gospels.* New York: Macmillan, 1973.

Via, Dan. *Kerygma and Comedy in the New Testament: A Structuralist Approach to Hermeneutic.* Philadelphia: Fortress, 1975.

Violet, Bruno. "Zum rechten Verständnis der Nazareth-Perikope Lc 4:16–30." *ZNW* 37 (1938) 251–271.

Walasky, Paul. *"And So We Came to Rome": The Political Perspective of St. Luke.* Cambridge: Cambridge University Press, 1983.

Wanke, Joachim. *Die Emmäuserzählung: Eine redaktionsgeschichtliche Untersuchung zu Lk 24, 13–35.* Leipzig: St. Benno, 1973.

Wartensleben, G. von. *Begriff der griechischen Chreia und Beiträge zur Geschichte ihrer Form.* Heidelberg: Winter's Universitätsbuchhandlung, 1901.

Weinert, Francis. "The Meaning of the Temple in the Gospel of Luke." Ph.D. dissertation, Fordham University, 1979.

Weiss, H.-F. *Der Pharisäismus im Lichte der Überlieferung des Neuen Testaments.* Berlin: Akademie, 1965.

Weiss, J. *Jesus' Proclamation of the Kingdom of God.* Philadelphia: Fortress, 1971.

————. *Über der Absicht und dem literarischen Character der Apostelgeschichte.* Göttingen: Vandenhoeck & Ruprecht, 1897.

Wellhausen, Julius. *Die Pharisäer und die Sadducäer: Eine Untersuchung zur inneren jüdischen Geschichte.* Greifswalk: Bamberg, 1874.

Wenschkewitz, Hans. *Die Spiritualisierung der Kultusbegriffe: Temple, Priester und Opfer im Neuen Testament.* Leipzig: Pfeiffer, 1932.

Wensinck, A. J. *The Ideas of the Western Semites Concerning the Navel of the Earth.* Amsterdam: Müller, 1916.

Wikenhauser, Alfred. *Die Apostelgeschichte: Übersetzt und erklärt.* Regensburg: Pustet, 1961.

————. "Doppelträume." *Bib* 29 (1948) 100-111.

Wilson, Stephen. *The Gentiles and the Gentile Mission in Luke-Acts.* Cambridge: Cambridge University Press, 1973.

————. *Luke and the Law.* Cambridge: Cambridge University Press, 1983.

Winter, Paul. "Miszellen zur Apostelgeschichte." *EvT* 17 (1957) 398–406.

————. *On the Trial of Jesus.* Berlin: de Gruyter, 1961.

Wrede, Wilhelm. *Über Ausgabe und Methode der sogennanten neutestamentlichen Theologie.* Göttingen: Vandenhoeck & Ruprecht, 1897.

Wright, G. Ernest. "The Significance of the Temple in the Ancient Near East. III. The Temple in Palestine-Syria." *BA* 7 (1944) 41–44, 65-77.

Zahn, Theodor. *Das Evangelium des Lucas.* Leipzig: Deichert, 1913.

Zehnle, Richard. *Peter's Pentecost Discourse.* Nashville: Abingdon, 1971.

Zeller, Edward. *The Contents and Origin of the Acts of the Apostles, Critically Investigated.* London: Williams and Norgate, 1875.

Ziesler, J. A. "Luke and the Pharisees." *NTS* 25 (1978–79) 146–157.

Index of Passages Cited

Biblical Books (with Apocrypha)

Index of Authors Cited

Modern Authors